Y0-DYJ-057

*Cambridge Imperial and Post-Colonial Studies Series*

General Editors: **Megan Vaughan**, Kings' College, Cambridge and **Richard Drayton**, Corpus Christi College, Cambridge

This informative series covers the broad span of modern imperial history while also exploring the recent developments in former colonial states where residues of empire can still be found. The books provide in-depth examinations of empires as competing and complementary power structures encouraging the reader to reconsider their understanding of international and world history during recent centuries.

*Titles include:*

Sunil S. Amrith
DECOLONIZING INTERNATIONAL HEALTH
India and Southeast Asia, 1930–65

Tony Ballantyne
ORIENTALISM AND RACE
Aryanism in the British Empire

Robert J. Blyth
THE EMPIRE OF THE RAJ
Eastern Africa and the Middle East, 1858–1947

Roy Bridges (*editor*)
IMPERIALISM, DECOLONIZATION AND AFRICA
Studies Presented to John Hargreaves

L.J. Butler
COPPER EMPIRE
Mining and the Colonial State in Northern Rhodesia, c.1930–64

Hilary M. Carey (*editor*)
EMPIRES OF RELIGION

T.J. Cribb (*editor*)
IMAGINED COMMONWEALTH
Cambridge Essays on Commonwealth and International Literature in English

Michael S. Dodson
ORIENTALISM, EMPIRE AND NATIONAL CULTURE
India, 1770–1880

Ulrike Hillemann
ASIAN EMPIRE AND BRITISH KNOWLEDGE
China and the Networks of British Imperial Expansion

B.D. Hopkins
THE MAKING OF MODERN AFGHANISTAN

Ronald Hyam
BRITAIN'S IMPERIAL CENTURY, 1815–1914: A STUDY OF EMPIRE AND EXPANSION
Third Edition

Iftekhar Iqbal
THE BENGAL DELTA
Ecology, State and Social Change, 1843–1943

Brian Ireland
THE US MILITARY IN HAWAI'I
Colonialism, Memory and Resistance

Robin Jeffrey
POLITICS, WOMEN AND WELL-BEING
How Kerala became a 'Model'

Gerold Krozewski
MONEY AND THE END OF EMPIRE
British International Economic Policy and the Colonies, 1947–58

Sloan Mahone and Megan Vaughan (*editors*)
PSYCHIATRY AND EMPIRE

Javed Majeed
AUTOBIOGRAPHY, TRAVEL AND POST-NATIONAL IDENTITY

Francine McKenzie
REDEFINING THE BONDS OF COMMONWEALTH 1939–1948
The Politics of Preference

Gabriel Paquette
ENLIGHTENMENT, GOVERNANCE AND REFORM IN SPAIN AND ITS EMPIRE 1759–1808

Jennifer Regan-Lefebvre
IRISH AND INDIAN
The Cosmopolitan Politics of Alfred Webb

Ricardo Roque
HEADHUNTING AND COLONIALISM
Anthropology and the Circulation of Human Skulls in the Portuguese Empire, 1870–1930

Michael Silvestri
IRELAND AND INDIA
Nationalism, Empire and Memory

John Singleton and Paul Robertson
ECONOMIC RELATIONS BETWEEN BRITAIN AND AUSTRALASIA 1945–1970

Aparna Vaidik
IMPERIAL ANDAMANS
Colonial Encounter and Island History

Kim A. Wagner (*editor*)
THUGGEE
Banditry and the British in Early Nineteenth-Century India

Jon E. Wilson
THE DOMINATION OF STRANGERS
Modern Governance in Eastern India, 1780–1835

---

**Cambridge Imperial and Post-Colonial Studies Series**
**Series Standing Order ISBN 978–0–333–91908–8 (Hardback) 978–0–333–91909–5 (Paperback)**
(*outside North America only*)

You can receive future titles in this series as they are published by placing a standing order. Please contact your bookseller or, in case of difficulty, write to us at the address below with your name and address, the title of the series and the ISBN quoted above.

Customer Services Department, Macmillan Distribution Ltd, Houndmills, Basingstoke, Hampshire RG21 6XS, England

# The US Military in Hawai‘i

## Colonialism, Memory and Resistance

Brian Ireland
*Senior Lecturer in American History and American Studies, University of Glamorgan*



palgrave
macmillan

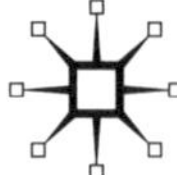



First published 2011 by
PALGRAVE MACMILLAN

Palgrave Macmillan in the UK is an imprint of Macmillan Publishers Limited, registered in England, company number 785998, of Houndmills, Basingstoke, Hampshire RG21 6XS.

Palgrave Macmillan in the US is a division of St Martin's Press LLC, 175 Fifth Avenue, New York, NY 10010.

Palgrave Macmillan is the global academic imprint of the above companies and has companies and representatives throughout the world.

Palgrave® and Macmillan® are registered trademarks in the United States, the United Kingdom, Europe and other countries

ISBN 978-0-230-22782-8 hardback

This book is printed on paper suitable for recycling and made from fully managed and sustained forest sources. Logging, pulping and manufacturing processes are expected to conform to the environmental regulations of the country of origin.

A catalogue record for this book is available from the British Library.

Library of Congress Cataloging-in-Publication Data

Ireland, Brian, 1966–
The US military in Hawai'i: colonialism, memory, and resistance / Brian Ireland.
p. cm.
ISBN 978–0–230–22782–8 (hardback)
1. Hawaii–History, Military. 2. United States–Armed Forces–Hawaii–History. 3. Collective memory–Hawaii. 4. Memorialization–Hawaii. 5. Hawaii–In motion pictures. 6. Vietnam War, 1961–1975–Press coverage–Hawaii. I. Title. II. Title: United States military in Hawai'i.
DU627.5.I74 2011
355.009969–dc22 2010034136

10 9 8 7 6 5 4 3 2 1
20 19 18 17 16 15 14 13 12 11

Printed and bound in Great Britain by
CPI Antony Rowe, Chippenham and Eastbourne

*This book is dedicated, with love, to Mary Ellen Ireland*

# Contents

# List of Illustrations

# Acknowledgements

This book would not have been possible without the help of the American Studies department at the University of Hawai'i at Mānoa, particularly David Stannard, Robert Perkinson and Floyd Matson (1921–2008). Thanks also to my colleagues in the History division at the University of Glamorgan, especially to Chris Evans for his continuing support, and Jane Finucane for her help in preparing the images used to illustrate this book. Thanks also to Holly for her patience and assistance, and to Morgan and Myles. The Hawaiian Historical Society granted permission to use material in this book which previously appeared in the *Hawaiian Journal of History*. Press Americana granted permission to use material that previously appeared in *Reel Histories: Studies in American Film*, edited by Melissa Croteau. I would like to gratefully acknowledge the assistance of Ted Pollard and Steve Pendergast of the Radnor Historical Society; Lisa Laughy of the Ohrstrom Library, St. Paul's School, Concord, NH; Louise Airlie of the Museum of Islay Life, Port Charlotte, Isle of Islay; Timothy Woodbury of the US Naval Academy Alumni Association; Kyle Kajihiro of the American Friends Service Committee; Summer Nemeth; Kathie Fry; Denby Fawcett; Dougal Watson and Palgrave's anonymous reader.

Cover image. Honolulu, Hawaii: Entering Honolulu Harbor, Hawaiian hula dancers and musicians boarded the transport *Waterbury Victory* off Diamond Head and entertained the troops of the famed 442nd Regimental Combat Team upon their return home. Pictured is Lieutenant Unkei Uchima of Kauai, of the 442nd Combat Team doing the hula with Leonetta Osorio. Courtesy of University of Hawai'i at Mānoa Library.

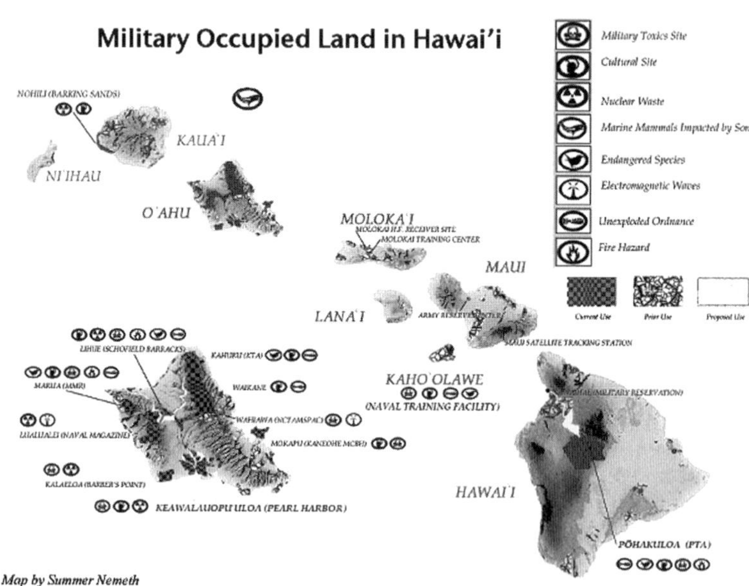


*Figure 0.1* Military Occupation and Its Impacts in Hawai'i. Created by Summer Nemeth for DMZ-Hawai'i Aloha 'Aina, 2007.

# Introduction

On 21 August 2009, a new exhibit called *Creating Hawai'i* made its debut at the Smithsonian Institution's National Museum of American History. According to museum publicity, the exhibit's purpose is to examine the gulf in perception between how Americans perceive Hawai'i, exemplified by 'aloha shirts, hula girls, surf boards, and leis,' and the reality of 'exploitation' and American 'annexation' (*Creating Hawai'i*). The gap between perception and reality is considerable: whereas the popular tourism-orientated image of Hawai'i is an idyllic paradise, the islands are also, in fact, home to one of the largest military arsenals in the world. There are 161 military installations in Hawai'i (Kajihiro, 'No Peace' 301), the largest of which are Schofield Barracks, Tripler Army Medical Center, Hickam Air Force Base, Wheeler Air Force Base, Kaneohe Bay Marine Corps Air Station, Fort Shafter Military Reservation, Fort Ruger Military Reservation, and Pearl Harbor Naval Base (Ferguson and Turnbull 1). The military controls 236,303 acres in Hawai'i, including training grounds at Pōhakuloa on the Big Island (Albertini *et al* 7), the Makua Valley on O'ahu, and Barking Sands on Kauai, which has been home, since 1966, to the US military's Pacific Missile Test Range Station. In total, the military controls almost 6 percent of the total land area in the state. On O'ahu, the most densely populated island, the military controls around 22 percent of the island's 382,148 acres (Kajihiro, 'No Peace' 272). Over 78,000 military personnel and their dependants comprise almost 7 percent of the population, and when added together with 112,000 veterans residing in Hawai'i (Schmitt, *Hawai'i Data* 1), the military-connected population comprises approximately 15 percent of Hawai'i's total population, making them a potentially powerful voting block and influential special interest group.[1]

Hawai'i is a vital American strategic possession: according to Colonel Mike Lundy, commander of the 25th Combat Aviation Brigade, Hawai'i is 'the optimal power projection platform. It gives us an unbelievable ability to project forward. That's why it will always be important to maintain a presence here' (Tsai). In other words, the islands offer the American military a mid-Pacific base of operations, from which it can enforce US foreign policy decisions and protect American economic interests in the region. Hawai'i is the home of the US Pacific Command (PACOM), whose area of responsibility 'stretches over more than 50 percent of the earth's surface from the west coast of North America to the east coast of Africa, from Alaska to Antarctica, encompassing 43 countries, 20 territories and possessions and ten US territories, 60 percent of the world's population, the world's six largest armed forces, and five of the seven worldwide US mutual defense treaties' (Kajihiro, 'No Peace' 301), making it '[p]ossibly the largest unified military operation in the world' (Albertini *et al* 2).

Contrary to popular belief, which holds that the United States has no history of colonialism, and that its overseas territories were acquired almost as an afterthought (Drinnon 307–32),[2] the militarization of Hawai'i did not occur by accident. In fact, American military involvement in Hawai'i has been evident from as early as 1826, when the USS *Dolphin* arrived in Honolulu with orders to investigate and recover debts owed to American merchants by Hawaiian *ali'i* (those of high-rank). In 1893, US Marines supported the overthrow of the Hawaiian monarchy, an event which paved the way for American annexation in 1898. Between then, and 7 December, 1941, the US fortified the islands by constructing Army camps, gun emplacements, airfields, and, of course, the iconic naval base and shipyard at Pearl Harbor. During World War Two, Hawai'i served as a base for military operations in the Pacific, as millions of men passed through the islands on their way to historic battles at Guadalcanal, Burma, Saipan, Guam, Iwo Jima, and many others. In the decades following World War Two, Hawai'i played a vital role in Cold-War conflicts in Korea and Indochina. For example, Tripler Army Medical Center treated around 65,000 casualties of the Korean conflict, and by 1960 the US Army alone had around 30,000 personnel and dependents stationed on O'ahu, and the US Navy, many more (Theimer 11–12).

In July 1960, soon after the US made Hawai'i its 50th State, *National Geographic* assured Americans that Hawaiians welcomed the US military. The magazine stated, 'The community, having gone through one Pearl Harbor, gains reassurance from the presence of these combat ready forces' (Simpich 6–7). However, islanders' views on the subject are more complicated than this. As Kyle Kajihiro, head of the Hawai'i chapter of the American Friends Service Committee, points out, some are patriotically supportive while others tolerate the military, or are indifferent. Some see the military as an 'obnoxious patron who pays the bills and puts food on the table' ('No Peace' 300), while others view US forces with the hostility of people under military rule. Native Hawaiian political activist Haunani-Kay Trask is in this latter group: she has compared the predicament of Native Hawaiians to that of 'other displaced, dislocated people, such as the Palestinians' (*Native* 18).

While no one section of the community in the islands holds a monopoly on any of these views, Native Hawaiians have a particular grievance against the US military, due to its role in taking away their status as an independent nation. Subsequent American rule did not bring with it the promised 'American Dream,' and the economic and social gap between Native Hawaiians and non-Natives remains large. On the eve of first contact with Captain James Cook in 1778, there were perhaps 800,000 to 1,500,000 natives in Hawai'i. By mid-nineteenth century, however, only 40,000 remained (Stannard, *Before* 37–45). Today, after two centuries of disease and diaspora, there are only around 10,000 people in the state who classify themselves as 'pure' Hawaiian, and a further 220,000 who are of 'mixed' Hawaiian lineage. Native Hawaiians suffer disproportionately from a variety of social ills compared to other inhabitants of the state. For example, life expectancy in Hawai'i is approximately 78 years but for Native Hawaiians it is closer to 68. Infant death rates for Native Hawaiians are double the overall state average. In fact, as Professor David Stannard of the University of Hawai'i points out, 'In every age category up to age 30 the Hawaiian death rate is never less than double, and often is triple, the equivalent general mortality rate in the islands' ('Hawaiians' 16).[3]

Native Hawaiians compose approximately one-fifth of the state's population but rent or own only one-tenth of its housing units. Over a quarter of those domiciles have reported incomes below the state's poverty line, probably because Native Hawaiians have the highest unemployment rate of all the ethnic groups in Hawai'i. Property-owning Native Hawaiians tend to live in poor quality homes in the more unfashionable neighborhoods, and are almost twice as likely to be below the state's poverty threshold than non-Native property owners. The State's education system also disadvantages Native Hawaiians. They have the highest rates of drop-out in the school system, and less than 50 percent have high school diplomas (Blaisdell 369). At the University of Hawai'i, Native Hawaiians compose less than nine percent of the student body and a Native Hawaiian earns only one out of every 200 graduate degree awards. In the criminal justice system, Native Hawaiians 'persistently rank at the bottom of virtually every index of social well-being' (18) comprising almost 40 percent of state prison inmates even though Native Hawaiians comprise only 20 percent of the state's population and are arrested only in proportion to that ratio. It is, therefore, difficult to find fault with Haunani-Kay Trask's conclusion that Hawaiians remain a 'politically subordinated group suffering all the legacies of conquest: landlessness, disastrous health, diaspora, institutionalization in the military and prisons, poor educational attainment, and confinement to the service sector of employment' ('Settlers' 3).

However, few of these details have made their way into the American consciousness: for most Americans, Hawai'i is, as the tourist board says, the land of discovery, adventure, indulgence and romance ('Hawai'i, the Islands'). Hawaiian sovereignty activist, Kekuni Blaisdell, claims there is a 'deliberate, intentional, purposeful miseducation and disinformation by the government, by the schools, and by the communications media' to hide the exploitation of Native Hawaiians (369). The same might reasonably be said of the government and media's attitude to the US military presence in the islands. Normally, the accoutrements of war would not sit comfortably with the Edenic imagery propagated by the tourist industry: in fact, they should work to shatter it. However, militarism has been so ingrained in Hawai'i that, to a large extent, its presence has come to be seen as natural and necessary. Non-natives have traditionally written the histories of Hawai'i, built its war monuments, constructed its museum exhibits, and depicted its people in Hollywood films. In these mediums, militarism is often presented as beneficial and normal, and the US military presented as a welcome, protective force, providing security and order. How and why this seemingly natural state of affairs came to be, will emerge over the course of this book.

What follows is a thematic rather than a narrative history of the US military in Hawai'i: it is, nevertheless, structured chronologically, in part, to illustrate the growth and impact of militarism in the islands, but also to enable those unfamiliar with Hawaiian history to better follow the course of events. Each chapter examines how the military's image of itself is replicated through different mediums in different eras. For instance, Chapter 1 discusses how the history of the military in Hawai'i has been shaped and imagined by museum curators and historians; Chapter 2 examines a World War One memorial; Chapter 3, military and civilian cemeteries; Chapter 4, Hollywood movies; and Chapter 5, underground and mainstream newspaper coverage of the Vietnam War era. These mediums convey information, and engage their audiences, in a variety of ways: for example, a war memorial is a permanent marker on the landscape, solid and unchanging, which provides tactile and visual cues as to how the sacrifice of our fallen warriors should be remembered. Movies encourage the temporary suspension of disbelief, entertaining audiences with visual and auditory stimuli. Museums use a variety of visual, audio, and tactile methods to persuade visitors to trust their version of history, whereas newspapers use a combination of the written word and visual images in asking their customers to trust the authority and honesty of news reporters and feature editors. Added together, they form a powerful advocacy for the benefits of militarism in the islands.

Chapter 1, 'War Stories,' is based on the premise that, in their choice of language and labels, historians do not just describe or retell the past, they also shape it. Until relatively recently, when a new wave of Native Hawaiian scholarship began to unveil Hawai'i's history from a native perspective, the dominant historical lexicon was that of the colonizer. For example, historians often use the term 'gunboat diplomacy' as a metonymy for British imperialism. However, American historians rarely use that term to describe US policy towards Hawai'i in the nineteenth century.[4] Instead, the military is presented as a positive force in Hawai'i's development into a modern state, and this is reflected in such prominent themes as 'restoring order,' 'progress,' 'creating civilization in the wilderness,' 'patrolling the frontier,' 'protecting American interests,' and 'teaching the natives American values.' This chapter exposes some of these linguistic practices, which have obscured American colonial ambitions in the Pacific, and excused the US military's role therein.

Chapter 2, 'Remembering and Forgetting,' focuses on the Waikīkī War Memorial Park and Natatorium, one of many military *lieu de mémoire* on the island of O'ahu. Situated in Kapi'olani Park, the memorial is comprised of a natatorium with a 100-meter salt water pool, a 20-foot tall entrance arch with four stone eagle sculptures, and an adjacent stone plinth featuring the names of 101 men from Hawai'i who died in the Great War (79 with American forces, and 22 with British). There is, however, considerable doubt as to the accuracy of those casualty figures, continued unease about the appropriateness of its *beaux-arts* design in a Pacific Island setting, and an ongoing debate whether to renovate the now-dilapidated natatorium or demolish it.

The memorial has been beset with problems since it opened in 1927. Although popular with locals and tourists alike, design flaws meant that seawater would not flush away or be replenished from the ocean. Before long, the water became stagnant, and a health hazard. Salt water erosion caused concrete walkways and viewing stands to crack, and the diving board tower began to rust. Periodic renovations could not solve the original design flaws, and in 1973 the City and County of Honolulu and the State of Hawai'i announced plans for its demolition. However, local people opposed the idea, formed a Natatorium Preservation Committee and eventually succeeding in getting the structure listed on the State Register of Historical Places. In 2001, the City and County of Honolulu decided to repair the Natatorium at a cost of almost $11 million. The façade was renovated, but the interior remained unsafe and unusable.

Much of the debate has been characterized by patriotic feelings about the need to remember Hawai'i's war dead, or by economic pragmatists who point to the memorial's cost.[5] Thus far, however, the debate has been uninformed by detailed historical analysis. War memorials do not simply recollect past sacrifices: they also shape how conflicts are remembered, and provide instruction about future conduct. It took nine years from when the memorial was first proposed in 1919, to its inauguration in 1927. During this time, competing groups fought for control over the project, including where it would be situated, and what form it would take. Like the current discussions, patriotic groups wanted no expense spared in honoring the dead, while others fretted over how the memorial would be funded. Hawai'i was, however, a much different place in the first two decades of the twentieth century. American patriots, concerned about the islands' inter-racial make-up, championed the '100% Americanism' of its inhabitants. The Waikīkī War Memorial Park and Natatorium is the product of this patriotic campaign.

Chapter 3, 'Unknown Soldiers,' builds on the previous chapter by extending the discussion of remembrance and memorialization to Hawai'i's burial sites. In its scale and design, the Waikīkī War Memorial Park and Natatorium offers a narrowly patriotic way of remembering Hawai'i's Great War dead. This simple story of sacrifice and duty is replicated in military graveyards on O'ahu, for example at the Post Cemetery, Schofield Barracks, and the National Memorial Cemetery of the Pacific (Punchbowl National Cemetery). Military and national burial rituals impose conformity and order on the dead, creating a sense of common purpose and shared sacrifice. In contrast, remembrance and memorialization at civilian cemeteries can offer a less ordered, and more personal memory of the dead. The headstones and markers, which dot the cemetery landscape, are engraved with information about the dead. Sometimes, they provide only basic, factual information; at other times, however, more personal messages offer insight to a culture's belief system and, on occasion, a family's personal view of the conflict in which their loved ones died. This chapter unearths the forgotten stories of Hawai'i's Great War dead, and examines the differences between private and public remembrance of these men, and that war.

Chapter 4, 'Hooray For Haolewood?,' focuses on cinematic representations of Hawai'i, and situates the islands in what writer Tom Engelhardt calls the 'American war story,' a cycle of sneak attack, retributive military victory, and a period of identity crisis. Movies about Hawai'i can be divided into three categories: (1) Pre-Pearl Harbor, (2) 1942–1955, (3) 1955–1973. In the first period, Hollywood movies emphasize the otherness of Hawai'i and provide stereotypical and racist views of Hawaiians. In period two, Hollywood films portray Hawai'i as part of America, to emphasize the fact that the Japanese attacked 'America,' not just a US possession. In period three, films about Hawai'i utilize images of the melting pot and 'rainbow state' as a paradigm and lesson for American race relations on the US mainland.

Chapter 5 is a comparative analysis of mainstream and underground Hawai'i newspaper coverage of the Vietnam War era. The mainstream press in Hawai'i is represented by the *Honolulu Advertiser* and *Honolulu Star-Bulletin*, and the underground press by publications such as *Carrion Crow*, *Roach*, *Hawaii Free People's Press*, *Gathering Place*, *Liberated Barracks*, and *Another Voice*. The mainstream media in Hawai'i has a comfortable and sympathetic relationship with the US military, and this is illustrated by mainstream newspaper coverage of the Vietnam War, which was supportive of the official reasons for going to war, and often acted as a conduit for the official Washington perspective. Contrary to the myth that Hawai'i was a docile home to US troops in the 1960s, analysis of underground newspapers published during this time reveals a vocal anti-war movement, whose activities often went unnoticed by the mainstream press.

# 1
# War Stories: A Militarized History of Hawai'i

Mention the United States military in Hawai'i and no doubt the first thing that comes to mind is the 'date which will live in infamy,' 7 December 1941, when the Imperial Japanese Navy launched a devastating attack on US military facilities in the Territory of Hawai'i, causing America's entry into World War Two. Daniel Martinez, a historian at the USS *Arizona* Memorial, refers to the attack as a life-changing event '[f]or the people of Hawaii, the United States and the world' (White 512). This was such a significant moment in American history that it tends to overshadow all other aspects of the US military presence in the Islands. Non-Natives have traditionally been privileged to write the history of Hawai'i, and in these history books, the US military is normally portrayed as a beneficial, protective presence, which provides security, order, and economic prosperity. Discordant counter-narratives are minimalized, trivialized, misrepresented or completely ignored. It is tempting to describe this sanitized version of history as a form of amnesia. However, as cultural historian Marita Sturken points out, history is not as much about forgetting the past as it is about substituting some uncomfortable narratives with more tranquil and convenient ones:

> American political culture is often portrayed as one of amnesia, and the media seem complicit in the public's apparent ease in forgetting important political facts and events. However ... American culture is not amnesiac but rather replete with memory, [and] cultural memory is a central aspect of how American culture functions and how the nation is defined. The 'culture of amnesia' actually involves the generation of memory in new forms (*Tangled* 2).

This 'memory in new forms' is crafted and shaped by carefully chosen rhetorical devices. For example, the synecdoche 'gunboat diplomacy' has specific connotations about the use of military might to enforce the policies of imperial powers. Historians Anthony Preston and John Major define gunboat diplomacy as 'the use of warships in peacetime to further a nation's diplomatic and political aims.' By this definition, the authors claim, 'the whole of the nineteenth century was an age of gunboat diplomacy' (3). The term can be found in numerous texts about British and French foreign policy in the Pacific and it is, indeed a perfectly apt description of, for example, French naval Captain C.P.T. Laplace's threats to bombard Honolulu in 1839 (Daws 103) or of the tactics of the Royal Navy's Captain Lord George Paulet, who annexed Hawai'i to Great Britain in 1843 (Daws 112–18). However, in the histories of the United States military in Hawai'i, the term 'gunboat diplomacy' is notably absent. This is just one of many lacunae found in what philosopher Mikhail Bakhtin calls the 'unitary language' of power. As Bakhtin explains it,

> [u]nitary language constitutes the theoretical expression of the historical processes of linguistic unification and centralization, an expression of the centripetal forces of language. A unitary language is not something given but is always in essence posited — and at every moment of its linguistic life it is opposed to the realities of heteroglossia [a diversity of languages and voices] (270).

So powerful is the centripetal force of unitary language that it has the ability to dismiss dissenting voices. It imposes limits on what can, and cannot be said, because it possesses an internal monologic that has, according to author Peter Good, 'little need to enter into a dialogue with any language other than its own' (38).

As University of Hawai'i professors Kathy Ferguson and Phyllis Turnbull have revealed, there are two specific discourses that, together, comprise the unitary language often used in historical analyses of the US military in Hawai'i — 'war talk' and the 'discourse of national security' (78), both of which act to legitimize the militarization of the Islands. In the discourse of war, common recurring themes and images are of loyalty, victory, sacrifice, and brotherly masculinity. This is a world of duty and honor, where the dead are 'heroes' and not 'victims or killers or dupes or confused young men with mixed motives' (91). However, while talk of war may be attractive for a time, it inevitably leads to talk of peace, and those who do not accept that goal may be ostracized or stigmatized as belligerent, aggressive, irrational war mongers. This is when the discourse of national security is often employed, because it has no opposing dichotomy such as war/peace (there is not, for example, a goal of 'national insecurity'). The internal logic of this discourse is always that more national security is desirable, and that anyone who opposes this logic is irrational, weak, and possibly a threat. In the discourse of national security, common recurring themes and images are vigilance, strategic goals, maintaining order and stability, and restoring predictability in an unpredictable world. All of these practices are made to seem rational, because their opposite values — lack-of-preparedness, disorder, and instability — are pejorative and undesirable. These dual discourses combine to form a single self-referential, monoglossic language of discussion 'that acknowledges only itself and the object of its investigation carries the danger that the subject's voice is devalued, reduced, muffled, made silent' (Good 92).

Such a unitary language dominates the discussion of the US military presence in Hawai'i, overshadowing (but never quite silencing) the narrative-challenging counter-histories of Native Hawaiian sovereignty activists, some of whom call the US military an occupying army, instead of the more familiar patriotic terminology. According to political activist Haunani-Kay Trask, for example, their presence is an 'American military invasion,' which has led to a military 'occupation of Hawai'i' (*Native* 31). Such anti-colonial terminology is outside the discourses of war and national security, and, as a result, is often made to seem irrational (or in the case of women, hysterical) and dangerous, because such terminology opposes the hegemonic unitary language which posits that the US military is a welcome and necessary force in the Islands. Edward Said has written extensively on the connection between systems of power and the hegemonic discourses that produce and sustain them. He states,

> stories are at the heart of what explorers and novelists say about strange regions of the world; they also become the method colonized people use to assert their own identity and the existence of their own history. The main battle in imperialism is over land, of course, but when it came to who owned the land, who had the right to settle and work on it, who kept it going, who won it back, and who now plans its future — these issues were reflected, contested, and even for a time decided in narrative. The power to narrate, or to block other narratives from forming and emerging, is very important to culture and imperialism, and constitutes one of the main connections between them (xii–xiii).

In the history (or histories) of the US military in Hawai'i, opposing dualities such as them/us, safe/dangerous, benevolent/cruel, innocent/

suspicious, brave/cowardly, fanatical/reasonable, diabolic/humane and uncivilized/civilized are utilized to frame the discussion and restrict what can and cannot be said about the military (Ferguson and Turnbull 48). Careful exegesis of such stories reveals that such narratives perpetuate a monoglossic, self-referential, and sanitized version of history, which suggests militarization is a rational, honorable, sensible, and necessary state of affairs.

This chapter, which covers the time period of 1778 to 1898, focuses on two sources of history which utilize the afore-mentioned unitary language of power, the book *Pearl: the History of the United States Navy at Pearl Harbor*, co-authored by Lyndall and Daniel Landauer, and the Army Museum of Hawaii at Fort DeRussy, which occupies 38,500 square feet of prime real estate at the entrance to Waikīkī, and attracts around 100,000 visitors per annum. The Landauers' account of Hawaiian history and the US Navy's role therein, has been singled out for analysis because it is typical of historical accounts of the US military's role in Hawai'i in utilizing a unitary language which asks readers to identify with military values and reject the arguments of those who oppose the military presence in Hawai'i. The authors' goal in *Pearl* is, they state, 'to follow two streams of history: that of the People of Hawaii and that of the United States Navy' (intro). However, what *Pearl* primarily does is militarize the history of Hawai'i and its people, creating contentious reasons why Hawai'i 'needs' the US military, as it attempts to silence counter narratives. The Army Museum merits critical scrutiny due to its physical and psychological presence. Its location, in one of Honolulu's foremost tourist districts, is a reminder to tourists and locals that the freedom they enjoy is won by military sacrifice. Inside, the museum tells a version of history dedicated to the preservation and promotion of American militarism. Like *Pearl*, the language employed by the museum asks visitors to identify with military values and oppose those who disagree with military strategy.

## 'The History of the United States Navy at Pearl Harbor'

Lyndall B. Landauer holds a doctorate in history, and has taught as an associate professor of history at Lake Tahoe Community College; Donald A. Landauer (1927–2006) was a retired US Navy sailor, a member of the Lake Tahoe Historical Society, and taught business classes to sailors on US Navy ships ('Obituary'). In their collaborative book, *Pearl: The History of the United States Navy at Pearl Harbor* (1999), the authors claim to write *the* history of Hawai'i, the US Navy, and the history of

Pearl Harbor. It is evident this triple task was beyond them, and is, perhaps, beyond anyone's ability. All histories are contentious but one should be wary of a book that purports to tell *the* history of any place or people since 'what happened' is often a matter of perspective.

The book's purpose is, ostensibly, to put the US military operations in Hawai'i into historical context. In doing so, however, the Landauers wander into a minefield of scholarly controversy. They acknowledge, for example, the debate that has occurred about the size of Hawai'i's pre-1778 population, which has been estimated as low as 200,000 (the Landauers quote a figure of 300,000) and as high as 1,000,000 (Dye 1–2), saying that the figures they quote 'are estimates and vary widely among historians' (5). However, the Landauers either ignore, or are perhaps unaware, of the compelling evidence presented in historian David Stannard's monograph, *Before the Horror*, of a population of *at least* 800,000. Stannard's re-appraisal of pre-1778 population figures has, to a large extent, been accepted by anthropologists and historians. For example, Patrick V. Kirch has judged Stannard's arguments as 'reasonable and well-documented' (395), and Ann F. Ramenofsky has described his analysis as 'elegant' (Heckathorn). Reviews by Robert V. Wells in the *Journal of Interdisciplinary History*, and Char Miller in *American Ethnologist* were supportive of Stannard's revised figures. While not totally accepting Stannard's highest possible population estimate, Andrew F. Bushnell nevertheless accepts that the population must have been 400,000 to 500,000 — at least double the commonly-accepted estimate used until Stannard's work appeared. Native Hawaiians scholar Lilikalā Kame'eleihiwa supports a figure of at least one million (81), as does Haunani-Kay Trask (*Native* 8).

*Before the Horror* was published in 1989, and Stannard issued a challenge to future scholars, 'If ... the population of Hawai'i was less than 800,000 in 1778 it is now incumbent on those who would hold this position to demonstrate — *in specific scholarly detail* — precisely how it came to be less than what all the evidence suggests is a minimum' (80). It is this 'scholarly detail' that *Pearl* lacks. Instead, the Landauers remain non-committal about pre-1778 population, thus leaving open the possibility of a figure as low as 200,000. By the turn of the twentieth century, Western diseases had reduced the native population to only 40,000 (MacCaughey 41; Trask, *Native* 6). Assuming that the population would have remained stable if there had been no contact with Westerners, the population loss was either 160,000 (if we accept that the pre-1778 population was as low as 200,000), or 960,000 (if the population was as high as one million). The latter figure suggests a staggering, but entirely plausible, population loss of around 96 percent. In allowing for the possibility of a lower pre-1778 population, therefore, the Landauers reduce the probable extent of population loss and thus minimize the 'horror' natives suffered due to imported diseases, for which they had no immunity. In so doing, the authors condition the reader to accept a version of history which obscures the full impact of Hawai'i's colonization.

*Pearl* is a chronological history, covering the period from the first American military intervention in Hawai'i in 1794, when John Kendrick, captain of an armed merchant ship, helped Kalanikupule, an *ali'i nui* (chief of high status) on O'ahu, to defeat his enemy Kaeokulani (28), through to the modern era of nuclear powered submarines and missile test ranges. Early in the book, the authors create an external threat to Hawai'i, stating: 'It has been said that if Kamehameha had not united these islands under his strong rule when he did, they would have been swiftly grabbed and partitioned by foreign, mainly European nations or individuals' (20). Hawaiian scholar Noenoe Silva has, however, a different interpretation of events: 'Kamehameha uniting the islands was not about fear of American or English onslaught; Hawaiians were working out their own stuff in their own world' (Kelly A8). There is, in fact, no evidence that a united Hawai'i under Kamehameha's rule had any effect on the Pacific strategies of European powers such as England and France. Moreover, the notable exclusion of Americans from the authors' list of dangerous 'foreigners' deflects attention away from American ambitions in the Pacific. Instead, the authors paint a picture of an external threat to Hawai'i, that required a decisive military response by a powerful leader. Such imagery foreshadows and acts as a template for the US military's self-stated role in the islands.

While the authors praise Kamehameha for his strong leadership in uniting Hawai'i, they view many native customs as uncivilized and barbaric. For example, they believe the *kapu* laws upheld by Kamehameha were 'onerous and brutal' (22), 'oppressive [and] rigid,' and were applied in an 'arbitrary' way (50). Having thus established the barbarity of the Hawaiian system of justice, the authors then defend its supposed cruelty as 'the only law that existed in the islands and it curbed, if not controlled, the worst abuse that human beings bring on each other' (47). The only language the natives understood, according to this narrative, is brutality and violence. In listing the many ways that violators of *kapu* were killed, such as clubbing, strangulation or burial alive, the Landauers suggest that Hawai'i was a land in savage disarray, which required the order and stability the US military would later bring. The effect (if perhaps not the intention) of the authors' selective analysis of *kapu* laws is to make Hawaiian cultural practices appear brutal. However, some sense of scale and context can be gained by comparing Hawaiian laws to English criminal law in the early nineteenth century. Under English law, hundreds of minor offences were punishable by death. Strangulation at Tyburn Hill gallows was only one of a number of brutal ways in which English lawbreakers were punished. In earlier times criminals were tortured and hung, drawn, and quartered and then their heads were impaled and exhibited on a spike (Denning 36–7).

*Pearl* is written in the language of triumphant militarism. American sailors in the eighteenth and nineteenth centuries sailed in 'magnificent' or 'splendid' ships and 'triumphed' over adversity. They were acclaimed as 'the best, most accurate gunners in the world' (acclaimed by whom, we are not told) (65). American crews were 'gallant,' 'courageously sailed into danger,' and 'bravely carried the flag of the United States to all the ports of the world' (44–5). American sailors always act with the best of intentions and have impeccable morals. The Landauers' version of history is painted in broad strokes of good and bad, and they use only primary colors of red, white, and blue.

Historians using the unitary language of power frequently employ phrases such as 'imposing order' and 'bringing stability.' Order, of course, has positive connotations. Frequently, however, the noun masks policies of economic or military control. For instance, when General Leonard Wood was asked what exactly 'stability' would mean for the American colonial adventures in Cuba, he stated, 'When money can be borrowed at a reasonable rate of interest and when capital is willing to invest in the Island, a condition of stability will have been reached' (Jacobson 40). Historian Matthew Frye Jacobson notes this stability was secured 'by U.S. military might' (55). In *Pearl*, the Landauers use narratives of order and stability to justify US military interventions. For example, they insist the role of the US Navy in Honolulu was to 'assist ... local police in dealing with errant American seamen.' As a result of this 'service,' the Navy was supposedly 'respected for fair treatment and their decisions were generally popular' (80). According to the Landauers, the Navy 'settled' local disputes (81) or acted as 'arbiters' (112), and the role of the US Marines in Hawai'i was, 'quell[ing] trouble' in Honolulu and at Pearl Harbor (183). However, the authors do not cite sources to support their assertions, nor do they question the Navy's role in enforcing 'order' in a place which was not, at that time, a US possession. Many questions remain unasked: for example, what type of disorder occurred and what sort of order was subsequently imposed? There is an assumption here — made through the authors' choice of either neutral or misleading descriptors — that the US Navy was an impartial observer or fair negotiator, creating order out of the chaos of an uncivilized land. James Loewen calls this 'standard textbook rhetoric: chaos seems always to be breaking out. Other than communism "chaos" is what textbooks usually offer to explain the actions of the other side' (*Lies My* 223). In fact, as Haunanai-Kay Trask points out, 'peacekeeping was a superficial excuse for the continuing American military presence. As every US minister after the Civil War had argued, warships were needed to protect American *economic* interests' (9–10).

In military discourses of 'them' and 'us,' the 'other' tends to act barbarously, unthinkingly, and without apparent acknowledgment of the consequences of their actions. Political or nationalistic factors rarely invade military discourses about the behavior of supposedly unthinking savages. However, as there is little evidence of Native Hawaiians acting out these stereotypes in their interactions with Americans, the Landauers marshal data from other Asia-Pacific regions instead. For example, the authors describe a native attack on US sailors in Sumatra in 1832 as a 'massacre.' However, the sailors' revenge for that attack, in which 150 natives were killed, is described in a more neutral tone — the natives are 'chastised' and 'killed,' rather than massacred. The authors excuse this slaughter as being 'de rigour' [sic], which suggests that military slaughter of natives is necessary given the natives' obvious inhumanity, and also 'effective,' although the only evidence provided to support that assertion is the *post hoc ergo propter hoc* logical fallacy that no further 'unfortunate incidents occurred there' (80).

In fact, naval bombardments may not have been effective at all in influencing the outcome of disputes between natives and sailors. Historian Jane Samson questions the effectiveness of gunboat diplomacy, asserting that natives 'might acknowledge a warship's destructive potential, but they did not necessarily consider themselves either educated or defeated by it' (131). While such bombardments may not always have had the desired effect, they did, nevertheless, demonstrate the devastating effect of modern technology when used against native peoples. For instance, historian Greg Dening records that when Hawaiian warriors killed 22-year-old English astronomer William Gooch at Waimea Bay, O'ahu, in 1792, Gooch's shipmates launched indiscriminate cannon fire at the nearest available village (7–9). While their intention was to exact 'justice' for Gooch's death, they were eventually satisfied when three Hawaiians, who were probably not involved in Gooch's death, were sacrificed by *ali'i*. This suggests that revenge rather than justice was their motive. In such circumstances, notions of even-handedness or keeping order are almost irrelevant: this was reprisal, not justice, vigilantism, not order. However, in terms of the unitary language of power, which often dominates such historical writing about the military in Hawai'i, only the enemy behaves underhandedly. As Loewen puts it, '[c]ivilized war is the kind *we* fight against *them* whereas savage war is the atrocious kind they fight against us' [emphasis in original] (*Lies My* 116).

There is no clearer example of this than the Landauer's account of the early interactions between the US Navy and Native Hawaiians. For example, in January 1826, USS *Dolphin* arrived in Honolulu. It was commanded by Lieutenant John 'Mad Jack' Percival, who was under orders to investigate and recover debts alleged owed to American merchants by the *ali'i*. Percival, however, spent most of his short time in Hawai'i trying to coerce the Hawaiian monarchy and resident missionaries to revoke the *kapu* on prostitution. In this respect, Percival differed from many British Navy officers in the Pacific, who were inclined to take the side of British and Western missionaries in disputes with local business interests. As Jane Samson notes, 'even British consuls found themselves under attack by naval officers for sympathizing with British subjects rather than islanders' (5). Percival not only favored local business interests, but having already secured a native woman for himself, then demanded the *kapu* forbidding relations between native women and his crew be lifted. Percival, worked himself into a rage, and claimed the *kapu* was an insult to the honor of the United States. He threatened to shoot missionary Hiram Bingham and burn down all the missionaries' houses if his demands were not met (Smith 130–1). On Sunday, 26 February, a crowd of sailors surrounded the house of Kalanimoku, a friend of the regent, in which Bingham was preparing to hold a service. They demanded women, and smashed all the windows. Bingham made his way home, whereupon he was joined by some native supporters. When the sailors arrived, Bingham warded off blows with an umbrella. However, when one of the sailors struck the female *ali'i*, Lydia Namahana, the Hawaiians attacked and subdued them. When Lieutenant Percival and his officers eventually arrived, he locked up the ringleaders and apologized. However, when he again demanded that the *kapu* be lifted, Governor Boki relented, and boatloads of women resumed their trade with the sailors (Daws 78–80).

In most historical accounts, Percival is described as arrogant and boorish, and the encounter between the USS *Dolphin* and Native Hawaiians seen as an archetypal example of nineteenth-century gunboat diplomacy. Journalist Frank W. Gapp concludes, for example, that the natives relented, 'not only because of the violence of the sailors, but also because of the veiled threat that Mad Jack might turn his guns on the city' (*Commodore*

31). However, the Landauers ignore Percival's behavior, calling him a 'sailor's sailor,' who 'worked as hard as his crew' and 'shared wine with his men.' The authors transform Percival's faults into virtues, asserting, for example, that he had 'colossal pride' and that his 'fiery temper was legend.' Percival's actions were, according to the Landauers, a result of 'misunderstandings' and 'perceived insults' to both 'his honor' and that of the United States (70).

The authors even try to portray him as an American version of Henry II: King Henry, enraged at the Archbishop of Canterbury Thomas Beckett in a dispute over power, allegedly said, 'Will no one rid me of this turbulent priest?' Four of Henry's knights took him at his word and hacked Beckett to death. Henry claimed innocence, stating that although his words led to Beckett's death, he did not actually order it. According to the Landauers, Percival said to his men, 'the sailors would serve the missionaries right if they were to tear down their houses' (72). At a later court of inquiry, ship's master Alfred P. Edwards, testified that Percival said, 'I wish to Christ that they had murdered the damned rascal and torn his house down' (Gapp, 'Kind-Eyed' 103). The Landauers describe this as 'an offhand comment' that some sailors used as license to attack missionaries. In view of Percival's well-documented threats of retaliation, and his disrespect for regent Ka'ahumanu, whom Percival called a 'liar' and a 'damned old bitch,' it is difficult to imagine such a set of circumstances occurring in the way the Landauers describe. However, it does follow their recurring pattern of always ascribing the best possible motives to US military men.

The Landauers describe Percival's mission as a success: his assignment 'had been to rescue two marooned sailors and settle the disputes between the Hawaiian chiefs and the merchants. He did both,' the authors conclude. He was firm in dealing with 'easily manipulated island chiefs' (73) and resolute in dealing with missionaries who got in the way of hard-headed men like Percival and the western traders. According to Robert Stauffer, however, 'Percival never got very far with his orders and only managed to add to the general problems of the town' (46). Although Percival's actions led to a Navy court of inquiry, the Landauers insist, however, that '"Mad Jack" had done his duty' (74).

Later in 1826, the USS *Peacock*, commanded by Lieutenant Thomas ap Catesby Jones,[1] docked in Honolulu. Despite the presence of an American consul in Hawai'i, Jones' warship was the real power behind the enforcement of American authority. His orders were to reach agreement with *ali'i* (high-ranking Hawaiians, descended from *akua* or gods) to recover debts they allegedly owed to American merchants. Jones was a career sailor who had fought against the British on a number of occasions. He battled British smugglers and slave traders in the Gulf of Mexico, and at the Battle of Lake Borgne in December 1814 was seriously wounded and captured. Jones was a Virginian who used slave labor on his 140-acre farm. He also kept a slave as a servant aboard ship, as he was unable to dress himself due to injuries caused by the British (Gapp, *Commodore* 6–16). Jones was hostile towards the British and resented their perceived influence in Hawai'i. No doubt, also, his attitude to dark-skinned Hawaiians was colored by his views on owning slaves.

Engaging in what Mark Rifkin has called 'militarized diplomacy' (45), Jones asked the *ali'i* to take responsibility for debts owed by earlier rulers. Faced with the threat of a gunboat in the harbor, and with Jones' veiled warnings about trade agreements that the '[United States] has the will as well as the power to enforce' (Kelly M16), the *ali'i* had little choice but to agree to Jones' terms. Native Hawaiian commoners would collect sandalwood, half of which they would keep, and half pay as a tax to the *ali'i*. The *ali'i* would then use the valuable sandalwood to pay off debts. Jones also signed a 'commerce and friendship' treaty with the chiefs, what today might be called a 'most-favored nation' agreement, guaranteeing American commercial rights in the Islands (Rifkin 43). This agreement became known as the 'Convention of 1826' and was the first of its kind between the Kingdom of Hawai'i and the United States. Although it greatly favored US interests, the *ali'i* held to their part of the agreement, in part, due to the 'implicit and explicit threats of force by the US Navy' (Rifkin 43). As Marion Kelly explains,

> the very earliest experiences of the Hawaiian Nation with the sandalwood trade reveal a direct relationship between foreign investment and local indebtedness. The value of the goods received by the Hawaiian chiefs had been paid for, perhaps several times over. With sandalwood resources exhausted, recovery from debt within any foreseeable future was impossible (16).

The Landauers, however, paint a very different version of these events, and of Jones:

> he made a marvelous impression. His bearing, stature and manners bespoke the carriage and breeding of a gentleman. This impression was accurate. He was the product of an affluent family whose residence was a plantation in Virginia. His educated, intelligent manner pleased merchants. His attitude and restraint pleased the missionar-

> ies, and most of all, his quick smile and dark eyes pleased the natives...His manners were courtly, his dress impeccable, his penetrating eyes and dazzling smile marked him for Hawaiians as an *ali'i* in his own land (75).

The authors blame the 'chiefs' for their 'unwise indulgences in ships, uniforms, and other luxuries,' which were 'part of the legacy of profligacy left by Liholiho years before' (75). Rifkin suggests, however, that this debt was overstated — Hawaiians had little knowledge of western capitalism and were often hugely overcharged for goods they received — and used as an excuse to further American national interest in the islands. Rifkin suggests, for example, that Hawaiian debt was 'an interested invention by US merchants and military personnel in the 1820s rather than a measure of the excesses of Hawaiian chiefs in their accumulation of Euro-American goods' (44–5). *Pearl* makes no attempt to contextualize the Convention of 1826, and its authors ignore American threat of force. The terms of the agreements are glossed over and made to seem beneficial to both sides. However, as Robert H. Stauffer points out, these were one-sided agreements highly favorable to US interests. For example, they committed Hawaiians to provide protection for US citizens, expanded the rights of non-Hawaiian businessmen to lodge claims against Hawaiians, and circumvented local laws in favor of foreign. The result of these agreements, Stauffer insists, is that the impoverished Hawaiian government was now obligated 'to provide protection for American commercial interests,' and this left it vulnerable to further claims by foreign governments in the next decade (52).

For the most part, however, the Landauers insist that the US Navy acted as a disinterested and impartial arbiter of disputes. For example, in 1829 the USS *Vincennes*, commanded by Captain William Bolton Finch, arrived in Honolulu. According to the Landauers, the *Vincennes* sailed as if by accident into Honolulu Harbor. As if coincidentally, Captain Finch 'had in his possession' a 'complimentary, friendly, and cordial' letter from the Secretary of the Navy, Samuel Southard, which was to be given to the Hawaiian *mō'ī*. Just as Captain Jones had to play the paternal role by 'scolding' (75) the childlike *ali'i* for their inability to delay gratification, the Laundauers suggest such infantilization was an ongoing trait of the Hawaiian race. Instead of progress since the Jones encounter, Captain Finch, the authors state, was confronted with 'familiar problems' (80), namely the apparent inability of the Hawaiians to govern themselves, keep order, and pay off alleged debts to western merchants. In fact, the Hawaiians had not paid their debts as they had little understanding of what that entailed. As Rifkin has demonstrated, Hawaiians saw the exchange of goods and services as gifts between individuals, and as such, they had no conception either of debt being inherited when one *ali'i* replaced another, or of debt being owed to companies or nations (52). Unable to appreciate such cultural differences, it is little wonder that merchants sometimes denigrated Hawaiians as profligate and untrustworthy. It probably did not help, either, that in metaphors Hawaiians used to describe their relationship with westerners, they sometimes referred to themselves as 'children' (Smith 159). However, while that may, in part, explain why westerners once viewed Hawaiians as child-like, modern-day historians should not repeat the same mistakes.

Finch delivered Southard's condescendingly letter, which congratulating the *ali'i* for their progress towards civilization and Christianity. However, he then raised the issue of the allegedly outstanding sandalwood debts. Finch reminded the *ali'i*:

> The general objects of a cruising ship, or man-of-war, are the care and presentation of lives and property of our citizens, where governments do not exist for that purpose, or where governments are unmindful of their obligations ... I must urge the perfect liquidation of your debts, at the period promised; and a care not to contract others. Unless free of debt, or with ability to discharge it, no nation takes its equal place among others (Stewart 252).

The underlying threat of annexation in the last sentence was not lost on the *ali'i*. In November 1829, Finch persuaded them to accept responsibility for debts amounting to $50,000 and to 'liquidate the whole within the ensuing nine months' (Stewart 213). The ongoing enforcement by US warships of a 'militarized regime of free trade' (Rifkin 60) demonstrates that Hawaiians remained at the mercy of foreign powers, and the US was not a disinterested observer in these events, as the Landauers claim.

Those who employ the unitary language of power are often tempted to write of the inevitability of historical events, whether this is the 'natural' triumph of western values or the 'unavoidable' need for military involvement. James Loewen suggests that this is a typical pattern found in history textbooks, which present events 'so as to make them seem foreordained along a line of constant progress' (*Lies My* 172). The Landauers make tenuous, irrelevant and unimportant connections between past and present to make the US military presence in Hawai'i seem unavoidable. For example, when Governor Boki of O'ahu was invited onto the USS

*Dolphin*, Captain Percival greeted him with a gun salute and an announcement. The Landauers state, 'How the announcement was worded is not recorded, but today it would be the honorary "Oahu, arriving"' (71). This weak comparison suggests an unbroken line of military tradition, and invites readers to view history solely from a military perspective. The authors describe the course of events in Hawai'i as 'irreversible' (150), stating: 'Some observers may view these relentless changes as a series of debacles for the Hawaiian people. Others may recognize and accept the inevitable forces of change and describe the European and American influences as a better alternative to what might have been' (106). It is clear from their choice of the word 'recognize' that the authors support the latter point of view.

There is, of course, nothing inevitable about the course of historical events in Hawai'i or elsewhere. As the historian E.H. Carr once pointed out, 'Historians, like other people, sometimes fall into rhetorical language and speak of an occurrence as "inevitable" when they mean that the conjunction of factors leading one to expect it was overwhelmingly strong ... Nothing in history is inevitable except in the formal sense that, for it to have happened otherwise, the antecedent causes would have had to be different' (126). The Landauers' historical determinism avoids assigning blame and disregards consequences. Such an approach, anthropologist Sally Engle Merry insists, 'ignores the devastating consequences of the infusion of European guns, ships, and military technology into Hawaiian society' (43). Even Gavan Daws, a historian not known for his overly-sympathetic approach to Native Hawaiian concerns (Trask, *Native* 117), states, 'Without constant pressure from foreigners ... transformation [in Native Hawaiian society] would certainly not have come about so quickly' (107).

Hawai'i's attraction as a tourist destination is largely dependent on its image as a peaceful tropical paradise, so outward trappings of militarism, which suggest the opposite of peace, may be intrusive and myth-jarring. In order to overcome such discordant images, the discourse of national security is often employed. One of the most successful aspects of this practice has been in convincing Americans (and often Hawaiians themselves) that the military is needed to defend Hawai'i from foreign threats. For example, when discussing the American victory at the Battle of Midway, the Landauers state the American Navy 'had once again ... protected Hawaii from foreign interventions as it had before from the Russians, the British and the French' (277). By creating the threat of potential invasion, the Landauers provide justification for the American annexation of Hawai'i. However, while the French and the Russians may have had inchoate and vague designs on the islands at various points in the nineteenth century, the one major power with interests in the region that was likely to remove Hawaiian sovereignty was the United States.

The British, in particular, had no real interest in making Hawai'i a colonial possession. Native Hawaiians had long realized that they needed to make alliances with foreigners if they were to maintain control over their islands. In 1794, for instance, Kamehameha negotiated an alliance with Royal Navy captain, George Vancouver, that the British could have, but did not, use as an excuse for annexation. M. Paske-Smith comments that the attitude of the British 'was to encourage the different islanders to maintain their independence and to develop their lands along civilized lines' (230). Thus, when King Liholiho (Kamehameha II) traveled to Britain in 1824 his purpose was, according to Boki, to ask for British protection against *American* power:

> We have come to confirm the words which Kamehameha the First gave in charge to Vancouver, thus, 'Go back and tell King George to watch over me and my whole Kingdom. I acknowledge him as my landlord and myself as tenant; for him as superior and I as inferior. Should the foreigners of any other nation come to take possession of my lands, then let him help me.'

The British monarch replied, 'I have heard these words. I will attend to the evil without. The evils within your Kingdom it is not for me to regard, they are with yourselves' (Paske-Smith 231). Clearly the Hawaiians were negotiating their own interests, which at that time seemed to be served by an alliance with Great Britain. The Hawaiians saw they could only gain respect from westerners if they copied western ways. Thus, in his dealings with such foreigners, Kamehameha began referring to himself as a 'king' rather a *Mō'ī*, Hawaiian *ali'i* began to dress like European elites, and the Hawaiians adopted a flag that incorporated the British Union flag. [Fig. 1.1] These events contradict the Landauers' assertion that the United States 'protected' Hawai'i from British conquest. In fact, if anything, the opposite seems to be the case. In the middle of these great powers, the militarily powerless Native Hawaiians cleverly negotiated for their own interests by playing each side against each other.

That is not to say that the British were any less arrogant or condescending in their dealings than the Americans. One of the problems faced by Native Hawaiians in the nineteenth century was, as Daws points out, 'a self important foreigner could summon up a warship just by shaking his

*Figure 1.1* Flag of the Kingdom of Hawai'i over Iolani Palace, lowered to signify annexation by the United States, August 12, 1898. Hawai'i State Archives.

fist, or so it seemed to Hawaiians' (107). There was no one more self-important than the British Consul to Hawai'i, Richard Charlton. Bad tempered and haughty, he had once dragged a native behind his horse as a punishment for shooting one of Charlton's cattle, which had trespassed on and damaged the Hawaiian's property. Trouble arose when Charlton claimed in April 1840, that he had a lease dating from 1826 granting him some valuable waterfront land. When *Mō'ī* Kauikeaouli refused to give Charlton what he wanted, the Consul made veiled threats about British military action and wrote to the British Foreign Office asking for a warship be sent to enforce his claim.

After 18 months of inaction, Charlton sailed to England to press his case. His deputy Alexander Simpson was left to deal with one of Charlton's outstanding debts. He argued that Hawaiian courts had no jurisdiction in the matter and he too wrote to the British Navy asking for help. In Mexico, Admiral Sir Richard Thomas ordered the frigate HMS *Carysfort* to Honolulu to investigate. When the ship arrived on 10 February 1843, its inexperienced captain, Lord George Paulet, issued a series of demands to Kauikeaouli under threat of force. These included the recognition of Simpson as Consul, honoring Charlton's dubious lease, and a number of other directives limiting Hawai'i's rights to enforce laws against British subjects. When these demands were quickly met, Paulet and Simpson pressed for more concessions.

Paulet, though, had acted beyond his authority and against standing British orders in the Pacific, which were 'to refrain from interfering in local politics, even if requested to do so, and to demonstrate respect for indigenous society "strictly to the established Regulations & Customs of the Place" and by taking care that no offense be given "to the peculiar habits, religious ceremonies, or even to, what may appear to be the absurd prejudices of the Inhabitants"' (Samson 43). On 25 February, after seeking aid from France and America that was not forthcoming, the *Mō'ī* was forced to concede sovereignty of Hawai'i to Paulet. On 26 July, however, Sir Richard Thomas arrived in Honolulu aboard the British flagship HMS *Dublin*. Acting on delayed orders from London, Thomas restored Hawaiian sovereignty on 31 July. Suitably chagrined, Paulet left Honolulu on 23 August. However, he returned later in the year and, after being ignored by the *Mō'ī*, he had his crew fire blank shells close to Honolulu before leaving for Hilo. Paulet's actions brought discredit to the British: however, the Hawaiians rewarded Thomas for his quick restoration of sovereignty by naming of a park on Beretania (British) Street, 'Thomas Square.' The Hawaiians had a friendly, if wary, relationship with the British dating back to King Kamehameha's time. They were also aware that Hawai'i could only maintain its sovereignty by playing the great powers against each other. This incident showed, though, how essentially powerless Hawaiians were in the face of aggressive and militarily advanced westerners. However, it also shows, contrary to the assertions of the Landauers, that Britain had no strategic designs on Hawai'i, and that Hawaiians did not need to be 'protected' from Britain by the United States.

The French were another matter entirely: in September 1836, Father Arsenius Walsh, a British subject and member of a French missionary order, was ordered off the islands because the converted protestant *ali'i* wanted to halt the spread of Catholicism. Due to the coercive intervention of British Consul Charlton, and the coincidental arrival of HMS *Actaeon* and the French man-of-war *Bonité*, he was allowed to stay, but warned not to teach Catholic doctrine (Daws 94–5). On 9 July 1839, French frigate *L'Artémise*, commanded by Capt C.P.T. Laplace, arrived from Tahiti. Although the *Mō'ī* had already issued a directive that Catholics should no longer be persecuted, as Daws relates, '[w]ithout even coming ashore [Laplace] issued a "manifesto" demanding complete religious freedom for Catholics, a bond of $20,000 from the chiefs to guarantee compliance, and a salute to the French flag ... he threatened to bombard Honolulu if his terms were not met. Foreigners [except Protestant missionaries] were offered asylum aboard *L'Artémise'* (102–3). The *Mō'ī* was away, so the *ali'i* raised the cash. On 14 July, the *Mō'ī* returned and spent the next three days 'negotiating' a 'commerce and friendship' treaty with the belligerent Laplace. This treaty overturned the Hawaiian policy of total abstinence by forcing the *Mō'ī* to allow imports of French alcohol with low import duty. It also dictated that French nationals accused of crimes had to be tried by a jury handpicked by the French Consul.

This was not the last French military intervention in Hawai'i. In 1842, the warship *L'Embuscade,* commanded by Captain S. Mallet, visited the islands, and in 1846 the Captain of *La Virginie,* Admiral Ferdinand-Alphonse Hamelin, returned the $20,000 bond Laplace had collected. In 1849 Rear Admiral Leogoarant de Tromelin made a second visit to Honolulu in his flagship *La Poursuivante,* accompanied by a second ship, *Le Gassendi.* In 1846 Hawaiian foreign minister had been forced to renew the 'commerce and friendship' treaty with new French Consul Guillaume Patrice Dillon. Dillon, however, continued to make extreme demands from the Hawaiians. When Dillon explained these demands to de Tromelin, the Rear Admiral threatened to use force against the Hawaiian government. On 25 August French troops landed and proceeded to wreck the fort, free prisoners, spike cannons and destroy munitions. They ransacked the Governor's home and stole his possessions, and in the harbor; they confiscated the *Mō'ī*'s yacht. French troops were stationed at important buildings. However, the French commander backed down from opening fire on Honolulu.

The Landauers state it was a joint action 'show of force' by both the British and Americans that led to the French climb down. However, as Paske-Smith points out, it was almost entirely due to the diplomacy of British Consul Miller. In 1844, Britain asked both France and the United States to pledge 'never on any grounds, or pretext, to take possession of the Islands': the French agreed, but the Americans declined Britain's proposal (246). Miller defused the situation in 1849 by reminding the French of their non-aggression pact, and by offering asylum to the Hawaiian King in the British Consulate building. In view of Miller's actions, and the recognition by the French that any further aggression could then be seen as an act of war against Great Britain, the French backed off. De Tromelin and Dillon left Honolulu on 5 September, having accomplished little except the destruction of Hawaiian property valued at $100,000.

In spite of this, the Landauers insist that Hawai'i's sovereignty was maintained only by 'the protection of American naval forces' (101). In fact, the opposite was true: it was the United States which refused to accept Hawai'i's independent status. The United States ignored the British-French proposal to maintain Hawai'i's independence and instead insisted on maintaining a free hand in the Pacific. In December 1823, President James Monroe had warned European powers that the Americas were no longer open to European colonization, effectively declaring Central and South America as American spheres of influence. Nineteen years later, President John Tyler extended the 'Monroe Doctrine' to Hawai'i, declaring that if any nation sought 'to take possession of the islands, colonize them, and subvert the native Government,' such a policy would 'create dissatisfaction on the part of the United States' (Richardson 317). Tyler had visions of America's 'Manifest Destiny' to sweep westwards to the Pacific and beyond. Empire builders, though, require bogeymen to convince the masses of the need for military action, and to provide the emotional investment required to ensure the military is given a free hand to complete its task. Historian Lawrence Fuchs points out, for example, during the annexation crisis of 1873, 'Hawaiian planters ... sent a drumfire of rumors to friends on the mainland alleging growing British influence in the Islands and had them circulate a report in Washington concerning an alleged movement to import Hindus as plantation labor under British supervision' (20). In this way, Americans in Hawai'i attempted to create an internal and external British enemy that would require US Navy protection.

The US Navy was happy to go along with this charade. For example, Congressman Fernando Wood was in charge of the bill to implement the Hawaiian Reciprocity Treaty of 1875. When he asked Vice Admiral David D. Porter for his estimation of the situation in Hawai'i, Porter replied that the British 'have long had their eyes upon them [as] a principal outpost on our coast where they could launch forth their ships of war upon us with perfect impunity ... [T]he taking of the Fijis is but the preparatory step to occupation of Hawaii.' Echoing the sentiments of the Tyler Doctrine, Wood brayed, 'The Pacific Ocean is an American Ocean' and repeated his belief that Hawai'i was 'the future great highway between ourselves and the hundreds of millions of Asiatics who look to us for commerce, civilization, and Christianity' (Hagan 24–5). Clearly both the US Navy and US politicians regarded the Pacific in the same way the Roman Empire regarded the Mediterranean, as *mare nostrum*. In reviewing the effects of the Reciprocity Treaty, Fuchs concludes, ironically, 'Praise the British bogeyman' (21).

In the annexation and sovereignty crises that arose in the second half of the nineteenth century, *haole* residents of Hawai'i began pushing for the imposition of US territorial status for the islands. In 1854, with over 2000 US citizens residing in Hawai'i, US Commissioner David Gregg alarmed *Mō'ī* Kauikeaouli with threats of Californian pirates and land grabbers. Gregg hoped to force the *Mō'ī* to sign an annexation treaty. However, it was 'fought strenuously' by British Consul General Miller, who argued that the US was a racist, slave-owning country in which Hawaiians would be an oppressed minority (Paske-Smith 256). Of course, it is difficult to gauge just how genuine Miller's motives were: although Britain had turned against slavery in the 1790s, it was still the center of the largest empire the world had ever seen. Nevertheless, the presence of HMS *Trincomalee* and the French warship *L'Artémise* partially negated the threat from the USS *Portsmouth* and three other US warships in the Honolulu Harbor. The Landauers avoid any connotations of gunboat diplomacy by use of the passive voice style: '[s]uch a large concentration of U.S. ships *was seen as* [emphasis added] intimidating by islanders' (111), thereby suggesting that Hawaiians' mistakenly interpreted the US Navy's presence as menacing.

The sovereignty crisis was finally averted, however, only when *Mō'ī* Kauikeaouli died in December 1854, to be succeeded by his nephew, Prince Alexander Liholiho. Unlike Kauikeaouli, Alexander Liholiho and his wife Queen Emma were pro-British. Paske-Smith states, for example, that the 'reign of King Kamehameha IV [Liholiho] and Queen Emma marks a period when the influence of the English in Hawaii was as great as in the times of Vancouver' (258). In 1862, for instance, Church of England missionaries baptized Queen Emma, whereas American missionaries had always refused her that privilege. Queen Emma also helped build a branch of the Church of England in Hawai'i. Alexander Liholiho had a certain antipathy towards the United States, caused, in part, by treatment he received while travelling through the US after a successful royal visit to England and France. As historian Ruth Tabrah tells it, a 'conductor on a Pullman car had mistaken the Prince for someone's colored manservant and summarily ordered him to leave. Alexander reacted thusly: "Confounded fool! The first time I ever received such treatment, not in England or France, or anywhere else. But in this country I must be treated like a dog to come and go at the American's bidding … They have no manners, no politeness, not even common civilities"' (Tabrah 63–4). This incident is not mentioned in *Pearl*: instead, the Landauers say simply that Alexander Liholiho's anti-American sentiments 'led to serious problems,' but they do not say for whom. In fact, it was, in part, Alexander Liholiho's succession to the throne that quietened American demands for annexation for the next few years, so the 'serious problems' mentioned in

*Pearl* suggest the Landauers believe American annexation was a desirable course of events.

The authors use evasive language to avoid assigning responsibility to Americans for underhand or ignoble behavior. For example, they claim the Hawaiian League (a predominantly American group of planters and businessmen) was created 'to avoid government scandals and misadventures by taking control themselves' (127), thereby excusing the behavior of a power-hungry group of *haole* business men, who acted in secret because they knew their actions were illegal. The authors contend that the Hawaiian League wanted 'reform not revolt' — reform being a euphemism in this case for a power grab. They describe the plotters' march on the Iolani Palace as follows: 'Though they expected to have a reasonable conversation with [King Kalākaua], they made sure they had several units of the Honolulu Rifles at their backs when they arrived. This show of force may have intimidated Kalākaua and it may be one reason the resulting document is called the "Bayonet Constitution"' (127). Clarence Ashford, who was present at the encounter, states clearly however, that the threat of violence forced Kalākaua's hand: 'there was sufficient determination and force ... to persuade the dusky monarch into subjection ... little was left to the imagination of the hesitant and unwilling Sovereign as to what he might expect in the event of his refusal to comply with the demands then made upon him' (Osorio 240). Remarkably the Landauers claim the 'Reform Cabinet' (the cabinet imposed on Kalākaua by the Hawaiian League) 'knew it was imperative that order and tranquility be restored,' without mentioning it was the League that had caused the 'disorder' in the first instance.

The 'Bayonet Constitution' meant ministers were no longer responsible to the *Mō'ī*, and voting restrictions were imposed by way of property restrictions. Almost all Native Hawaiians were disenfranchised by a series of voting tests and qualifications similar to those that disenfranchised African-American voters in the American South. The Landauers are technically correct in saying Native Hawaiians were not actually disenfranchised due to their race, only that many were no longer 'eligible' because they did not own property or earn a sufficient income. However, this was the same tactic used by white supremacists in the American South to ensure ex-slaves could not vote or hold power. Although the Hawaiian League used the language of the US War of Independence, Gavan Daws explains that this was a conservative revolution of businessmen. He asks, 'where was liberty?' (251). An armed attempt to defeat the Hawaiian League began on 30 July 1889. Significantly, because they had declined to use this terminology in reference to the Hawaiian

League, the Landauers call this event a 'revolt' and those involved 'revolutionaries' (137), thus reversing the roles of legitimacy in favor of the League.[2] Under the leadership of Robert W. Wilcox, a group of armed pro-Kalākaua supporters took up positions in the grounds of Iolani Palace. The next day they opened fire on opposing government militia troops at the Opera House. After supplying the militia with 10,000 rounds of ammunition, 100 Marines from the USS *Adams* came ashore and took up positions around town (Silva 128). Wilcox's men were swiftly repelled and taken prisoner.

The 'rebellion' was over as quickly as it began, although its significance is far greater than its short duration, and certainly deserves more space in *Pearl* than the Landauers allow. It certainly cannot be dismissed as simply an 'armed riot or a pathetic revolution' (137). In fact, Wilcox's actions in support of the sovereign demonstrate the deep unpopularity of the Hawaiian League among Native Hawaiians. Furthermore, the US Navy did not intervene when the Bayonet Constitution was imposed on Kalākaua, yet swiftly moved to support it when threatened by Wilcox's men. This demonstrates complicity in the usurpation of a legally elected monarch (the only one in the world at that time), and military and political interference in the affairs of a sovereign state. By utilizing a unitary language of power, however, the Landauers attempt to dismiss such inharmonious narratives as trivial and illogical, describing Wilcox's efforts as 'pathetic' and 'harmless' (137).

In spite of his prominent role in the Hawaiian League, the Landauers insist that Sanford Dole was 'respected by Hawaiians, including many of the natives' (145), which is not only a dubious assertion but also illustrates the authors' problematic application of national or ethnic labels. When the authors want to minimize American connivance, they refer to those responsible by their national origins: for example, they point out that only two members of the 'Reform Cabinet' were American, and '[a]ll the rest [were] British' (127). However, when the authors want to legitimize American military actions, they refer to the alleged support of 'Hawaiians' when they really mean is 'haoles'. As Hawaiian historian Jonathan Osorio notes, describing those born in Hawai'i as Hawaiians, suggests a common identity between those of Hawaiian 'birth, parentage and affiliation,' but for *haole* to claim themselves Hawaiian is an 'appropriation of what had once been an exclusively native possession' (237).

In 1891, Queen Lili'uokalani became monarch on the death of Kalākaua. It quickly became apparent that she was a threat to the new ruling elite. Although she had sworn an oath to uphold the 1887

Constitution, she clearly wanted it abolished. When the new monarch began to impose her will on the legislature by appointing her own representatives, *haole* businessman Lorrin Thurston saw his chance, and organized a 'Committee of Safety' to overthrow the monarchy. With the aid of Marines from the USS *Boston* [Fig. 1.2] (they had earlier enlisted the support of its captain, G.C. Wiltse), who were used, as Clarence W. Ashford describes, 'for the purpose of overawing and disarming the forces of the Constitutional Government and of putting the Provisional Government, which was proclaimed under the protection of the American bayonets, in power,' Thurston and his supporters imposed martial law. As Marion Kelly, professor of ethnic studies at the University of Hawai'i, points out, Thurston, committed an act of treason against the Hawaiian government '[u]nder U.S. military protection' (19). The Queen was told by her advisors not to resist, and Lili'uokalani surrendered her authority to US minister John Stevens, declaring, 'I yield to the superior force of the United States of America, whose Minister Plenipotentiary, His Excellency John L. Stevens, has caused United States troops to be landed at Honolulu and declared that he would support the said Provisional Government' (Kuykendall, *Hawaiian* 603). She correctly gauged that he was behind the overthrow, but she expected it to be reversed once Washington found out exactly what had happened. Sadly for the monarch,

*Figure 1.2* USS *Boston* entering Nagasaki Harbour, Japan, 1897. Photo of John Seymour. Courtesy of Dougal Watson.

and for Hawaiian independence, this never took place. The United States declared Hawai'i a protectorate, and officially incorporated it as a territory in 1898. As Lawrence Fuchs notes, 'once again American rifles proved more effective than Hawaiian votes or legal decisions' (30) as 'military rather than popular rule prevailed' (33).

The Landauers excuse the overthrow of the popular Hawaiian Queen, however, because she had an 'imperious attitude' (140), was 'self-serving' (150), 'corrupt, inefficient and unreliable' (141). Furthermore, the authors state blandly that after the rebellion the US Navy 'was again ready to serve the legal government,' without commenting on the ethical issues raised by US support for the illegal overthrow, or 'end' (138) as they euphemistically call it, of the monarchy in Hawai'i (137). Hawai'i's annexation to the United States, is described by the authors in neutral terms, as a simple change of status in which Hawai'i was 'brought ... under the protection of the US' (138). Ironically, at this point in time, the United States was the only power in the region that Hawaiians required protection from. President Cleveland appointed James H. Blount to go to Hawai'i to report on the overthrow. Blount eventually condemned the American-backed overthrow, and recommended Lili'uokalani be restored to power. The Blount Report is generally seen as impartial and accurate. Haunanai-Kay Trask calls it 'the single most damaging document against the United States [and] the missionary descendants' (*Native* 13). However, the Landauers believe it has 'shortcomings' and is 'one-sided' (147). In view of these comments, and what has gone on before, the authors' remarks that they 'felt the anguish of the Hawaiians at the time of annexation, but could understand the reasons for it' (351) seem disingenuous and self serving.

Four decades earlier, in 1843, Captain Lord George Paulet of the British Navy acted beyond his authority and annexed the Hawaiian Islands to Great Britain. A few months later, however, the British returned sovereignty to Kauikeaouli. Queen Lili'uokalani expected the American government to do likewise. However, American strategic ambitions precluded such an altruistic act. To excuse these factors, the dominant, colonial discourse of annexation maintains that Native Hawaiians either actively welcomed or were simply uninterested in the loss of their national sovereignty. For example, the Hui Aloha 'Āina (Hawaiian Patriotic League) collected over 20,000 signatures on petitions against the annexation (Silva 151).[3] This represents over half of the estimated 40,000 native population at the time. This leads historian Ruth Tabrah to conclude that, for Native Hawaiians, annexation 'was a day of lamentation and despair' (5). The Landauers, however, question whether the petitions, 'constitutes an angry protest,' and suggest instead that Native Hawaiians welcomed annexation (157). Furthermore, they infer the militarization of the islands has been a marriage of toleration, rather than the more obvious colonizer-colonized relationship. They state, for example, 'the Hawaiian people are supportive of their neighbors, the US Navy' (349), that the Navy is a 'good neighbor to the citizens of Hawaii' (339), and that 'both the Navy and Hawaii ... benefit' from the US Navy presence at Pearl Harbor (330). To support these assumptions, the authors go to some length to list the supposed financial and economic benefits of the US military presence in Hawai'i. Their self-referential analysis refuses to acknowledge alternative viewpoints, nor do they discuss, in any depth, or with any real conviction, the many problems that the military causes, such as unaffordable housing, pollution, water and land use, to name only a few of the more obvious contentions (Kajihiro, 'No Peace').

As a work solely of military history, *Pearl* contains what one might expect — stories designed to boost military pride and to validate military actions. However, when the Landauers broaden their discussion beyond what the military thinks about itself, the weaknesses in their analysis become apparent. Page by page, they create a mythology about weak, defenseless islands, threatened by hostile Asian and European colonial powers. This myth-making portrays the United States as an innocent nation, interested only in bringing progress, democracy, and civilization to less enlightened natives. In doing so, the Landauers create a Hawai'i that the American military needs to justify its presence. Since the Hawaiian renaissance of the 1970s, scholarship about Hawai'i has been, as Paul Lyons notes, 'increasingly multi-vocal [and] contestatory' (543). Native Hawaiians have increasingly claimed ownership of their own history: new research by Hawaiian-speaking scholars allows them access to a crucial array of sources that English-only accounts lack (while my account is informed only by English language sources, it utilizes and benefits from this new scholarship). New approaches have challenged the prevailing historical accounts, in which the history of Hawai'i has been written as a triumphant story of progress towards shared goals, with the liberty to pursue those goals protected by the US military. The result has been a welcome remedy to historical writing that borders on national myth. The Landauers, however, act as if this new wave of scholarship had never broken.

## The U.S. Army Museum of Hawaii (Fort DeRussy)

The U.S. Army Museum of Hawaii is located incongruously amid the tourist beaches and hotels of Waikīkī. Its imposing physical presence in an area of Honolulu dedicated first and foremost to tourism and, therefore, the *ersatz* reproduction of Native Hawaiian culture, could be viewed from an anti-colonial perspective as a reminder of both militarism and colonial ownership. To the American tourists of Waikīkī, however, the museum, built on the site of Fort DeRussy artillery battery, is likely a welcome and familiar reminder of American power in the Pacific. This would affirm sociologist Steven Dubin's analysis that the main purpose of museums has always been 'displays of power,' the stories of 'great men, great wealth, or great deeds' including 'the spoils of war' and 'man as the crown of creation' (3). This is apparent before the visitor even enters the Army Museum, as its exterior is 'guarded' by imposing military vehicles such as a tank and an attack helicopter. [Fig. 1.3] Inside, the museum tells a version of history that is dedicated to both the preservation and promotion of American militarism. Just as colonial powers 'have clothed their acts of conquest in a rhetoric that aims both to justify and to disguise the consequences of their acts' (Wood 9), the museum uses rhetoric that justifies and excuses the US military presence in Hawai'i. In the controlled environment of the exhibition, staged as it is inside a former military base, the museum effectively silences counter-narratives by rewriting the history of the Islands as a tale of conquest and re-conquest.

*Figure 1.3* Exterior of US Army Museum. Photo by Brian Ireland.

Museums are in some ways the official depositories of history. Their versions of the past are given weight by the assumption that a museum is a permanent fixture and is thus anchored both in time and space. In a world where the past is often swept by the rough seas of revisionist history, this sense of permanence adds credence to the museums display of historical 'fact.'[4] Museums use a variety of methods of conveying information, including visual, audio, and tactile — whichever mode will best encourage visitors to respect and trust their version of history. James Mayo argues, for instance, that visitors 'expect public museums to present coordinated, accurate collections that record history, preserve objects, and further education. People trust that museum exhibits will be legitimate portrayals of history, because the museum serves the public history rather than itself' (*Landscape* 37). What happens then when that 'trust' is broken?

Historian Mike Wallace argues that history museums 'generate ... conventional ways of seeing history that justif[y] the mission of capitalists and len[d] a naturalism and inevitability to their authority.' Museums, Wallace argues, generate 'ways of not seeing' (24). In *Lies Across America: What Our Historic Sites Get Wrong*, James Loewen notes that our historic sites omit many pertinent historical facts and therefore present skewed views of historical events or characters. Contrary to the general public's view of museums as repositories of a supposedly official version of history, museum exhibits and narratives are often contentious.[5] Rarely though do museum controversies reach beyond the spheres of scholars and professionals.[6]

While the American public may assume and expect that other historical mediums such as movies, books or, to a lesser extent perhaps, television documentaries may be contentious, it does not normally expect controversy in its history museums. Museologist Duncan Cameron states, for example, '[t]he public generally accepted the idea that if it was in a museum, it was not only real, but represented a standard of excellence. If the museum said that this and that was so, then that was a statement of truth' (195). In fact, some research has shown that visitors come to historical sites not to learn but simply to be reassured. Museologists William Alderson and Shirley Low claim, for example, that 'nostalgia is one of the prime motivations' for visitors. They conclude,

> Many people have a romantic view of a past that they believe was less hurried and more relaxed than the time in which they now live. They minimize or ignore the hardships of the past ... For many visitors ... the historical site is a form of escape. Other visitors

> appear to be searching for their cultural roots and for a sense of belonging. They want to experience the sense of continuity that the site can help provide as a tangible link with the past (24).

However, museum exhibitions often generate controversy, and the most vociferous critics are often those who believe their story has been distorted or omitted from exhibition narratives. For example, indigenous peoples of the United States have contested the contents of museums, as well as other receptacles and mediums of historical and cultural knowledge. Native American writer Vine Deloria Jr. has criticized scholars who 'become very competitive with Indians, believing that because they have studied an Indian tribe they therefore know more than any of the tribal members' (65); Ward Churchill has taken issue with anthropologists, stating that their discipline 'churns out what might be best described as "disinformation specialists"' (172); and Haunani-Kay Trask has condemned the anthropologist as 'a taker and a user' (*Native* 127). The voices of indigenous peoples offer potent criticism of colonial practices. As these groups have been marginalized and their voices often silenced, they are therefore perfectly positioned to comment upon what Mike Wallace calls the 'unwritten understanding' that museums impose 'limits on what can be said, even if they have not been laid down explicitly' (123).

Formally a gun emplacement during World War Two, Fort DeRussy is an army post, now used as a rest and recreation centre for United States military personnel. The base also contained Battery Randolph, a gun emplacement built in 1911 for coastal defense purposes. Soon after World War Two, Battery Randolph was decommissioned and in the 1970s was converted by the Army into a military museum whose mission statement is: 'Collect, preserve, exhibit and interpret artefacts that reflect the history of the US Army in Hawaii and the Pacific Area, the military history of Hawaii, and the contributions made by Hawaii and Hawaii's citizens to the nation's defense' (*Operation* A25). The museum is funded by the Department of Defense, and is run by a board of trustees that includes serving and retired military officers (Ferguson and Turnbull 43). The museum does not charge an entrance fee and the latest financial figures available show that in 2007 its operating costs were $734,290 per annum (*Operation* B17), although some of this is offset by gift shop sales and a donation box, both of which are run by volunteers from the Hawaii Army Museum Society (*Operation* D19). The Department of Defense funds both the Army Museum and the Tropic Lightning Museum at Schofield Barracks. Together, their operational costs are over one million dollars per annum, representing a significant State investment in the promotion of military values in the islands (*Operation* B17).

The Department of Defense's Annual Report to Congress on the Operation and Financial Support for Military Museums states that the purpose of the Army Museum is to act as 'the steward of the Army's heritage assets' in Hawai'i. It also acts as an educator for military personnel and their dependents, and for the local community, and 'promotes *esprit de corps* for current and future generations of Soldiers' (A25). The last phrase is particularly revealing, as the Army clearly intends the museum to function as a recruitment tool. Its educational intentions must, therefore, be seen in this context. Sociologist Jacques Ellul argues that if propagandists are to be successful they must address their message to both the individual and to the masses. Ellul identified two 'routes' this might take, firstly through creation of 'conditioned reflexes ... so that certain words, signs, or symbols, even certain persons or facts, provoke unfailing reactions,' and secondly by creating a mythology which 'pushes man to action precisely because it includes all that he feels is good, just, and true' (31). The Department of Defense's admission that the Army Museum is a recruitment tool is evidence that one of the museum's roles is the distribution of propaganda to the individual and the masses — a task it attempts to accomplish by following a familiar patriotic narrative that both creates and reinforces the aforementioned conditioned reflexes and myths.

The museum exhibits artefacts that, according to its mission statement, 'reflect the history of the US Army in Hawaii.' However, as Ferguson and Turnbull astutely observe, Fort DeRussy mirrors only the military's understanding of itself. The museum accomplishes this primarily by creating an internal and external threat to the islands, and by rewriting the history of Hawai'i as a tale of the strong conquering the weak or the unprepared. In so doing, it interprets the society around it in ways that justify the retention in the islands of a significant US military presence. For example, in the museum's darkened halls, Hawai'i is transformed into a feminized and vulnerable place. The museum is replete with images of smiling Polynesian women, who dance the hula and welcome incoming soldiers with leis and smiles. This image of a dark skinned, seductive native consigns natives to stereotypical roles of passive children or sexual objects. Since children and women need to be 'protected,' the museum creates a reason for its own existence, by producing a history of Hawai'i the US military needs in order to justify its presence in the islands.

The museum employs three full-time professional curators (*Operation* C22) who choose the artefacts that are exhibited and also give context to those artefacts by providing text and labels to help visitors interpret what they see. The curators operate in an unusual environment: as it was originally designed for use as a fortified gun emplacement, the museum is unlike many modern museums, whose designs are planned out meticulously to enable maximum utilization of available space. In contrast, the Army Museum utilizes one long corridor to tell its story, with a series of side rooms used to hold larger artefacts. The museum's mission is detailed in the first text box in this extended corridor:

> Hawaii's military heritage is richly diverse. Military institutions, events, and technology have affected Hawaii's people since ancient times with political, social, and economic impact. Our story tells of the men and machines which shaped that heritage: warriors who built a kingdom, soldiers who defended an island, citizens who served their country and sacrificed to keep it free. Hawaii's many ethnic groups share this proud heritage. Each has contributed in some way to the fabric of Hawaii's military past. This is their story, and the story of the U.S. Army in Hawaii.

By claiming that what its visitors are about to see is 'their story,' the museum tries to speak not only for the military but also for Native Hawaiians and Hawai'i's 'many ethnic groups.' The museum thereby ensures that potential counter narratives to militarism and colonialism are marginalized. This process is 'hidden in plain sight' (to use Ferguson and Turnbull's apt phrase) by the assumed authenticity of a narrative which claims to speak for everyone. However, even a brief interrogation of the museum's approach reveals its inherent weakness. For example, who are the ethnic groups and citizens the museum claims to speak for? Are they the Native Hawaiians who fought with unscrupulous foreign traders in the post-Cook era?; the local Chinese merchants attacked by US soldiers in Honolulu in 1898? (Linn 9); the 1500 Americans citizens of Japanese ancestry who were interned during World War Two? (Ng 25); the Asians and Hawaiians attacked by 500 sailors in a Honolulu race riot in 1945? (Imada 336); the Native Hawaiians opposed to the military's occupation and utilization of Kaho'olawe island as a target range? (Kajihiro, 'No Peace' 277); or the residents evicted from the Makua Valley on O'ahu so that the military could use it as a training area? (Kajihiro, 'No Peace' 278). The museum's version of citizenship omits such discordant voices: instead, its narrative conveys the message that good citizens are either in the military, or are patriotic Americans who support the military. The freedom of Native Hawaiians to control their own destiny is thus submerged by the museum's claim to speak for them but also by visitors' association of 'freedom' with the success of America's armed forces rather than with anti-imperialist or anti-colonialist narratives.

Museum Director Tom Fairfull acknowledges that there is a 'degree of friction between the army and certain parts of the local community' (Burlingame). However, he denies that the museum is an instrument of propaganda. He wants it to be 'used to support the education, training and recreation of Army personnel, and as a community resource,' and the way to accomplish this is simply to 'show the way that it was' (Ferguson and Turnbull 45). However, historical narratives are always being revised, and Fairfull's claims of authenticity are open to dispute. James Mayo, for example, notes that '[b]y presenting [only] the facts, museums avoid controversy about war, and conveying honor enables museums to legitimize their designed scenes of war' (*Landscape* 43). Many of the Army Museum's 'facts' are presented without context, and some of its terminology is problematic. A display entitled 'Sugar and Soldiers: Reciprocity Treaty Of 1876,' states, for example:

> The American Civil War, 1861–1865, stimulated Hawaii's sugar industry. Reciprocity, duty-free export of sugar to the United States, became a goal for Hawaii. In 1872, General John Schofield reported the strategic value of Pearl Harbor to U.S. interests: reciprocity in exchange for cession of Pearl Harbor seemed mutually advantageous. King David Kalakaua granted the United States use of Pearl Harbor as a naval base and thus secured Congress' approval of reciprocity on August 15, 1876. Hawaii and the United States were linked formally by military and economic issues.

The text does not state to whom Schofield reported. In fact, he was an American spy, eying up Pearl Harbor for possible American military use. His 'report,' kept secret for 20 years, recommended that Pearl Harbor be acquired in 'whatever manner possible' (Tabrah 82).

According to the exhibit text, 'Reciprocity ... became a goal for Hawaii' but what or who does 'Hawaii' represent in this narrative? Is it the Hawaiian government of the time, the *mō'ī*, the people, or, perhaps more accurately, big business interests in conjunction with the US military? In fact, the Hawai'i legislature that negotiated the Treaty was representative only of the islands' 3000 haoles, and a few wealthy natives (Tabrah 83). Native Hawaiians disputed the authority of Kalākaua, who rubber-stamped the Treaty. When Lunalilo died, a dispute arose between David Kalākaua and Queen Emma over genealogy and, therefore, over who was next in line for the throne. Kalākaua apparently won the legislative vote and Emma's supporters rioted. Foreign Affairs minister Charles Bishop and O'ahu Governor John Dominis asked for help from three docked warships, USS *Tuscarora*, USS *Portsmouth*, and HMS *Tenedos*. Some 230 American troops landed and suppressed the protest. In effect, haoles asked foreign troops to interfere in a Hawaiian Royalty dispute because they feared Queen Emma's anti-Reciprocity, pro-British stance (Kent 45). The threat of US military intervention would remain as the warships *Tuscarora*, *Portsmouth*, *Benicia*, *Lackawanna* and *Pensacola* were assigned to visit Honolulu on a continual basis from then on. Clearly Fairfull's claim to 'show the way that it was' is only tenable if information such as this is omitted from the museum's version of events.

This becomes clearer when the museum is obliged to deal with the potentially narrative-disrupting issue of annexation. An exhibit entitled 'Annexation: Pacific Strategy' states, for example:

> The United States became a world power and acquired overseas holdings as a result of the Spanish-American War. Hawaii's strategic location made it critical to the military interests of the United States. Hawaii would serve as an outpost to protect the west coast from any foreign threat. Hawaii would also serve as a coaling station and naval base to fuel the Navy's steam-powered warships. Hawaii would be a crucial link to the United States' new possessions, Guam and the Philippines, ceded by Spain, and to the economic markets of Asia. On August 12, 1898 the United States ratified the treaty of annexation offered by the government of the Republic of Hawaii. Hawaii became a territory of the United States.

The opening sentence uses passive voice, as if the United States played no part itself in 'becoming' a world power and in 'acquiring' the coyly named 'overseas holdings' (colonies). As sociologist Lawrence Levine has noted, passive voice 'helps to insulate historical figures from their own unheroic or unethical deeds' (*Lies My* 25). The museum narrative suggests that the US acquisition of overseas territories happened almost accidentally, that it was an unwilling paternal benefactor, unexpectedly tasked with the 'white man's burden' of responsibility for the native peoples of Cuba, Hawai'i, the Philippines, and Guam. It is disingenuous for the museum to refer to the 'government of the Republic of Hawaii' without explaining that this was an illegal government, which existed only because of a conspiracy and rebellion which overthrew Hawai'i's last monarch, Queen Lili'uokalani. All of this was noted in the US government's official investigation, the aforementioned Blount Report. Investigator James H. Blount concluded that the overthrow was an illegal act perpetrated by big business interests with the help of US Minister to Hawai'i, John Stevens, and US Marines. To state ambiguously that the US ratified a treaty of annexation 'offered by the government of the Republic of Hawaii' without providing the proper context results in pseudo-history that the museum can only accomplish by ignoring major and well-documented historical incidents such as the Bayonet Constitution and later overthrow of Lili'uokalani. Indeed, a booklet published in 2000 by The Hawaii Army Museum Society seems, belatedly, to acknowledge this point. It reprints all the text of the 'Annexation: Pacific Strategy' exhibit except the last two lines about the treaty 'offered by the government of the Republic of Hawaii' (Mills 16). In the museum's chronological exhibit, this missing section of Hawaiian history is hidden in plain sight by the strategic placement of a fire escape door (Ferguson and Turnbull 59).

The museum utilizes a chronological rather than thematic structure for its exhibits. One advantage of using a chronological approach to describe historical events is that it can add coherence, without the excessive repetition that is, sometimes, the result of a thematic approach. Here, though, the chronological approach tends to obscure rather than enlighten. For example, although the museum purports to tell the story of Hawai'i's military heritage, missing from this story is the nineteenth-century gunboat diplomacy of the US Navy. While the museum displays images of Hawaiian warships from that period, and also discusses later American naval actions, it omits the actions of Captain 'Mad Jack' Percival, Captain Thomas ap Catesby Jones, or the Marines from the USS *Adams* or USS *Boston*. The museum chooses carefully its narrative of continuity, as it does not want to embed the US military in Hawai'i before 'the United States ratified the treaty of annexation offered by the government of the Republic of Hawaii.' To do so would suggest, correctly, that the American military was an agent of change. However, by portraying pre-1778 and early nineteenth-century Hawaiians only in the context of warfare and conquest, the museum indicates that Hawai'i was a militarized place when westerners arrived, and thus justifies the presence of US Armed Forces as being a 'natural' progression from earlier conflicted times.

Projecting a sense of continuity is clearly a major goal of the museum. A publicity leaflet states, for example:

> A little over two hundred years ago the young warrior Kamehameha dreamed of enfolding all of the Hawaiian Islands into one great lei

> — creating a nation which could take its place among the other nations of the world. Hundreds of canoes pierced the sands of Waikiki and thousands of warriors rushed ashore to commence the attack on the defenses of Oahu. Today a museum stands on the ground that could have been the very center of the gathering. (*U.S. Army Museum*)

To emphasize this point, at the front exterior of the museum are five carved wooden figures that represent Kunuiakea or Ku, the Hawaiian god of war. [Fig. 1.4] Furthermore, each chronological exhibit of Hawaiian history in the museum's long corridor is accompanied by a comparison with events that took place in the United States. For example, the 'Sugar and Soldiers' exhibit is accompanied by the text '1876 Custer defeated at the Little Big Horn,' 'Annexation: Pacific Strategy' is accompanied by '1898 Remember the Maine! — War with Spain,' 'Hawaiian Warfare — Ancient Military Systems' is accompanied by '1492 Columbus sails to the New World,' and so on. While curators could argue that a comparative narrative is necessary if visitors are to get some sense of a world timeline, an alternative hypothesis is that the museum aims to create

*Figure 1.4* Carved wooden figures representing Kunuiakea, the god of war. Photo by Brian Ireland.

links to the United States where none previously existed. Many foreign powers had interests in Hawai'i, and the American annexation is sometimes justified by the argument that Hawai'i is better off as an American colony than, for example, under Japanese or British colonial rule. By making these textual connections between events in Hawai'i and seemingly unrelated historical events on the United States mainland, the museum seems to be retroactively and metaphorically planting an American flag to counter the one raised by Captain Cook in 1778.

Military continuity is maintained also by painting the ancestors of today's Native Hawaiians as a warlike race. The museum first displays native weapons such as sling stones and then later in that exhibit shows how the natives have become 'civilized' by appropriating and utilizing flintlock muskets. The 'Sling Stones' exhibit states, 'Before the arrival of western technology, Hawaiian warriors used slings to hurl missiles at the enemy. Range and accuracy were limited by the strength and ability of the slinger.' The text's focus on the physical attributes of Native Hawaiians, the brute strength needed to hurl the fist-sized stones exhibited,

*Figure 1.5* Sling Stones exhibit at the Army Museum of Hawaii. Photo by Brian Ireland.

is unfortunately typical of centuries of racist discussion of 'backward' races whose intellect was supposedly inferior to that of Westerners and who could only be admired for their physicality. The contrast between a supposedly stone-age civilization and the sophistication of European weaponry is underlined by the image that accompanies the 'Sling Stones' exhibit, a drawing of a primitive-looking Hawaiian. [Fig. 1.5] To the uninformed tourist, the message of the exhibit is demeaning and misleading, that Native Hawaiians were violent, Stone-Age barbarians, and the arrival of Western technology and ideas acted as a catalyst for civilization.

The exhibit entitled 'Flintlock Musket,' for example, contrasts the sophisticated technology of European warriors with the previously shown primitiveness of the natives. The text states, 'A typical firearm adopted by Hawaiians after 1775 is the British "Brown Bess" .69 caliber. Sparks from flint striking steel ignited the gunpowder primer. Accurate range for this smooth-bore muzzle loader was only about 50 yards, but the blast, fire, and smoke were terrifying.' As if to underline this superiority, the text is accompanied by a cutaway diagram of the gun, which serves to further contrast the technical design of Western warfare with that of natives who, it seems, simply picked up stones and threw them. In fact, a sling stone was probably at least as good at short range as the musket. The text suggests, however, that guns terrified Native Hawaiians, who were too primitive and superstitious to understand such advanced technology. There is, however, some evidence that Native Hawaiians quickly got over the novelty of guns. In 1778, for example, Captain Cook fired point blank into the chest of a native, but the bullet failed to penetrate the Hawaiian's heavy protective matting (Daws 20). This is hardly the awe-inspiring technology suggested by the museum.

In a display entitled 'Hawaiian Warfare: Ancient Military Systems,' the museum highlights the supposedly primitive and savage nature of natives:

> Hawaiians sailed to their islands nearly a thousand years before Columbus' time, and developed military systems. Preparations for war were elaborate. Temples were built and the gods were consulted for auspicious times to fight. Trained warriors, armed with weapons of wood, stone, sharks' teeth, and bone, deployed on open ground in dense crescent formations. Before battle was joined, sacrifices, prayers, and orations were offered to the gods. At the attack signal, the armies rushed forward, throwing spears and sling-stones to loosen the enemy's formation. They met with daggers, clubs, and fists, using brute strength

> in hand-to-hand combat. The army whose formation broke, took flight. The victors' pursuit was intense and deadly.

This description is accompanied by an engraving of a fierce-looking Hawaiian warrior. The text seems to suggest that the first thing Hawaiians did when they discovered the islands was to establish 'military systems.' The focus of the museum's gaze is on warfare and not, for example, the incredible accomplishments of ancient Hawaiians in navigation and agriculture. The reference to Hawaiian religious practices ('gods were consulted and temples were built') is off-hand and dismissive. There is no attempt to explain Hawaiian religion, and the visitor is likely to dismiss ancient Hawaiian society as heathen and barbaric. If the museum had chosen here to compare European or American events of that time period to the events taking place in Hawai'i, it could have mentioned, for example, the Euro-American destruction of Native American culture. However, only those comparisons that serve the overall narrative of 'primitive' Hawai'i are displayed. Hence, the only reference to Native Americans in the museum is at the 'Sugar and Soldiers' display where it states, '1876 Custer defeated at the Little Big Horn.' Just as Custer's death has been told in the language of 'savages' and 'massacres,' one get the impression that the museum wants to surround its American visitors with images of savage, warlike Hawaiians, as if to remind those visitors that a US military presence is still required at 'Fort Hawai'i' if such massacres are to be avoided in the future.

One of the major difficulties of claiming that the museum 'just want[s] to show the way that it was,' is the museum's interpretation of Hawaiian society. In the 'Ali'i: Ruling Chiefs' display, for example, the museum claims 'Captain Cook found a feudal society in Hawaii, like Europe of the Middle Ages.' However, in her authoritative book *Native Land and Foreign Desires*, Native Hawaiian scholar Lilikalā Kame'eleihiwa makes a compelling case that westerners tend to interpret the Hawaiian system using a western frame-of-reference, and that such comparisons between western social systems and pre-1778 Hawaiian are based on superficial similarities only. Kame'eleihiwa demonstrates the relationship Hawaiians had to their land was not feudal but, in fact, symbiotic. She states, 'Control of *'Āina* is not the same as ownership of *'Āina,* in the Western capitalist sense. In traditional Hawaiian society, *'Āina* was given from one person to another, but was never bought or sold' (51).

In theory, the *Mō'ī* was the head of a land distribution system dedicated to the welfare of all Native Hawaiians. Land was parceled out in various sizes such as *Moku* (the biggest land division) *'Okana* (an area containing several *ahupua'a*), *ahupua'a* (a triangular area of land usually running from the mountains to the sea), *'ili* (an area of land smaller again), *Mo'o'āina* (smaller than an *'ili*), *paukū'āina* (smaller again), *kīhāpai* (smaller again) and several other divisions of land such as, *ko'ele* and *hakuone* which were parcels of land cultivated by the *kama'āina* (literally, child of the land, but here it means Native Hawaiians) for the *ali'i*. Although land could be redistributed at any time at the whim of the *Mō'ī*, for example if a land owner broke a *kapu* (sacred or prohibited) law, or through *Kū* (war) or *Lono* (marriage/love), the main division or perhaps sharing of land took place at the *kālai'āina*, the distribution of land at the death of a *Mō'ī*. Kame'eleihiwa makes it clear that the *Mō'ī* and *ali'i* did not decide who should own the land but instead who would be its guardian, and who would best use it (that is, who had the most *mana* or power) for the benefit of all Hawaiians. It was not only *pono* for the *Mō'ī* to be generous with his gifts of land, it was also sensible. For example, if a series of natural disasters happened in the islands, this could be used as a weapon against an unpopular *Mō'ī*. If he was not *pono* he could be removed.

There was, therefore, an amount of give and take in the relationship between the rulers and their people. For example, in the time of Liholiho the system for distribution of lands was in flux, partially resembling a Western capitalist system in that the large amounts of land were now in the hands of the *ali'i* without any input from the *Mō'ī*.[7] Because Liholiho had few lands to distribute, he could not be generous and could not gain *mana*. Kame'eleihiwa claims these factors 'further undermined his ability to be *pono*' (84). In this respect, Hawai'i was not a feudal society as many historians, military and otherwise, have maintained. In feudal societies it was impossible — short of rebellion — for a peasant living on land owned by a noble to seek redress for grievances. In fact, the closest Hawai'i came to feudalism was after the *Māhele*, when the 'Big Five' owned most of the land and wealth, and Native Hawaiians, and other disenfranchised non-westerners, were valued only for their labor. As Lawrence Fuchs points out, in this period Hawai'i resembled 'the post-Civil War South, with a small and powerful oligarchy in control of economic and social prerequisites, and large masses of dark-skinned laborers whose direct contact with Caucasians was limited to working under *haole* overseers in the field' (22).

The issue of whether or not Hawaiian society used to be feudal is not simply some ivory tower academic debate. Instead, it is a way of thinking that continues to pigeonhole pre-1778 Hawaiians as culturally less advanced than Europeans or Americans, and also suggests that the extant capitalist economic system, which is European in origin, is somehow a natural progression from earlier feudal times. Haunani-Kay Trask berates historians for 'characterizing our chiefs as feudal landlords and our people as serfs' as being 'malevolent in design.' This invention 'degrade[s] a successful system of shared land use' and transforms 'a spiritually based, self-sufficient economic system of land use and occupancy into an oppressive, medieval European practice of divine right ownership' (*Native* 115). The museum continues this 'malevolent design' by painting Native Hawaiian *ali'i* as dictatorial tyrants who conscripted their serf-like 'tenants' into military service against their will:

> Ali'i, powerful warrior chiefs, controlled the islands through heredity and kapu, a rigorous system of socio-religious rules. Wars were fought for land, wealth, and power. The ali'i required military service from the tenants on their land, and trained them regularly in the arts of war. Powerful ali'i mustered armies of several thousand men: alliances added more. There was a constant struggle among the rival chiefs and kings for advantage and dominance.

In case the point is missed, the *ali'i* are made comparable to King George III by a reminder that, as the events above played out, in the United States the 'U.S. Army [was] born in Boston.' Further references to 'chiefs' and 'kings' are misleading in that they impose European cultural labels on a society that was very different to feudal Europe. In addition, the museum cannot resist comparing Kamehameha with George Washington in a display entitled 'The Rise Of Kamehameha The Great.' Although there are no obvious connections between the two men beyond superficial comparisons of them as 'nation founders,' the exhibit creates one. Visitors are asked to contrast America's greatest hero and military strategist — '1789 Washington inaugurated as President' — with 'King' Kamehameha, whose victory, we are told, was ensured only by a stroke of good luck 'when Keoua's army, marching past Kilauea volcano, was decimated by a timely eruption.'

One of the more prevalent tactics of military discourse is to designate an area in need of protection in order to justify military intervention. Hawaiians, of course, had every reason to fear foreign intervention in their affairs. However, the museum incorporates Hawaiian fears of foreign influence with the fears of the United States that the French, British, or Japanese would establish a colony in Hawai'i. The museum labels the French, British, and Japanese as foreign, but declines to include the

United States in that category. Its description of Honolulu Fort is, therefore, somewhat misleading:

> As a statement of independence for the Hawaiian monarchy, Kamehameha directed the construction of a fort to protect Honolulu Harbor and symbolize his strength. Honolulu Fort, was built of coral blocks, completed in 1817, and mounted forty canons of various size, to deter foreigners, English, French, and Russian, from attempting to seize control of the island. It remained a viable fort until 1857 and served as a military garrison, police station and a prison. Honolulu Fort foreshadowed the Coast Artillery of the U.S. Army in the defense of O'ahu.

A color diagram of the fort, surrounded by grass huts, accompanies this text. While European ships are also shown, the large ship in the foreground flies the Stars and Stripes flag of the US Navy. Punchbowl Fort is shown in the background. Both forts are shown out of proportion to their actual size, as if to exaggerate the threat faced from European powers. The final sentence imposes a fake continuity between past and present military usage: by the time the Coast Artillery of the US Army was plying its trade, Hawai'i was a colony of the United States.

Despite its air of disinterested authenticity, the museum is under the same pressure to draw in visitors as other tourist attractions in Hawai'i. Mayo notes that commercially minded museums such as this 'must have a legitimate appearance to attract customers. Such museums must be located near historic sites not only to capture the attention of those who wish to visit an actual place associated with a war but also to attempt to legitimize their own existence' (*Landscape* 47). The Army Museum attempts to make this connection by reminding its visitors on a publicity leaflet entitled *The U.S. Army Museum of Hawaii: A Most Unusual Glimpse into the Past* it was ON THIS VERY BEACH [sic] that Kamehameha and his warriors arrived 200 years ago. The title of this leaflet is worth noting: there is nothing too 'unusual' about the museum except, perhaps, that it is located in a disused gun battery. The leaflet is obviously designed to pique the curiosity of visiting tourists in the same way that 'unusual' freak shows or displays of death attract those with a morbid disposition.

To be successful, a museum must know what its visitors expect from it. Edward Relph asserts that 'for many people the purpose of travel is less to experience unique and different places than to collect those places' (Mayo, *Landscape* 46). The museum therefore attempts to create what it calls a 'you were there' experience to cater to these tourists (*U.S. Army*

*Museum*). This authenticity includes actual weapons and documents but also miniatures of ships and a model of Battery Randolph. Mayo notes that in such scenes, 'tourists are expected to accept that the quality of toy soldiers is equivalent to authentic history' (*Landscape* 48). Because Hawai'i is a tourist-driven economy, and the number of tourists fluctuates depending on national economic trends, the museum also needs to attract local residents. Visitor numbers have, in fact, fallen from 140,000 annually in 1999 (Ferguson and Turnbull 44) to 100,000 by 2001 (Ting 50). According to Peter Schall, senior vice president and managing director of the Hilton Hawaiian Village, and a financial contributor to the museum, 'It's very important for the people in the community to show their appreciation to the military and to support them because, after all, they are very generous and very loyal' (Ting 50). For his services, the Hawaii Army Museum Society rewarded Schall with an *Ihe* award, which is 'given to the person who supports the military' and who is 'alert and concerned about his people' (Ting 50).

The Army Museum's exhibits of the pre-1778 to 1898 period in Hawaiian history are, to use Mike Wallace's phrase, 'inescapably political' (122). The museum mixes pseudo-history and entertainment with propaganda and commercialism. James Mayo claims military museums that cater to tourists are 'inauthentic experiences of war memory. Facts of battle may be told, but it is dramatized history without the intricacies of real events. These places develop and fine-tune their acts according to what the public will buy. They are parasites of authentic landscapes and have the atmosphere of a circus sideshow rather than a museum of authentic artefacts' (*Landscape* 49). The Army Museum tries to be all things for all people: it wants to lionize the US Army in Hawai'i. However, because that military narrative may appear out of place on a supposed 'island paradise,' the museum also wants to minimize the impact of American militarism by recounting Native Hawaiian military displays. After all, militarism seems natural if an area is designated as hostile, fought-over, savage, and vulnerable to attack. The museum claims to speak for everyone — Hawai'i's 'warriors ... soldiers [and] citizens.' In doing so, it silences counter narratives and justifies American militarism. Military museums need to reach a wide audience: they do not want to appeal only to aficionados — 'button collectors and rivet counters' (Ferguson and Turnbull 45). In imposing a military interpretation of events on non-military affairs, however, the danger is that militarism, rather than peace and democracy, is seen as the natural state of affairs. Mayo notes, for example, that in military museums, 'War is not questioned, and it is often treated as inevitable' (*Landscape* 43). The Army Museum makes the

American military presence in Hawai'i seem not only inevitable, but also necessary, and fun for all the family.

## Conclusion

Military versions of history are often self-referential to the point that they reflect only a militarized view of the world. They create a climate wherein a military presence is deemed necessary for 'protection' or 'keeping order.' Counter-narratives, or uncomfortable historical events that threaten military discourses of protection and order, are either ignored or glossed over. The Army Museum of Hawaii overlooks American gunboat diplomacy in the nineteenth century, for example, and Landauer and Landauer's *Pearl* maintains a pretence that the British, French, Russians and Japanese are foreign to Hawai'i, while Americans, somehow, have an innate affinity for the islands, and justly deserve stewardship over them. *Pearl* and the Army Museum employ a self-referential unitary language, in which the construction of a solely American national narrative subsumes or appropriates Native Hawaiian cultural difference. Alternative narratives can only be exposed when historians challenge these misleading and expedient accounts of the US military in Hawai'i.

# 2
# Remembering and Forgetting at Waikīkī's Great War Memorial

On the western slope of Diamond Head, commanding a majestic view East towards Waikīkī, Honolulu, and further towards Pearl Harbor, there once stood a Native Hawaiian structure known as *Papa'Ena'Ena Heiau*. Clearly visible from nearby Waikīkī village, the *heiau* or place of worship measured 130 feet in length and 70 feet in width. It consisted of a *mana* (supernatural or divine power) house approximately 50 feet long; an oven house (*hale umu*); a drum house (*hale pahu*); a *waiea* or spiritual house; an *anu'u* or tower; a *lele* (altar) and 12 large images. The *heiau* was bordered by a rectangular wooden fence approximately six to eight feet tall with an eight-foot wide base which narrowed to three feet at its apex. On the western side of the *heiau* there were three small terraces, on the highest of which was planted five *kou* trees at regular distances from each other. The *heiau* was the center point of an area of land considered sacred or spiritual to Native Hawaiians, which may have stretched across what is now Kapi'olani Park as far as to the Kupalaha *heiau* situated near the present day intersection of Kalakaua and Monsarrat Avenues.

It is likely that the *heiau* was built in 1783 by Kahekili, the *mō'ī* or ruler of Maui, as part of a victory celebration following Kahekili's conquest of O'ahu. After Kamehameha's victory at the Battle of the Pali in 1895, Kamehameha ordered the sacrifice of the defeated *ali'i* of O'ahu at *Papa'Ena'Ena Heiau*. The *heiau* was used for sacrificial or sacred purposes for around 35 years. However, following the death of Kamehameha and the subsequent diminishment in status and practice of Hawaiian religious beliefs the *heiau* was leveled along with many of the other traditional religious *heiau* and monuments. Its ruins lay relatively undisturbed until the 1850s when the stones that comprised the *heiau* were removed to build roads in Waikīkī and walls at Queen Emma's

*Figure 2.1* The Waikīkī War Memorial Park and Natatorium. Author's personal collection.

estate. (Weyeneth 48–52, 62, 67; 'Heiau'; 'Major Heiau'; Chan and Feeser 17).

In sharp contrast to *Papa'Ena'Ena Heiau,* and nine other sacred structures in and around Kapi'olani Park, there now stands an incongruous *beaux-arts*-style, neoclassical memorial, another *lieu de mémoire,* called The Waikīkī War Memorial Park and Natatorium, which opened in 1927. [Fig. 2.1] Although it has fallen into disrepair, in its prime the memorial was an impressive structure. The swimming pool was over 100 meters long, twice the size of an Olympic pool, and the *mauka* (mountain-facing) wall was composed of an arch at least 25 feet high, flanked by two 12-foot arches each topped with four large eagle sculptures. Approximately 9800 of Hawai'i's citizens served in the US Armed Forces after America's entry into World War One in 1917 and the names of 101 of those who died are inscribed on a plaque attached to the 'Honolulu stone' situated *mauka* of the Natatorium and unveiled in 1931 (Burleigh 13). [Fig. 2.2]

There is, however, some considerable doubt as to the veracity of those casualty figures. According to the *Hawaiian Journal of History,* of the 9800 Hawai'i residents who served in World War One,

> 102 died — 14 overseas during the war, 61 in Hawai'i or North America or after the armistice, and 27 in unknown circumstances. Twenty-two of the 102 recorded deaths occurred among Island resi-

*Figure 2.2* Honolulu Stone, Waikīkī War Memorial Park and Natatorium. Photo by Brian Ireland.

> dents serving with the British. Actual battle deaths of persons in the US armed forces whose preservice residence was Hawai'i numbered six: seven others were wounded (Schmitt 172–3).

These figures are not entirely correct: 101 names are listed on the memorial not 102; eight soldiers were 'actual battle deaths,' not six. Nevertheless, these figures raise questions about the purpose of the Memorial. Since only eight Hawai'i residents died by enemy action under the US flag — the others having died of other causes before and after the war's end — the Memorial obviously exaggerates the death toll, thus magnifying the sacrifices made by 'Hawai'i's sons.'

Memorials are an important way of remembering. They are not just part of the past, they help to shape attitudes in the present and thus act as a guide for the future. Philosopher Charles L. Griswold argues that memorials are 'a species of pedagogy' that 'seeks to instruct posterity about the past and, in so doing, necessarily reaches a decision about what is worth recovering' (689). In *Lies Across America,* Loewen asks, 'Where ... do Americans learn about the past?' He argues persuasively that it is 'surely most of all from the landscape' (15). One recurring theme is the importance of memorials as a political statement. Although many memorials outwardly project discourses of 'remembering' or 'honoring,' they may also have covert and hidden meanings. Rather than simply paying tribute to the dead, the Waikīkī War Memorial actually promotes militarism. It is a triumphalist monument to the glory of war and dishonors the dead by masking the horror of mechanized trench warfare behind a pretty façade and noble but misleading words.

Furthermore, when one adds the memorial's architectural style, which is so incompatible with its Pacific Island setting, to the discrepancy between actual casualty figures and those listed by the memorial, it becomes clear that the War Memorial was built also to further the '100% Americanism' of Hawai'i. It commemorates not only those who died in World War One, but also Hawai'i's colonization by the United States. The memorial constitutes a political statement of ownership. It is a symbol of the dominance of Western culture over Polynesian, a solid, concrete and unchanging reminder that Hawai'i is a colonial possession of the United States, and a channel through which Hawai'i's American settler community can express their nationalistic pride. Patriotic groups have used the Waikīkī War Memorial Park and Natatorium to further the cause of Americanism and to glorify war as a noble and heroic sacrificial act. Conveniently forgotten in this narrative, however, are the stories of the soldiers actually named on the Memorial. Why did they enlist? How and where did they die? This chapter addresses how and why these soldiers are remembered by the Memorial and evaluates if the extant structure is either the best or only way to remember their deaths. It questions who benefits from the existing memory practices, and asks that these soldiers be remembered as individual human beings rather than as ciphers in militarized memories.

## Consolidating empire

In first two decades of the twentieth century, Hawai'i was adjusting to its new, enforced status as a US territory. This was a time of American empire building and Hawai'i acted as an important stopping-off point for US troop ships on their way to the Philippines to suppress a Filipino uprising against American rule. Indeed Hawai'i became an essential element in US military thinking about the region. In 1890, Captain Alfred Thayer Mahan of the US Navy published *The Influence of Sea Power Upon History*. He believed that whichever country controlled the sea-lanes would also lead the world economically. Mahan, who predicted war between East and West, and believed Hawai'i would be vital to US interests, said: 'Hawaii ... possesses unique importance — not from its intrinsic commercial value, but from its favorable position for maritime and military control' ('Hawaii' 39). He therefore supported a large US Navy, and fortification of American possessions in the Pacific. This became known as the Mahan Doctrine (Okihiro 17–18).

The Mahan Doctrine provided US policy makers with another reason to expand the US Navy's role in the Pacific and to begin fortifying its new colony in Hawai'i. Fort Shafter, which opened in 1907, was the first permanent US military base in Hawai'i. Evelyn Winslow, US Corps of Engineers, was assigned to O'ahu in 1908 to design and construct coastal fortifications at Diamond Head (Fort Ruger) and Waikīkī (Fort DeRussy). Fort DeRussy comprised an area of 72 acres, which was acquired by the government in a series of 12 land purchases between 1904–15. The major armament of the fort was Battery Randolph — two 14-inch guns that could shoot 'a 1560 pound projectile to a range of 14 miles' (Winslow xii). Other coastal defense guns were placed along the southern coast at Forts Armstrong, Kamehameha, and Weaver. A new infantry base was built on O'ahu to house ever growing numbers of American troops. The new base, named Schofield Barracks, would eventually become the biggest army base in the United States and is now the home of the 25th Infantry Division. The US military dredged the Pearl River and from humble beginnings as a coaling station in 1908, the site eventually became the biggest military installation in the Pacific, occupying over 1200 acres of valuable real estate adjacent to Honolulu. Pearl Harbor would become the home of the US Pacific Fleet and, to the Japanese Navy, also, of course, the biggest US military target in the Pacific. Hickam Air Force Base was completed in 1938 and Wheeler Air Force Base in 1939. Kaneohe Bay Marine Corps Air Station opened in 1939, and Barber's Point Naval Air Station, west of Pearl Harbor, was commissioned a year after the Japanese attack. Tripler Army Medical Center has occupied a commanding view from the Monalua Ridge since 1948 (Cragg).

This military build-up went hand in hand with continuing 'development' and 'Americanization' — two terms that are, in fact, almost interchangeable. Lawrence Fuchs describes Americanization as 'going to Christian churches, playing American sports, and eating apple pie; there was nearly complete accord that it did not mean labor unions, political action, and criticism of the social order in the Islands' (51). Part of this effort was connected to the 'City Beautiful' movement that was inspired by the 1893 Columbian Exposition (Mayo, *Landscape* 80). Civil War and Great War memorials provided young, inchoate cities like Honolulu, Cleveland and Indianapolis with 'way[s] to express civic improvement'

(Mayo, *Landscape* 181). However, another motive of developers was profit, mixed with ideas of civilization and progress that were specifically associated with Western notions of expansion. For example, Honolulu Harbor was dredged in 1908 to encourage further trade. A lighthouse was built at Makapuu to facilitate a new inter-island steamer, the *Mauna Kea*. Mānoa Valley became the first residential area in Hawai'i to get electric lighting. By 1910 the Nuuanu Dam and Beretania pumping stations were established to bring water to parched Honolulu (Grant, Introduction xi). Much of Waikīkī's wetlands were to be dredged to provide reclaimed land for construction. A 1920 article in the *Pacific Commercial Advertiser* outlined Territorial Governor of Hawai'i, Charles J. McCarthy's vision of the future of Honolulu:

> I have looked down on Honolulu from the hills and observed the shining rice fields, taro patches and duck ponds; and I have imagined how soon all these will be done away with, and in their place shall arise alternative, wellkept [sic] homes, the handsome mansions of the wealthy and the comfortable cottages of those who are making good livings in a prosperous country ('Actual Work').[1]

McCarthy's plans for the area were supported by notable local civic, educational, and religions organizations, many of which were also involved in the plans for the Waikīkī War Memorial and Natatorium. ('Governor's Plan').[2]

From the late 1800s to the mid-1900s the 'Big Five,' a consortium of business corporations comprised of Alexander & Baldwin, Amfac (American Factors), Castle & Cooke, C. Brewer & Co. and Theo. H. Davies & Co., controlled most of the economic activity in the Islands, in areas such as banking, insurance, the construction industry, shipping, large-scale agriculture, and wholesale and retail trade.[3] The founders of these companies had made their fortunes initially in the sugar industry. In the main, they were of European or American descent, although some married into Native Hawaiian nobility. They considered themselves *kama'āina* — children of the land — different due to their wealth and class from haoles outside their exclusive social group.

Sugar is a labor-intensive crop so sugar planters recruited foreign workers from Japan China, the Philippines and Korea to work the land, in the process, permanently altering Hawai'i's ethnic make-up. In 1872, Native Hawaiians constituted nearly 83 percent of the plantation work force. However, by 1882, Chinese immigrants composed the largest group at 49 percent. They were replaced as the largest group in 1890 by Japanese workers who constituted 42 percent of the plantation work force. However, by 1922 it was Filipinos who comprised the highest percentage of plantation workers at 41 percent (Okihiro 59). Sugar bosses used this diversity as a method of control: one stated, 'We lay great stress on the necessity of having our labor mixed. By employing different nationalities, there is less danger of collusion among laborers, and the employer, on the whole, secures better discipline' (Kuykendall, *Hawaiian* 147). This policy worked: there are few instances of workers from different ethnic groups acting in concert for better wages or conditions. However, there was also very little inter-racial strife among these new immigrants to the Islands and the resident *haole* community. Partly this was due to the rigid system of social, political and economic control exercised by the elite. However, it seems also that non-white immigrants in Hawai'i prospered to an extent inconceivable in the continental United States. Historian Ronald Takaki notes, for example, that the Chinese suffered more racial discrimination and violence in California than they did in Hawai'i. Takaki attributes this to demographics: in California, the Chinese were a minority among whites, with whom they were in competition for jobs. In Hawai'i, however, whites were a minority without a 'predominantly white society to preserve or defend' (40). Furthermore, non-whites in Hawai'i, were in competition with each other for jobs, not with the small number of *haole* laborers, and certainly not with the *haole* elite.

This situation changed with increased militarization in the early years of the twentieth century. The arrival of tens of thousands of US military personnel and their families — many of them from America's southern states, where the doctrine of white supremacy reigned — created not just the usual friction that such an influx of young men causes with locals, but also a level of racial hostility previously unknown in Hawai'i. These *malihini* (newcomers) were inclined to view Native Hawaiians according to American racial classifications, that is, they equated the dark-skinned natives with the subordinate and supposedly racially inferior 'niggers' they were already familiar with (Daws 319). They knew little of Hawai'i or Hawaiians, and what little information they had gleaned from press reports only supported their racist perspective. For example, an American political cartoon from the Spanish-American War era caricatured Native Hawaiians as 'black-skinned pigmies with kinky hair and big lips' (Desmond 55). Local haoles, while still paternalistic and condescending in attitude to the 'inferior' Native Hawaiians, judged themselves able to distinguish between well-bred natives (those descended from royalty or from good families) and the lower class of natives who had interbred with other ethnic groups. Furthermore, their attitude towards the latter group was sometimes guided by a sense of *noblesse oblige*, similar to the paternalism of the slave owners and their descendants in the American south (Kent 83). The more open prejudices of the *malihini haole* military quickly led to confrontations: a riot in Downtown Honolulu in 1919, involving 200 or so *malihini* military men and Native Hawaiians, erupted when the uniformed men 'appl[ied] the term "nigger" to two natives who were seated on their doorsteps playing ukuleles' ('Sailors, Soldiers').

It was in this social, racial, economic and political context that the Waikīkī War Memorial was envisaged and constructed. Western ways were being imposed at the expense of Native Hawaiians and other non-Caucasians and non-Americans. Great efforts were made to eradicate non-American customs and to instill instead American practices, symbols, flags, emblems, and traditions. In this period of American history, all the forces of a modern Western state were utilized to suppress what remained of Native Hawaiian culture and to Americanize Hawai'i's inhabitants. The Waikīkī War Memorial and Natatorium was part of this propaganda and Americanization effort.

## Origins of the Memorial

Local citizens formed a War Memorial Committee in 1918 in response to the promptings of a group called 'Daughters and Sons of the Hawaiian Warriors.' A number of civic, educational, and religions organizations took an interest in the project.[4] Notable interested individuals included former territorial Attorney-General W.O. Smith and territorial tax collector Colonel Howard Hathaway (Peek 108).[5] As historian Kirk Savage has noted, they were following a relatively new trend in monument building that began in the nineteenth century:

> In the expansive era of the nineteenth century, monuments were not bestowed by the state on the citizenry, or at least they weren't supposed to be ... What gave monuments their particular appeal in an era of rising nationalism was their claim to speak for 'the people' ... Most monuments therefore originated not as official projects of the state but as volunteer enterprises sponsored by associations of 'public-spirited' citizens and funded by individual donations. These voluntary associations often had direct links to officialdom, but they

> received legitimacy only by manufacturing popular enthusiasm (and money) for the project (6).

Who were these organizations and individuals and what was the political outlook? Some clues can be gleaned from various *Advertiser* articles of the period: on 13 August 1919, for example, the Rotary Club had as Guests of Honor at one of its receptions, 'Four of the principal officials of the government of the Republic of Hawaii who participated in the transfer of the sovereignty of the Hawaiian Islands to the United States,' namely President Sanford Dole, Minister of Foreign Affairs Henry E. Cooper, Attorney-General W.O. Smith, and Hawai'i's representative to Washington, F.M. Hatch. (The *Advertiser*'s coy phrase, 'transfer of sovereignty,' sanitizes what was, in reality, a military-backed overthrow.) Also present at the reception were Governor McCarthy, Mayor Fern, and two military officials Major-General Morton US Army, and Rear Admiral Fletcher US Navy. At the Fourth of July celebrations in 1919, representatives of both The Rotary Club and the Ad Club sang 'America' and participated fully in a parade in which,

> the white gowns of the girls representing Uncle Sam's children were seen through the trees. Headed by Uncle Sam, the representatives of the states, beginning with Virginia and Massachusetts, marched in single file, each girl carrying a state flag. After the 48 states came Alaska and then Hawaii with her ensign ... The girls made a pretty sight as they circled the bandstand and then crossed the platform in single file, each maid placing her flag on a table before Uncle Sam. Then grouping themselves on either side and behind him, they repeated the pledge of allegiance to the flag. The Star Spangled banner, sung by the entire audience, was the closing number of the program ('Birth of Nation').[6]

In September 1919, military representatives including Colonel Howard Hathaway, addressed the Ad Club. Hathaway warned, 'men of responsibility and thought must organize to meet the rising tide of Bolshevism and anti-Americanism' ('Ad Club'). The YMCA provided a forum for American nationalists, for example, when it invited Federal Judge Horace W. Vaughan to speak. Vaughan voiced his opinion that, 'foreign language schools [in Hawai'i] must be abolished' ('Vaughan'). In October of that year, the YMCA also asked Hathaway to give a talk on the dangers of organized labor and of 'unprincipled aliens who are not and never can catch the spirit of Americanism' ('Men of Action').[7]

Not every organization involved in the advocacy or planning of the Waikīkī War Memorial and Natatorium did so solely out of a sense of American patriotism. However, it appears they all took very practical and concrete measures to establish American customs and institutions in Hawai'i, and to foster the narrative of Hawai'i's willing participation in US colonial expansion.

The first designs for the memorial had no connection whatsoever to the extant construction. In fact, there was considerable support at one stage for either a memorial designed by Roger Noble Burnham[8] to be erected in Palace Square close to the statue of King Kamehameha or for a Memorial Hall of some kind ('Proposes Aid'). Burnham suggested that his design would 'symboliz[e] Hawai'i's contribution to Liberty. It consists of three figures, the central one typifying Liberty while beneath are a Hawaiian warrior and a Hawaiian maiden. The warrior offers his spear, while the maiden extends in outstretched hands a lei' ('Proposes Aid'). As Burnham explained it, the monument would be the 24-foot high central figure of a 50-foot long structure. Perhaps as a compromise to those seeking the erection of a memorial hall, Burnham also made allowances for a rostrum or stand enclosed on three sides by a wall, where an audience might be situated to hear a public speaker. Inscriptions on the wall would include Hawai'i's civilian population and their contribution to the war in buying bonds and helping the Red Cross, and the other walls would depict military activities. On two foreground pillars there were to be representations of both a sailor and soldier. A tablet with the names of war casualties was to be placed in the center of the monument at its base. Burnham was also conscious of the question of race, and he assured his listeners that the sculpture 'would be large enough ... to depict the activities of the various nationalities in the Islands who had given their sons for the cause of Liberty' ('Proposes Aid').

Burnham's modest design was championed by Mrs. Walter (Alice) Macfarlane. She was born Alice Kamokila Campbell, daughter of wealthy landowner James Campbell and Abigail Kuaihelani Maipinepine, who was from a mixed Native Hawaiian and *haole* family from Lahaina, Maui. When James Campbell died in 1900, his estate was held in trust for his wife and daughters. Alice Macfarlane, who in later years would become a voice against statehood for Hawai'i, was a respected and influential woman. She opposed notions of a memorial hall, an auditorium or civic center, as she was concerned that a 'memorial hall would commercialize the memory of the men who had paid the supreme sacrifice.' Supporters of the memorial hall design, however, believed that it would become a center of civic life where 'people could go and hear enlightening talks and entertaining music' ('Proposes Aid'). One other suggestion at this time, by the Chamber Of Commerce, was for the memorial either to be placed in a prominent position at the entrance to Honolulu Harbor or on Sand Island, where 'it would be the first thing that would greet the arriving traveler, and the last thing he would see' ('Promotion Body'). These early deliberations about the site of the monument, and its design as either a traditional monument or a usable, 'living' structure, would characterize the nature of the debate for many months.

In early February 1919, further designs were considered; Burnham exhibited sketches of a design that incorporated his original sculpture into a larger design that also included a memorial hall. The *Advertiser* provided details of Burnham's proposal:

> The monument utilizes the Burnham model, to be treated as an archway leading to the memorial hall rotunda. The sketch showed a triumphal arch. There would be life-size figurants, also, of Hawaiian soldiers and sailors on the arch pedestals, while the panels would disclose suggestions of Hawaii's chief industries which the young men defended. Entrance to the building would be through two outer archways. In the rotunda arrangements would be made to display war relics, tablets containing names of the dead heroes and other places wherein the history of Hawaii's participation in the war would be shown. Behind the rotunda would be two halls, one an auditorium with a capacity of 2000, arranged for large assemblies. Adjoining would be a smaller hall. This would be equipped with a stage so that the hall could be used for lectures and small gatherings. A pipe organ would be so arranged that its music could be played directly intone half or the other. In the upper story would also be a lecture hall ('Mass Meeting').

The cost of this project would be somewhere in the region of $750,000 ('Rotarians Interested'), the equivalent today of $7,674,333.33 (*Economic History*). Another suggestion at this point was for a very practical memorial that would comprise one new wing of the Queens Hospital ('Mass Meeting'). Yet another design by T.H. Ripley & Davis architects envisaged an impressive memorial hall surrounded by large Grecian columns, which would feature a large rotunda containing 'statuary tablets' ('Proposed Memorials').

By the end of February 1919, the general consensus of the War Memorial subcommittee had shifted towards the idea of both a monument and memorial hall, although nothing definite had yet been agreed. At one point, however, someone raised the idea of erecting a memorial fountain instead of Burnham's memorial design. Mr. J.D. McInerny, spokesman for a promotion committee, supported this particular plan. He had been influenced by a letter from Avard Fairbanks of Salt Lake City, Utah, who had designed part of the Mormon Temple at Laie on O'ahu. Fairbank suggested that a fountain be erected at the entrance to the Capital grounds, and the *Advertiser* provided a forum for his views:

> The theme I have worked out is a fountain with the central figures representing the 'Liberty of the World' being upheld and sustained by the efforts of the Allied Nations. Then the fountains that are placed around the central group represent the fountains of Knowledge, Faith, Life and Energy, all putting forth their strength to the development of the World. Around the pool of water will be groups of sculpture that will represent the devotion of the different islands in the recent great struggle. These groups will be placed in such a manner that they will beautify and complete the setting for the central figures. I would suggest that each island be given an opportunity to present a sculpture group, and that each also keep a replica of the same for the adornment of its own island. This will bring more prominence and feeling of respect for the large memorial. I would also suggest that Liberty should be executed in marble and that the other groups be in bronze ('Memorial Project').

Some dismissed Fairbanks's design for being too common, the type of monument that might be suitable in Washington, perhaps, but not one that represented local involvement in the war. It was suggested instead that 'Hawai'i's memorial should have sculpted themes which symbolize her own participation, using Hawaiian figures principally for the main group and using the other nationalities as studies for bas reliefs on panels' ('Want Sculpture'). Since only The Daughters of Warriors and the Rotary Club had, by this stage, offered definite proposals for the memorial's design, the subcommittee felt unable to offer a proposal to the main War Memorial Committee. They therefore decided once again to ask for views from representatives of local institutions ('Memorial Project').

On 24 March 1919, it was reported in the *Advertiser* that the War Memorial Committee would finally announce that a general design had been agreed upon for a monument and memorial hall to be situated on a 'strip of land along Punchbowl Street, between King and Queen Streets.' This was to be the majority report's proposal. A dissenting minority report, led by Alice Macfarlane, questioned the cost of the proposed memorial and suggested once again that it be limited solely to a monument without the additional expense of a memorial hall. Macfalane reiterated her view that the monument should 'emphasize the spiritual side of victory, rather than ... show the wealth of the community' ('Final Decision'). The next day, however, the *Advertiser* reported that the memorial would not be situated on Punchbowl and that proposals had been made to approach the Irwin estate to buy property at Kapi'olani Park instead. For some time John Guild, chairman of the Beach Park Memorial Committee, had been in correspondence with the Irwin Estate about buying the property for use as a Pan-Pacific Peace Palace. However, at the War Memorial Committee meeting, Guild suggested that the land be purchased for a war memorial park instead. Guild was particularly effusive about the proposed beach site:

> The tropical settings are expressive of the country, the background of Diamond Head and its fortifications is appropriate to a military memorial and the sea on which the property fronts is a constant reminder of those who served in the naval establishment. The surf which beats upon the reef is a constant reminder of the manly sports of the island boys which they turned into such good account in their war endeavors ('Irwin Property Makes').

The Legislature of the Territory of Hawai'i sided with Guild and in 1919 passed Act 191 to appropriate $200,000 for the purchase of the land (CJS Group 2).

The site of the memorial had now been resolved but the debate over its design had not. Guild championed a memorial consisting of an 'arch or statue' as opposed to a memorial hall ('Memorial Park'). He was insistent that the memorial plans be given due consideration should not be rushed:

> We do not want to erect a monument which shall at some future date be looked upon as a thing of bad taste. Too many of the soldier's [sic] monuments of the past have been of this character. I believe the memorial should take a form that will express the spirit of Hawaii and be in harmony with the wonderful tropical surroundings of the proposed site ('Irwin Property Makes').

At this point, Burnham stepped up efforts to publicize his design, by presenting it to the Pan-Pacific Committees of Artists and Architects

*Figure 2.3* Burnham's design: 'Young Hawaiian warrior and maiden.' Hawai'i State Library Newspaper Collection.

and also by placing a model in the Pan-Pacific window of Thrum's Bookstore. The image was reproduced in the *Advertiser* with the legend, 'Hawai'i's offering to Liberty ... a young Hawaiian warrior and maiden ... giving themselves' ('Burnham Design'). [Fig. 2.3] Like Burnham's earlier proposed inscription of a Hawaiian warrior 'offer[ing] his spear,' his latest inscription had both salacious and colonial implications: the terminology of 'offering' and 'giving themselves' suggests submission and emasculation. It underpins American imagery of Hawai'i as an erotic locale, and sanitizes the sorrow of death in war. Nevertheless, the *Advertiser* furnished Burnham's design with lavish praise, stating:

> it would be difficult to express, artistically, in any more vital or beautiful way, the passionate enthusiasm and patriotic devotion with which the people of these Islands throw themselves into the cause of liberty and justice. [Burnham] took advantage of the opportunity to use Hawaiian figures and symbols and thus have a monument that would be distinctly expressive of this locality and that could not be duplicated anywhere else in the world, nor designed by anyone to whom conditions and types of Hawaii were unknown ('Burnham Design').

The *Advertiser* also noted, correctly, that throughout the various discussions and proposals for design of the war memorial, it had always been generally accepted that Burnham's sculpture would form a centerpiece. Furthermore, the paper argued that the Pan-Pacific Committees of Artists and Architects had rejected the idea of a memorial arch in a park setting as unsuitable and they had, instead, endorsed Burnham's design as the most appropriate yet available. The design would also include various tablets or panels that would:

> bear inscriptions and data giving a general history of all that Hawaii did in the war, such as the numbers enlisted and drafted from the different islands and from the great variety of nationalities and races represented in this Territory. There would also be a record of our going 'over the top' in all Liberty Loans and other drives and the accomplishments of the women in Red Cross work ('Burnham Design').

However, when the War Memorial Committee met once again on 28 May 1919, with no consensus as to what would be the most appropriate design, and with some even suggesting once again that a memorial hall be built in Downtown Honolulu, the committee decided that the only way to break the impasse was to appoint yet another committee, this time simply to choose a site in Kapi'olani Park within the borders of the newly-purchased Irwin estate on which the memorial would be sited. The decision to form another committee only gave the appearance of progress without actually accomplishing anything. After all, how could it first be decided where the memorial would be situated if its dimensions and form were unknown? What the Committee did agree upon was that Burnham's design was the most appropriate so far, but that a design by Avard Fairbanks for a memorial including a fountain would also be considered as soon as Fairbanks could present it. Fairbanks, who had studied at Paris's *École des Beaux Arts,* had recently been commissioned by the Church of Jesus Christ of Latter-Day Saints to erect four sculpture friezes for the temple in Laie, Hawai'i (Fairbanks 50). In the event, Fairbanks' design was first aired in the *Advertiser* when J.D. McInerny, a long-time advocate of the young sculptor, submitted sketches. The *Advertiser* entitled the design, 'Mother Hawai'i Sending Forth Her Sons to Battle on Sea and Land.'

## Colonialism by design

Of particular interest in some of the designs submitted thus far is their hieratic scale. The word 'monument' comes from the Latin *monere,* 'to remind, admonish, instruct' (Loewen, *Lies Across* 43). This 'instruction' can be racial in nature — Caucasians in dominant positions over non-Caucasians perhaps — or it can be gender-inspired, with male images dominating female. While Burnham's original design manages to include both of these traits, Fairbanks' 'Mother Hawai'i' reverses the traditional male dominance but instead substitutes a maternalistic Mother Hawai'i/Lady Liberty image. Fairbanks' phallic design — he called it an 'imposing shaft of lava' ('Mother Hawai'i')[9] — is also a symbol of American masculinity in a place traditionally designated by foreigners as a female-gendered paradise. Ferguson and Turnbull assert that Westerners viewed Hawai'i as a 'welcoming feminine place, waiting with open arms to embrace those who come to penetrate, protect, mold, and develop, while simultaneously lacking that which would make it fully realized (and which the intruders conveniently believe themselves to possess). Maps of Hawai'i from Captain James Cook's expeditions represent Hawai'i with soft, curved, breast-like mountains and mysterious coves and bays ... Missionary accounts of "the natives" emphasize their darkness; naked, unashamed, promiscuous' (6).

'Hawai'i is "she",' declares Haunani-Kay Trask, 'the Western image of the Native "female" in her magical allure' (*Native* 136–7). In the American imaginary, Hawai'i was both an extension of the primitive, feminized New World — a 'virgin land' vulnerable to conquest — and also another step in their manifest destiny to sweep forever west, brushing aside native peoples in the process of 'civilization.'[10] Historian John

Higham points out, for example, that although it was the artistic convention of sixteenth-century Europeans to illustrate the world's continents as female, but only the New World female was portrayed as a primitive:

> To differentiate America from Africa and Asia, artists relied chiefly on her partial or complete nudity. Asia was always fully clothed, often sumptuously so. Africa, attired in sometimes revealing but always elegant dress, was supposed to look Moorish, since Europeans were most familiar with the Mediterranean littoral. America alone was a savage (Stannard, *American* 229).

Fairbanks envisioned a memorial park with a lagoon, a block of lava, and an *ali'i* 'of the ancient Hawaiian regime decked in his feather cloak and helmet of war.' In creating this seamless historical narrative, Fairbanks implied that the Hawai'i residents who enlisted in the US military during World War One were spiritual descendants of the warlike 'ancient Hawaiians.' Like many other narrators of Hawaiian history, Fairbanks coded Native Hawaiians solely as noble warriors and ignored other aspects of their culture and history.[11] Furthermore, his 'noble warrior' narrative suggests the US military is a continuation of this tradition, rather than oppressing and appropriating it.

Fairbanks wanted a monument of 'majestic proportions,' set in a large lagoon and framed against a backdrop of Diamond Head Crater. It would 'tower above the trees, making it visible from many points of interest about Honolulu.' The centerpiece of the memorial was to be a boat whose prow was in the shape of an American eagle, in which 'youths from the Hawaiian Islands' would be situated posing with an American flag, symbolizing their readiness 'to defend the rights of mankind.' Fairbanks' boat would symbolize 'the crossing of the seas when the sons of Hawaii assisted in fight for the freedom of their fellow mankind over there.' On the shaft itself, Fairbanks envisaged a relief of 'an Alii [sic] of the ancient Hawaiian regime decked in his feather cloak and helmet of war. He will be in low relief which will suggest that the spirit of the ancient warriors breathes from the very rocks of the Islands, and that they prompt and inspire the youth of today to struggle for universal liberty.'

Fairbanks' design also had a pseudo-religious element. He foresaw the memorial as an altar-like formation around which pedestals representing 'each island's loyalty to the cause of freedom' would be placed. He hoped that this would lead to 'feelings of reverence to the big monument from the people of the different islands.' To ensure that everyone for miles around would be reminded of the importance of the monument and all it represented, Fairbanks suggested that it be illuminated at all times by a 'battery of lights' screened by reflectors of stained glass decorated with the Hawaiian coat of arms. Maintaining his Biblical allusion, Fairbanks spoke of the monument as 'a pillar of light.' This proposed monument of 'colossal proportion' was designed to memorialize the combat deaths of, at most, eight people.

Like most of the proposed memorials, including the extant one, Fairbanks insisted on the inclusion of some Hawaiian words. In this case he wanted the memorial inscribed with the words *'Hawai'i nei,'* which, in one limited sense can be seen as a tribute to Native Hawaiians, but in the wider context of colonization can be interpreted as Western appropriation of the image/language of the 'savage' or of the supposed noble masculinity of the native. Social historian Eric Lott's work on blackface minstrelsy is instructive here: Lott argues that such mimicry was both a 'formal public acknowledgment' (*Love and Theft* 4) that black culture existed, but also arose due to white 'obsession' with dark-skinned bodies ('Love and Theft' 23). More insidiously, blackface minstrelsy comforted whites by catering to their sense of white supremacy. It was also accompanied by what Lott calls 'an aura of illicit sexuality' ('Love and Theft' 25), which is a facet of white appropriation of non-white culture that is particularly revealing in a Hawaiian context, given the aforementioned connections Americans tend to make, linking the islands with sexual wantonness. Utilizing Hawaiian language in such a way is an ongoing process in the transformation of power from Hawaiians to Americans.

The period between the end of Reconstruction and the start of America's Great Depression was perhaps the nadir of race relations in the United States. The change in the social and economic order caused by the Civil War, and the perceived threat to white hegemony led, for example, to a record number of lynchings — 49 African-American men were lynched in 1882, for instance, and 161 in 1892 (Bederman 47). While whites feared the supposedly 'primitive' nature of African-American men, especially the 'black beast rapists' (Bederman 47), whites were, at the same time, appropriating the nobler aspects of the primitive. Historian Gail Bederman notes, for example, that whites joined fraternal groups such as the Improved Order of Red Men 'in order to perform elaborate weekly rituals imitating their fantasies of American Indian adventures. Interest in camping, hunting, and fishing — seen as virile survival skills of primitive man — flourished ...' (22–3).[12] This 'back to nature' trend manifested itself in Hawai'i also: in 1918, for example, an 'Aloha Parade' organized by *haole* businessmen as a patriotic send off for a contingent of local volunteers featured 'The Daughters of Warriors of Hawaii' — an all–*haole* group — which, according to Kuykendall, 'gave a distinct touch of Hawaii of olden days' by dressing in 'the feather cape or robe of royalty' (*Hawaii* 89). Author Houston Wood argues that such appropriation 'often masqueraded as a validation of Native traditions, when the actual effect was to encourage their destruction' (166).When seen in that light, the inclusion of some Hawaiian words on a statue benefits only the dominant American culture, since their part of this 'arrangement' enables them to associate themselves with what they perceive to be the better, more manly aspect of the 'noble savage.'

Fairbanks' design was out of all proportion to the relatively minimal casualties sustained or the sacrifices made by the people of Hawai'i in the context of either the overall casualty figures World War One (excluding civilian deaths) of over six million or even those solely of the United States, which amounted to 116,000 (Schaefer 161). The proposed construction of such an imposing structure therefore must have had underlying motives unconnected to the war. Fairbanks' proposal that the 'monument will tower above the trees, making it visible from many points of interest about Honolulu, and in the distance, appearing as its back-ground, will rise the famed crater of Diamond Head,' is symbolic not only of man's general conquest of nature but also the triumph of technological Western civilization over Native Hawaiian culture, while pretending to honor it. Fairbanks' intention to 'prompt and inspire the youth of today to struggle for universal liberty' is an obvious reminder that the monument was meant to *monere,* to remind, admonish, instruct the people of Hawai'i that in the future their role was to 'defend liberty,' which of course meant the United States.

## 100 percent Americanism

Early deliberations over the erection, placement and design of the memorial took place solely within the American civilian community in Hawai'i. However, in August of 1919 the newly-formed American Legion entered the fray ('Veterans Plan'). Colonel Theodore Roosevelt (son of the ex-president), and other senior officers, created the Legion in France to direct disaffected soldiers away from the lure of socialism. Journalist Marcus Duffield states, 'The American General Staff was seriously concerned about how to keep up morale. American bankers and business men [sic] who visited Europe returned filled with anxiety.

What would be the attitude of returning troops?' (5). By early 1921, the Hawai'i branch of the Legion had wrested control of the Memorial scheme out of the hands of the citizens' War Memorial Committee. There is no suggestion of conflict or dispute in the historical record — a *Paradise of the Pacific* editorial noted simply that the 'American Legion ... has charge of the projected War Memorial' ('A Suggestion') — but it would have taken a very brave or foolish citizen indeed to stand up to military veterans who had so very comprehensively wrapped themselves in the US flag.

Despite the many different ideas as to what design would constitute a fitting memorial and where it should be situated, by early 1921 the American Legion's views held total sway. CJS Group Architects note in their *Final Historical Background Report* on the memorial, that, 'This concept of having a memorial [i.e. one that included a swimming pool] was originally initiated by the American Legion Chapter of Hawai'i' (2). This despite the fact that the Legion was not involved, in fact did not even *exist*, when some of Hawai'i's citizens were submitting plans and raising interest and money for the memorial in 1918. Of course, arguments over control of projects such as memorials are not unusual: The Daughters and Sons of the Hawaiian Warriors were complaining as early as January 1919 that 'they proposed the memorial first and then later on another element steps in and crowds them' ('Proposes Aid').

However, even given that expected bickering, the question still remains, why did such a new and untried organization quickly gain such a hold over the Memorial project? Perhaps the answer can be seen in the preamble to the Legion's Constitution, in which the Legion pledges not only to 'preserve the memories and incidents of our associations in the Great War' but also to 'foster and perpetuate a one hundred percent Americanism' (Rumer intro). Coming so soon after the end of a devastating World War in which approximately 116,000 Americans lost their lives (Schaefer 161), it is hardly a surprise that a veterans' group would quickly attain a position of influence. However, what made the Legion so powerful was that its aims coincided with those connected to the powerful US military presence in Hawai'i, with some of the *haole* elite who were pushing for statehood, and with others who did not want statehood but did want to make Hawai'i less alien to their American sensibilities.

In this time period, the Legion advocated unquestioning patriotism towards the United States, a policy it called '100 percent Americanism.' For instance, in March 1920, a spokesman of the newly-formed Legion addressed the Ad Club and 'outlined the plans of the Hawaii Americanism

Commission ... and called for the cooperation of the Ad Club in the effort to make Hawaii 100 percent American' ('Legion Objects'). On a national level, it actively campaigned for an increase in the size of the US military and against Peace Conferences and arms reductions talks. It worked to exclude Japanese immigrants, deport foreigners, and prosecute 'slackers,' draft dodgers and conscientious objectors. It also attacked those it considered as 'Red,' 'Bolshevik,' or indeed anyone it saw as acting in an un-American way.

Whereas today one view of the Legion might be that it is a harmless institution, comprised mostly of elderly men dedicated to remembering their dead comrades, in the 1920s the Legion's members were young and tough, recent veterans of a vicious World War. They quickly became involved in some rather unsavory incidents. For example, in Centralia, Washington on Armistice Day, 1919, the American Legion set out to destroy the union hall of the left wing, staunchly working class, International Workers of the World (IWW) — also known as the 'Wobblies.' However, when the attack came, IWW members responded with gunfire that killed three Legionnaires and wounded eleven others. One of the gunmen, Wesley Everest, was later dragged from a police cell and taken to the edge of town where Legion members 'cut off his testicles, then his penis ... hanged him from a bridge and then shot him' (Loewen, *Lies Across* 79). The Legion actively campaigned against freedom of speech for those whose views differed from their own. On one infamous occasion the Los Angeles branch of the Legion considering taking action to stop Albert Einstein from visiting California, calling him 'a pacifist traveling in the guise of a mathematician ... a propagandist against the best interests of the country' (Duffield 218). The Legion's National Commander from 1922–3, former Texas assistant attorney general Alvin Owsley said, apparently without irony or any sense of foresight, 'Do not forget that the Fascisti are to Italy what the American Legion is to the United States' (Duffield 169).

There were no 'Wobblies' in Hawai'i, however, and the economic power of the 'Big Five,' backed by the authority of the police and criminal justice system, were enough to ensure both social control and, for the most part, worker cooperation. The Legion therefore used its contacts with local power bases to influence local politics and achieve its patriotic goals. Since its inception in Honolulu on 4 September 1919, the Legion was faced with what the *Advertiser* called 'some knotty problems, conditions found nowhere else in the United States' ('Hawaii to Have'). Those 'knotty problems' were, of course, the various non-Caucasian races that were perceived as a threat to the continuing

Americanization of Hawai'i. The Legion therefore enthusiastically, and with military discipline and planning, set about undermining the status of those groups. Called 'an outpost of Americanism in the Pacific' by the ever-supportive *Advertiser* ('American Legion To Meet'), the Legion concentrated its efforts 'to develop and maintain a thoroughly American civilization in Hawaii, and for the securing of legislation to insure that result including the encouragement of immigration to these Islands of Americans and races whose loyalty to and assimilability in American institutions is sure' ('100 Percent').

Many in Hawai'i did not meet the high standards of the Legion, especially in one the most obvious manifestations of difference, the ability to speak fluent English. The Legion therefore advocated the abolition of non-English language schools, 'favoring the passage of legislation locally and nationally preventing the operation of schools in any language other than English' ('100 Percent'). The Legion also demanded favorable treatment for its members in Territorial civil service jobs stating openly that 'We favor preferment to ex-service men and women for all civil service positions and that liberal provisions be made to permit them to secure public lands' ('100 Percent'). In Hawai'i at this time, when both land and respectable employment opportunities were in short supply, these demands were particularly important and especially harmful to both non-veterans and the Islands' already disadvantaged non-*haole* majority. By 1935, for example, Fuchs records that 'haoles, comprising about one-fifth of the population of the Islands, constituted less than 1 percent of the agricultural labor force and filled more than 40 percent of the professional services' (59). Not every member of the Legion was *haole*, of course, but they did constitute a significant majority. Furthermore, despite Legion claims that a member's former military rank played no part in the hierarchy of the organization, in practice those Legion members who were formerly of officer rank tended to get deferential and preferential treatment. Not by coincidence, all those officers were *haole*. While Filipinos, Native Hawaiians and Chinese were acceptable as rank-and-file soldiers, to act as laborers and occasionally cannon fodder in the Great War, only Caucasian officers were trusted to comprise the officer class.

On a national level, the Legion was concerned about the education of America's youth. Specifically, they wanted to introduce their brand of military-inspired patriotism into the school system by supporting ROTC programs. However, this was just the tip of the iceberg: at the Legion's first National Convention it was recommended that 'all schools be required to devote at least ten minutes each day to patriotic exercises, and to fly the flag whenever weather permitted' (Gellermann 200). In 1933 the Legion urged its members to get involved in their local school systems, 'to cause to be adopted in the schools of their communities regular courses of study in patriotism ... Make it your business to see that the schools of America are American' (Gellermann 202). The Legion introduced a National Essay Contest in 1922, with a suitably patriotic subject chosen beforehand. It even went as far as to condemn many American history books as unpatriotic and even subversive, and to commission its own history book, *The Story of Our American People*, 'to express to the rising generation a faith in our country and a BELIEF [sic] in it that shall inspire confidence in our laws and loyalty to our Government' (Duffield 273).

The Hawai'i branch of the Legion adopted many of these national policies, and when implemented in Hawai'i they were particularly damaging. In a national setting they can perhaps be considered as harmlessly patriotic. However, in Hawai'i, with its rich, multi-cultural history, the Legion wanted to impose a monoculture, and it saw the school system as an ideal place to start its own 'children's crusade.' For example, in a letter to the territory's Superintendent of Public Instruction in March 1920, Henry J. Ryan, a Legion official from Massachusetts responsible for spreading Legion cant in America's schools, asked 'if there is any law on the statute books making the study of American history and civics compulsory' ('American Legion Wants'). In May 1920, Miss Mary Lawrence, children's librarian of the Library of Hawai'i, wrote an article in the *Advertiser* entitled 'Americanism is Part of Library Work.' Described by the *Advertiser* as her 'contribution to American Legion's propaganda for 100 percent [Americanism],' Lawrence's article describes the aim of the Americanization of Hawai'i's 'foreigners' to be 'to create in this inner soul life of the individual a feeling of loyalty for America and a desire to work toward accomplishing the ideals for which it stands.' She personally hoped to encourage this by utilizing the library and ensuring that there 'should be branch libraries in the schools with enough books *of the right kind* [emphasis added] for every child' ('Americanism').

As well as the aforementioned action the Legion took against foreign language schools, it also actively campaigned against Hawai'i's foreign language press. The issue was first raised publicly as the Legion prepared for its Territorial Convention in February 1920 ('Legion Convention'). On 18 February, the Honolulu branch agreed to propose a resolution at the Convention 'demanding federal legislation requiring the publication of English translations of matter appearing in foreign language newspapers and territorial laws properly regulating such papers' ('Legion to Demand'). While not going so far as to advocate abolition of foreign language newspapers (as it did foreign language schools), the Legion did want them brought under control. At the Convention, where in his keynote address Departmental Commander Leonard Witherington referred to Hawai'i as 'a great military and naval base on the last frontier of civilization,' the Legion not only adopted the foreign language newspaper resolution as policy, but also such other colonialist policies as anti-alien land laws forbidding foreigners from owning land in Hawai'i, and anti-alien labor laws ('Americanization'; 'American Legion Urges'; 'Lightfoot is Told').

These were not simply ineffectual resolutions passed by some insignificant pressure group. Within days of the end of the Territorial Convention, the Territory's Acting Attorney-General Joseph Lightfoot invited Legion members to a conference to discuss how these resolutions could be adopted and implemented ('Lightfoot Calls'). Such was the import of the Legion's propaganda and influence in this area that the British Consul in Honolulu, William Massy Royals wrote both to Hawai'i's Acting Governor, Col. Curtis P. Iaukea and also to the British diplomatic mission in Washington to ask what action was going to be taken about the Legion's proposals to discriminate against foreigners, including a significant number of Britons ('Legion Action'). Eventually, the British protest was withdrawn without explanation. One can speculate, however, that assurances were received that such discriminatory actions would only be applied to non-haoles.

Legionnaires in Hawai'i had many of the same traits that sociologist Albert Memmi noted of European colonists in Africa:

> He loves the most flashy symbols, the most striking demonstrations of the power of his country. He attends all military parades and he desires and obtains frequent and elaborate ones; he contributes his part by dressing up carefully and ostentatiously. He admires the army and its strength, reveres uniforms and covets decorations. Here we overlap what is customarily called power politics, which does not stem only from an economic principle (show your strength if you want to avoid having to use it), but corresponds to a deep necessity of colonial life; to impress the colonized is just as important as to reassure oneself (59).

No one wanted to impress the colonized in Hawai'i at this time as much as the American Legion. However, their actions were not totally unopposed, and the local population did not sit idly by while the Legion, the US military, and Hawai'i's *haole* population asserted control. Locals fought these powerful interests in the courts and sometimes with their fists in the streets. Despite a century of population decline, the destruction of their religion, theft of their land, and attacks on and appropriation of their culture, Native Hawaiians fought for and retained many of their traditions and practices. And in 1927, perhaps not coincidentally the year in which the war memorial opened, lawyers for Hawai'i's Japanese language schools won a US Supreme Court victory over the Territorial Legislature's attempts at regulation (*Japanese in Hawaii* 65).

## The Legion and the Memorial

It was in the midst of these battles over Americanism that the American Legion became involved in the war memorial debate, and the final design of the memorial itself has to be seen in the context of this conflict. At the Memorial Park's formal dedication on Armistice Day, 11 November 1919, the same day as the Legion attack on the IWW hall in Centralia, Governor James McCarthy symbolically handed over possession of Park to the Legion whose Honolulu Branch had only been formed barely two months earlier. The Legion's chaplain, Father Valentin, read prayers at what the *Advertiser* described as a 'semi-military ceremony not without its lessons to present and future generations' ('Beautiful Park'). Although those lessons were supposed to be anti-German in nature, perhaps the real lessons being taught were ones of colonialism: this was a show of force promoting the 'excessive patriotic ardor' that Memmi noted as a trait of colonialists (64). These men were setting an example in their 'pure fervor for the mother country' that the Natives were supposed to follow (59).

At this time, however, the War Memorial Committee was still no closer to coming to a decision on the actual design of the Memorial itself. In the summer of 1919, however, a swimming carnival was held on O'ahu, which was described as 'the biggest and most successful ever held anywhere. It served to put Honolulu more conspicuously on the map' ('Boost The Game'). Swimming was a major attraction for Hawai'i, made popular in part by local man, and Olympic gold medallist, Duke Kahanamoku. This was important to the city's businessmen who saw the promotion of the islands as a tourist destination as essential for their future wealth. It may well have been as a result of this carnival, and the forces of the tourist industry, that the first thoughts of building a Natatorium at Kapi'olani Park emerged.

Why, the question may be asked, would anyone want to build a natatorium on a swimming beach? Firstly, it was an attempt to manipulate and conquer nature — a major theme of the European conquest of North America. Westerners associated Native Hawaiians with the natural landscape, as if they were an element of nature alongside animals and vegetation. Just as surely, Westerners viewed themselves above such things on the Great Chain of Being. As historian Jill Lepore notes, 'When John Foster engraved a map of New England to accompany William Hubbard's *Narrative*, he marked English territory with tiny houses and church steeples, and Indian territory with trees' (83). In a similar vein, in early twentieth-century *National Geographic* photographs, haoles in Hawai'i would be photographed in poses and clothes that contrasted with the natural background whereas Native Hawaiians would be photographed as if they were part of nature. Desmond describes, for example, Americans 'pictured as Lilliputian hikers amid gigantic ferns or as plantation experts [whereas] the photographs of Hawaiians show "natives" in grass huts, grass skirts, fishing in brief loincloths, or, in the case of three children, lying naked on the beach' (85–6).[13] Desmond refers to these portrayals of Native Hawaiians as 'a tone of celebratory primitivism — bronzed skin, near nudity ..., imitations of natural (native) physical prowess, the surfer at one with the forces of nature ... In tourist discourse there were rarely any competing representations of Native Hawaiian men, no natives in suits, no Natives working' (125). Other races would also be photographed with nature as a backdrop — Filipinos or Japanese working on a plantation, for example. When seen in this light, the Natatorium can be viewed as another conquest of Western Manifest Destiny, as Americans rescued underutilized 'virgin land' from less civilized races, taming nature in the process.[14]

Although the Legion had endorsed the natatorium project, they had no vested interest in the proposal beyond a shared interest in the geographical link between the natatorium and the War Memorial Park ('Legion Decides'). Less than three months later, however, the Legion offered prizes for proposed designs which might include 'the development of Memorial Park at Waikiki ... an open air auditorium, a natatorium built out into the sea, and a dignified monumental feature which shall emphasize the memorial nature of the park' ('American Legion Plans'). Although the Legion may have had plans to develop the park, it clearly had not solved the problem of the design of the war memorial itself. In that respect it had made no more progress than the War Memorial Committees from which it had ousted control.

In this one sided power struggle, the Legion attempted to disarm its critics with the help of the *Advertiser*. It assured its readers that:

> [the Legion] desires to work out its plans in cooperation and with the full approval of the public, and without the appearance or reality of forcing its own ideas on the people. Nevertheless it is felt that the comrades of the war dead, and those whose living sacrifice is also commemorated, should have a large part in the decision as to the nature of the memorial ('American Legion Plans').

The Legion, however, ignored previous designs and schemes and published a rough outline of its own proposals:

> ... an arch or other memorial feature at the shore. To the landward would be an open space under the trees, carefully landscaped and prepared for seats so that memorial exercises, band concerts or other similar events may be held with the arch or monument as the stage and background. To the seaward would be a natatorium, but with its concrete walls rising only high enough above the waterline to keep their tops above the surf ... By the plan suggested the views along the beach would not be obstructed in any way and yet all the features of other plans, and more, would be preserved ('American Legion Plans').

Clearly the Legion was trying to defuse any potential protests by stating that it was incorporating other designs in its proposals, However, there is no evidence of either Burnham's or Fairbanks' designs in their plans. It is telling that although the Legion was offering prizes for new designs, it had already established what the rough outline of the memorial should be. Unlike Burnham's earlier design, this would be a memorial dedicated only to the military, with no recognition of the contribution made to the war effort by Hawai'i's civilian population. In fact, the Legion's outline is remarkably close to the extant memorial, the only real differences being the incorporation of the arch into the actual natatorium and the omission of the landscaped area on which now stands the Honolulu Stone and plaque. Instead of the main arch that currently stands, the Legion's plan would also have included a large portico leading to the entrance of the Natatorium with a roof supported by four columns. Lastly, in the Legion's design, the *mauka*-facing wall would have been in arcade style, with 15 arches topped by a decorate cornice. It is interesting that in the extant memorial the *mauka* wall is much higher than the Legion's original stated intent. This wall also obstructs the view of the beach, breaking another Legion promise. Obviously when the plan was for a simple natatorium the Legion was free to make aesthetic promises of this sort. However, when the memorial became an integral part of the natatorium's structure, aesthetic promises that would have served to diminish the stature and grandeur of the memorial were quickly forgotten

At a Legion meeting on 24 August, plans were further crystallized. There now appeared to be three main options:

1. A lofty monument with sculpture as one of its features.
2. A municipal organ in an architectural memorial.
3. A natatorium in the ocean just off the park area ('Threefold Plan').

However, after those proposals were aired, a structure combining all three designs was contemplated. It was hoped that it might be 'an artistic and dignified structure ... built at the edge of the water, forming a background for the natatorium on the sea side, and for the great organ on the other side, with a greensward arranged for seats for those attending the concerts' ('Threefold Plan'). This was perhaps the first time that the natatorium and the memorial were envisaged as being part of the

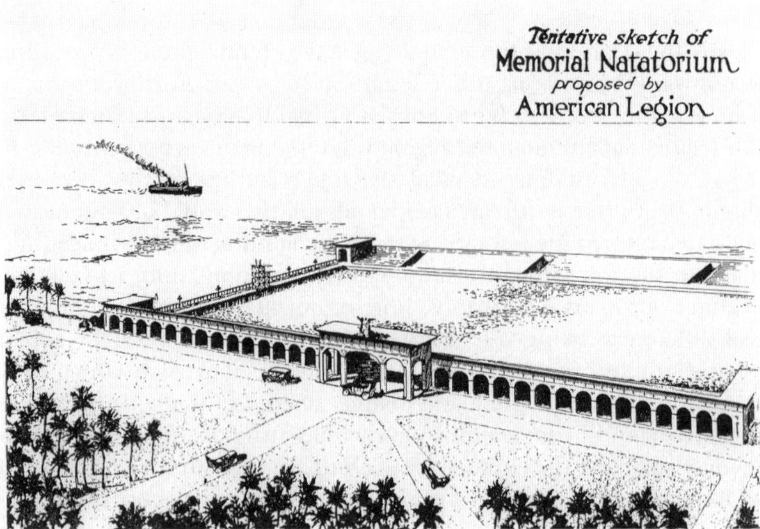


*Figure 2.4* The American Legion's plan for a memorial. Hawai'i State Archives.

same structure, and from this point on, the Legion's design for the combined memorial and natatorium became the only real option on offer. [Fig. 2.4] When, in 1921, the Territorial Legislature authorized the appointment of a Territorial War Memorial Commission to hold a competition to find an appropriate design for the memorial, the Legislature insisted that a swimming pool be part of the project. Governor McCarthy asked the Legion to put together the Memorial Committee, effectively handing it total control over the project.

## The competition

In 1921, Act 15 of the Territorial Legislature authorized the construction of a memorial that must include a 100-meter swimming pool. The Territory was to pay for the memorial, with no contribution from the public expected. The budget for construction was $250,000. Act 15 also authorized the appointment of a 'Territorial War Memorial Commission,' which would hold a competition under the rules of the American Institute of Architects to find an appropriate design for the memorial (CJS Group 2–3). Governor McCarthy asked the Legion to submit names for the Memorial Committee and the Legion responded on 25 March 1921, in a letter to the Governor asking him to appoint A. Lester Marks, John R. Gault and A.L.C. Atkinson (Butler). McCarthy asked Louis Christian Mullgardt to be the Territorial War Memorial Commission's advisory architect.[15] In choosing Mullgardt and, later, the other architects who would judge the competition, Governor McCarthy and the American Legion, virtually ensured that a neoclassical-style memorial would win the design competition as all the architects had previously favored neoclassical designs. For example, Mullgardt designed the Panama-Pacific International Exposition's *beaux-arts* 'Court of the Ages' and 'Tower of the Ages.' While the Exposition's purpose was, ostensibly, an 'expression of America's joy in the completion of the [Panama] Canal ... commemorating the peaceful meeting of ... nations' (Macomber 5), art historian Brian Hack questions, however, if there were other, perhaps more sinister, themes underlying Mullgardt's design:

> American figurative sculpture, equally infused with idealized forms embodying human perfection, is typically perceived as classical or as Beaux-Arts-inspired rather than as emblematic of current biological thought. Representational sculpture in the age of Modernism was, however, not merely a carryover from the century past, but an active response — albeit one of desperation — to what was

> perceived as the degradation of form. Its advocates — convinced that the cubist and futurist butchers were mentally and morally degenerate — worked in silent collusion with the promoters of eugenics. The Panama-Pacific International Exposition, held in San Francisco in 1915, served as one of the clearest national expressions of eugenic philosophy. Promoted as a celebration of the completion of the Panama Canal, the exposition showcased the decade of human progress since the 1904 Louisiana Purchase Exposition in St. Louis. Among the advancements noted by one exposition reporter were the wireless, the aeroplane, the automobile, and 'selective breeding.'

Matthew Frye Jacobson calls the Exposition 'one great paean to evolution and hierarchy' which 'popularized current anthropological, psychometric, and eugenic thinking on questions of race and the relative merits of the world's peoples' (151, 181). Of Mullgardt's Court of Ages (later known as the Court of Abundance), Hack notes it was:

> centered on the theme of evolution through natural selection ... Mullgardt's Tower of Ages, adorned with Chester Beach's Altar of Human Evolution, illustrated the progress of humankind from the primordial muck to the Middle Ages and upward to the age of mortal divinity. Finial sculptures of Primitive Man and Primitive Woman by Albert Weinert traversed the top of the tower, which Mullgardt had ornamented with sculpted tadpoles, crawfish, and other forms of aquatic and floral life.

Clearly, there was more at stake here than a simple argument over architectural styles.[16] In the Gilded Age, many white Americans felt threatened by the massive influx of immigrants into the United States. Most of these 'tired ... poor ... huddled masses' originated from Eastern and Mediterranean Europe, and were considered to be inferior peoples when compared to the Nordic or Aryan northern Europeans — the ruling class in the United States. In choosing neoclassical styles of architecture instead of modernist — which was based on the idea that 'form follows function,' that American architecture should be based on American function, not European traditions — the white American elite was, in a sense, joining the American Legion in its efforts to push back the tide of the undesirable 'foreign' influence on American life. In following American ideas of a new 'democratic' style of architecture, and abandoning classical Greek and Roman designs, the modernists were rejecting those very races upon which America's ruling class derived their supposed authority. The problem inherent in choosing a neoclassical design, especially in Hawai'i, is that it evokes outdated notions of chivalry and honor, concepts that the slaughter of World War One might have consigned to the past. As architectural historian, James Mayo, explains, 'Classical symbolism gave architects the historical remembrance and notions of valor that they wished to depict, but in so doing it virtually ignored the reality of modern technological warfare' (*Landscape* 96).[17]

The Territorial War Memorial Commission nominated three architects from the mainland, Ellis F. Lawrence of Portland, Bernard Maybeck of San Francisco and W.R.B. Wilcox of Seattle, to judge the competition ('Memorial Architects'). However, the winning design would have to conform to Mullgardt's plan for the Memorial Park, with a memorial consisting of 'a temple of music, plaza, and collosseum [sic] with swimming basin' (Kuykendall, *Hawaii* 451–2). It is clear at this stage that the Legion had in mind a certain style of architecture for its memorial, a mode in the neoclassical or Greek Revival tradition, both of which were inspired by the *beaux-arts* style.[18] The architects chosen by the Territorial War Memorial Commission were practitioners of that style. For example, Lawrence established the Department of Architecture at the University of Oregon, which, from 1914 to 1922, was heavily influenced by the *beaux-arts* style (*University of Oregon*). Maybeck is the most well known of the trio, and has been described as 'a truly monumental figure, ranked with Louis Sullivan and Frank Lloyd Wright' (Chapman). Maybeck too, was a noted *beaux-arts* devotee, having studied at the *École des Beaux Arts* in Paris. He utilized that style in such constructions as the First Church of Christ, Scientist, in Berkeley, California, and Palace of Fine Arts at the Panama-Pacific International Exposition in San Francisco in 1915.

When the judges arrived in Hawai'i in June 1922 to award the prize, they were greeted by officials of the American Legion under whose auspices the memorial was to be built. Within a few days the judges awarded the first prize to Lewis Hobart of San Francisco ('Successful Architects'). [Fig. 2.5] Neither Burnham's nor Fairbanks' designs were considered. Between 1922 and 1927, when the Waikīkī War Memorial and Natatorium was finally opened, Hobart's original design, described as a 'dream plan' by Maybeck, was twice pared down to stay within the $250,000 budget The original plan for a natatorium, temple of music, ticket booth, dressing rooms, and some very elaborate friezes, busts and murals could not be built within the budget, and after attempts to appropriate more money failed, the temple of music became the

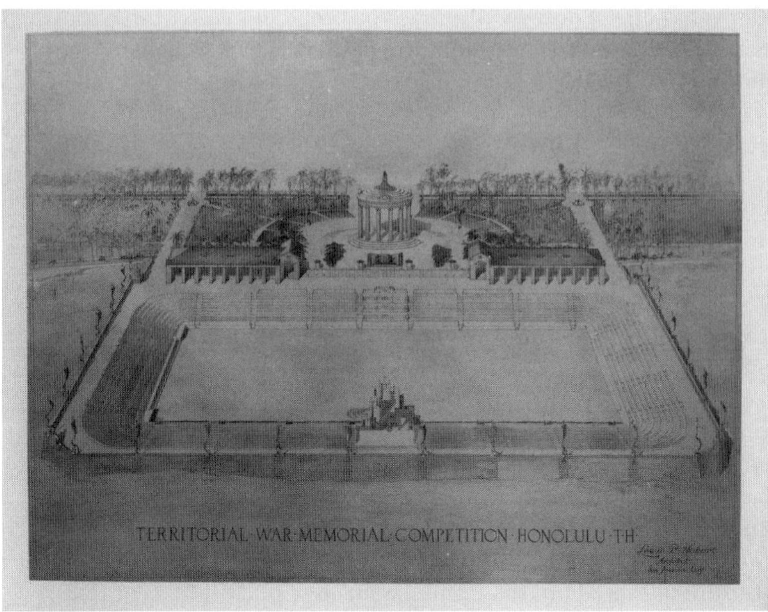


*Figure 2.5* Louis Hobart's winning design. Hawai'i State Archives.

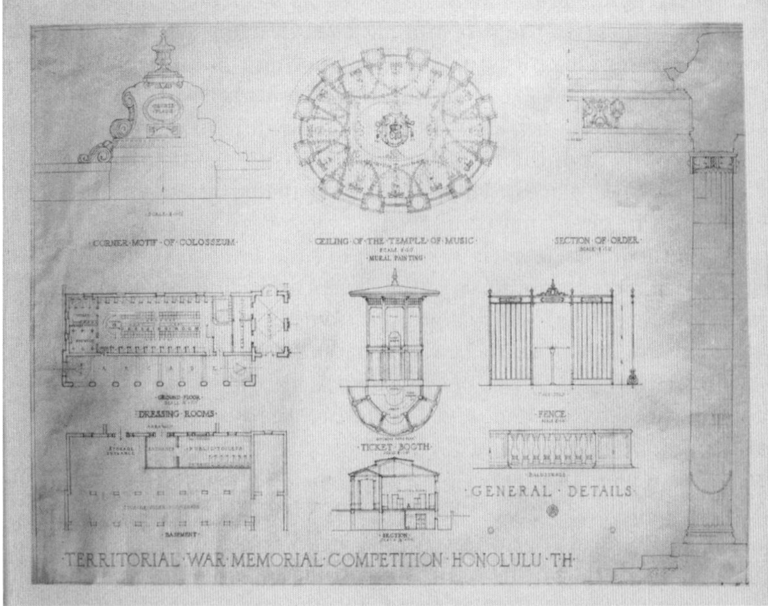


*Figure 2.6* Hobart's 'Temple of Music.' Hawai'i State Archives.

cost-cutters' main casualty [Fig. 2.6]. As a result, Hobart's extant memorial is less like his award-winning design and more like the Legion's earlier guiding sketch.

## Hobart's folly

Like most *beaux-arts* constructions, the Waikīkī War Memorial Park and Natatorium is grandiose and pompous. The entrance is composed of a grand arch flanked by two pilasters projecting slightly out from the wall (pilasters are rectangular supports resembling a flat column). The top of the arch features typical classical ornamentation — a medallion and frieze topped with a round pediment in the Greek Revival style. Two large symmetrical eagles on either side flank the medallion. Adjacent to the main entrance arch are two smaller arches, above each of which is a decorative cartouche set into the wall, topped with elaborate cornices. The effect of the entrance is to present a symmetrical façade, an imposition of order, structure, and planning into the natural disordered surroundings of sea, beach, and parkland. In its imperial grandeur, it means to instruct viewers of the benefits of the stability and order that European civilization can provide. Architectural historian William Jordy states, 'the idea of stability was ... implicit in the traditionalism of the Beaux-Arts esthetic; in other words, its academic point of view which held ... that the past provided vocabularies of form and compositional themes from which the present should learn' (279).

Memorials can only work as designed when the shared memory of the past is uncontroversial. As historian Kirk Savage points out, for example, memorials to the American Civil War avoided controversy by memorializing soldiers from both sides instead of the disputed causes they fought for. In the process, these memorial makers erased from their reconstructed history images of slaves and slavery. Conversely, the Vietnam Veterans Memorial is controversial because its design reflects the arguments over the war it commemorates.[19] American World War One memorials avoided such controversy by narrating that war as a noble cause, a clear-cut fight between good and evil, freedom and despotism — the evil 'Hun' verses the freedom-loving, democratic nations of England and the United States. Historian G. Kurt Piehler explains: 'After the Armistice, national leaders rushed to build monuments and create rituals honoring America's victory. Through these monuments and rituals, they hoped to camouflage the divisions caused by the war (93–4).

While comparisons between war memorials dedicated to different wars can be problematic, some use can be made of comparing and contrasting the Vietnam War Memorial in Washington to the Waikīkī War Memorial. It should not be expected, of course, that the Waikīkī War Memorial should in any way resemble the Vietnam Wall: the former is a product of a victorious war with relatively few American casualties (compared to other Allied losses); the latter is a product of a bitterly divisive war, which America lost. However, rather than making any comparison between the two memorials inappropriate, those differences in historical context can actually serve to illustrate the functions of memorials in a society at any given time.

Unlike, the self-reflective Vietnam War Memorial, the imposing entrance of Hobart's structure has most of its decoration and inscriptions well above eye level, and thus demands that its audience step back, crane their necks and look up to the two American eagles. The Vietnam War Memorial is made with black reflective granite instead of the triumphant white marble or stone of *beaux-arts* monuments. Whereas the façade of the Waikīkī War Memorial insists that viewers remain passive in contemplation of its majesty, onlookers at the Vietnam War Memorial can see themselves reflected in the stone, which seems to mirror the introspective mood associated with the 'Vietnam Syndrome.' The names on the Honolulu Stone are arranged in a rigid and anonymous way: top and center is an eagle holding laurel leaves. Below that there is a five-pointed star in whose center is a circle with the letters 'US.' Below that on a banner is the legend 'FOR GOD AND COUNTRY.' Below that is the legend 'ROLL OF HONOR' and below that again is the line [in quotation marks] 'DULCE ET DECORUM EST PRO PATRIA MORI.' Below that are the words 'IN THE SERVICE OF THE UNITED STATES.' The names are listed in three columns and split into Army and Navy. Below that, also in three columns are the names of those who died 'IN THE SERVICE OF GREAT BRITAIN.'

These categorizations group the soldiers together as if they died in a common cause, and to make them anonymous servants to the greater glory of war. Compare that to the Vietnam Veterans Memorial, where the soldiers' names are arranged chronologically by date of death instead of country, rank or regiment. This has the effect not only of verisimilitude — making it real — but also of making it a more democratic 'people's' memorial, rather than a regimented military monument. Memorial designer Maya Lin's initial intention was that visitors wanting to find a name on the memorial would need to already have a certain amount of historical information about the war, including the date of the death of the soldier. In this way, the wall's design would require interactivity between the memorial and the visitor. However, after some discussion with veterans, telephone book-style directories of names were placed on nearby podiums so that visitors could locate individual casualties (Sturken, *Tangled* 56). Whereas most war memorials function as designed only if they remain vague about actual details of a war and its causes, in contrast, the intention of the Vietnam Veterans Memorial was that it would work only when precise historical details are present. Unlike the interactive Vietnam Veterans Memorial, which asks visitors to reflect on the causes of the war and the folly and waste that war entails, the façade of the Waikīkī War Memorial and Natatorium means to inspire awe and respect for Euro-American achievements, to excuse warfare as a legitimate and honorable way of solving disputes, and to glorify the US military and its role in the conflict.

The Waikīkī War Memorial and Natatorium is dedicated to war, not peace. However, it is also dedicated to victory. The memorial contains, for example, three triumphal arches (an entrance arch, flanked by two smaller arches). In a 1919 *Advertiser* article, architect C.R. Ripley had warned of the inappropriateness of utilizing such celebratory imagery. Ripley argued, 'Surely we want no memorial arches. The watchword of the war has been, "To make the world safe for democracy." Where does the victory arch typify that inspiration? We want no memorials to glorify war and victory' ('Proposed Memorials'). Hobart, however, relied heavily on the American legion's arch-dominated design ('Tentative Sketch'), and thus ensured the memorial would be dedicated to vanquishing America's enemies.

James Mayo describes war memorials dedicated to victory as 'trophies,' which 'assure us that the war was honorable. God was on the side of the victors, and therefore their cause was righteous' (*Landscape* 61). The Waikīkī War Memorial fits neatly into Mayo's analysis of victory monuments: it is made to be 'steadfast and solid,' of those 'good materials [that] are practical expressions of permanence.' The main design on the *mauka*-facing wall is above head level, a technique, Mayo notes, that 'works as a metaphor, since we look "up" to people we respect' (*Landscape* 61). A major theme of this memorial is the sacrifice that Hawai'i and its citizens make for the greater glory of America. Advocating 'peace' instead of victory was seen as weakness; war was a rite of passage to manhood transmitted 'through inscriptions on war memorials which lauded martial virtues by accompanying the names of the fallen with adjectives such as "brave" or "courageous"' (Mosse 48).

The Waikīkī War Memorial does not make any bold or precise statements about those it commemorates. There are no phrases, for example, like 'killed in action' or 'killed by enemy fire.' Instead, the memorial is coy and evasive about where and why these soldiers died. It utilizes non-specific phrases such as 'For God And Country,' 'Roll Of Honor,' '*Dulce Et Decorum Est Pro Patria Mori*,' 'In The Service Of Great Britain,' and 'In The Service Of The United States,' all of which could refer to a number of wars. Clearly the overall impression the memorial wishes to convey is that the soldiers died for a noble cause, which is why the legend does not linger on any specific reasons for the war, or mention any particular battles. The effect of this is, as Mayo notes, 'facetious,' as the high-minded and abstract ideals mentioned 'are not grounded in the ugly realities of war' (*Landscape* 88). In this respect, the memorial is ahistorical. This narrative is, as historian Paul Fussell points out,

> typical of popular histories of the war written on the adventure-story model: they like to ascribe clear, and usually noble, cause and purpose to accidental or demeaning events. Such histories thus convey to the optimistic and credulous a satisfying, orderly, and even optimistic and wholesome view of catastrophic occurrences-a fine way to encourage a moralistic, nationalistic, and bellicose politics (*Wartime* 21–2).

Whereas the British public knew by the end of the war that the battlefields of Belgium and France were slaughterhouses, an epiphany which led to the disillusioned literary style of the period, Americans, who had suffered far fewer casualties, and had been fighting for only about six months, from March 1918 until the Armistice in November, were still inclined to think of the war as a 'noble cause.' Historian David Kennedy states, 'Almost never in the contemporary American accounts do the themes of wonder and romance give way to those of weariness and resignation, as they do in the British' (214). This desire by Americans, to remember the war as dignified and purposeful, is also why Latin was chosen as the language of the most forthright statement on the tablet. Such raised and 'essentially feudal language,' as Fussell calls it, is the language of choice for memorials (*Great* 21).

By the end of the war, British writers left behind the 'high diction' of nineteenth-century literary tradition — words and phrases like 'steed' instead of 'horse,' 'strife' instead of 'warfare,' 'breast' instead of 'chest,' and 'the red wine of youth' in place of 'blood' — and instead described events in a more down-to-earth and realistic way (Fussell, *Great* 21). However, memorials were a different matter: whereas it seemed appropriate, given the high death tolls and brutality of World War One, for writers to change to a more factual and graphic idiom, 'high diction' remained the language of monuments and memorials. It seemed somehow inappropriate and disrespectful, given the solid dignified presence of a concrete or marble memorial, to tell the undignified truth about wartime deaths, a truth that would involve grisly descriptions of severed limbs, burst intestines, decapitations, and other bloody injuries. Moreover, if the purpose of Waikīkī War Memorial was to inspire Native devotion to the greater glory of the state (the United States) — to be, as historian John Bodnar puts it, 'reminded of "love of country" and their duty to their "native land"' — it would be self-defeating to remind Hawaiians of the butchery of Flanders ('Public' 78).

The purpose of the Waikīkī War Memorial and Natatorium is only superficially a tribute to Hawai'i's Great War dead. In fact, the dead were used in death as they were in life, as sacrifices to the gods of war, to militarism, colonialism, and nationalism. This is evident in the memorial's scale and in its deliberately vague and guarded inscription. James Mayo argues that war memorials 'represent failure, the failure to prevent war' (*Landscape* 58). However, the American Legion and its supporters chose to build a huge neoclassical structure that exaggerates Hawai'i's role in the Great War. Given the relatively small number of casualties and minor role played by Hawai'i, a more honest memorial would surely have been the small token affair envisaged by Burnham and championed by Macfarlane.

## Conclusion

The Waikīkī War Memorial and Natatorium represents a grand, overstated tribute to the relatively small number of casualties sustained by residents of Hawai'i. However, that, of course, is not its true purpose, as is evident in its design and scale. The message that it evokes is one of submission to imperial forces and glorification of both war and the American military. This is exemplified by the legend on the Honolulu stone which reads, '*Dulce et decorum est Pro patria mori*,' or 'it is sweet and noble to die for one's country,' from Horace's *Odes*. This phrase would not only have been familiar to those with a classical education, but also to a wider audience who had read popular war novels. As David Kennedy points out, 'one of Edith Wharton's characters [in her 1918 book *The Marne*] tearfully meditate[d] on the ancient phrase from Horace: "dulce et decorum est pro patria mori"' (179). However, at that time, the more topical and relevant use of that quotation was by British soldier and war poet, Wilfred Owen. His poem entitled *Dulce et decorum* cautions against the very same triumphant patriotism that the Waikīkī War Memorial Park and Natatorium represents:

> *My friend, you would not tell with such high zest*
> *To children ardent for some desperate glory,*
> *The old Lie: Dulce et decorum est*
> *Pro patria mori.*

Both Hobart and the American Legion probably knew of Owen's poem. Like Siegfried Sassoon, he was well known and widely publicized at that time. They chose, however, to use the quote in its original context — as an obsequious and jingoistic tribute to war.

One-hundred-and-one persons from Hawai'i died during the Great War. Who can know now what their motivations were in enlisting? Certainly for some it was not to defend the United States, as 22 of them enlisted with the British forces before the US even entered the war. On 31 July 1917, a military draft was introduced that applied to all residents of the United States between the ages of 21 and 30, whether native born, naturalized, or alien. The draft was expanded in October 1918 to all male residents between the ages of 19 and 40. In total, 4336 of those who registered for the draft were called up to serve in the 1st and 2nd Hawaiian Infantry (Warfield 78). Of the 79 non-Navy US deaths recorded on the memorial, 40 men served with the 1st or 2nd Hawaiian Infantry. These units were, in effect, the Hawai'i National Guard, federalized and sent to Fort Shafter and Schofield Barracks for garrison duty to release other, more professional troops for war service. Soldiers in these units had little chance of being sent to France. Many of them worked in the sugar plantations and, as scholar Charles Warfield notes, Washington recognized that Hawai'i's sugar was more important than any contribution in terms of manpower that it could make to the war:

> The National Guard had been organized with the idea that it would be used only for the defense of the Islands and would never be sent overseas. A large proportion of its ranks was composed of men who were indispensable to the sugar industry of the Islands, which had been greatly expanded during the war in Europe. If the National Guard of Hawaii were mobilized when the United States went to war it would seriously cripple the sugar industry (Warfield 72).

Twenty-five of the non-Navy soldiers who are named on the memorial enlisted after July 1918, and 36 of the 67 men enlisted in non-naval forces were attached to the 1st and 2nd Hawaiian Infantry. In other words, nearly one-third of those who died while serving in the US military may have been unwilling draftees, not volunteers, and almost one half may have joined up to avoid having to go overseas to fight in the World War.[20] It is also possible that some 'aliens' (non-US citizens) went into the draft believing that it offered a route to US citizenship, or, at least, some kind of social acceptance. Historian Lucy E. Salyer reveals, for example, the Selective Draft Act of 1917 meant only aliens who had declared their intention of becoming US citizens were eligible for the draft. Nationwide, of the half a million men who were either enthusiastically or reluctantly inducted in the first draft in 1917, 123,277 were aliens, and between 1918 and 1920, almost a quarter of a million soldiers were naturalized as US citizens (851–2).[21]

Of the 72,000 residents of Hawai'i registered for the draft as eligible to fight, 29,000 — or 40 percent — were *issei* and *nisei*. Of the total that actually did serve in the US Armed Forces, 838 — approximately 9 percent — were of Japanese descent (Odo and Sinoto 208). Since Japan was at war with Germany at this time, who can say, with any certainty, where their loyalties lay? In 1921, for instance, journalist Joseph Timmons of the *San Francisco Examiner*, questioned whether military service was an appropriate measure of loyalty to Americanism. Referring specifically to the Japanese of Hawaii, Timmons concluded, somewhat caustically, 'none of them volunteered; they were in the National Guard and had no choice, or they were drafted' (Salyer 863). If they did intend to fight for the US, as did the Japanese volunteers of the famous 442nd Regiment in World War Two, how many enlisted to prove their loyalty in an unwritten test that should never have been enacted? Undoubtedly, those involved in the advocacy, planning, design, and building of the War Memorial were mostly *haole*. There is little evidence, for example, of the involvement of Native Hawaiians or Japanese residents of Hawai'i. Indeed, it is ironic that 838 Japanese residents of Hawai'i served in the American military, yet it was military that asked the Hawai'i State Legislature in 1919 to pass a bill regulating Japanese language schools, and the American Legion, which gave that bill its full support, were hostile, in both rhetoric and action, to Japanese culture in Hawai'i (Okihiro 108).

Most newspaper accounts of Hawai'i during the Great War paint a picture of a dedicated, patriotic populace, eager to do 'its bit' for the war effort. Occasionally, there was some slippage in this narrative. For example, a 1919 *Advertiser* headline complained, 'not enough Hawaiians are on hand at the railroad depot when the mustered-out soldiers arrive there each day from Schofield Barracks to form a real welcoming committee. Representative citizens are in a feeble minority in the crowds.' This was in contrast to the US mainland where 'every town that has a railroad depot has its crowds on hand when a train comes in and the returning boys are given the biggest kind of welcome' ('Weak Welcome').

Sociologist Albert Memmi has noted that it is the colonialist's 'nation's flag which flies over the monuments' in a colonized country and that the colonialist 'never forgets to make a public show of his own virtues, and will argue with vehemence to appear heroic and great' (13, 54). Both of these descriptions aptly fit the Waikīkī War Memorial and Natatorium. It glorifies war and acts to consolidate the American colonial presence in Hawai'i. Its celebration of the deaths of men for 'freedom and democracy' masks the fact that the Great War was fought between imperial powers, many of which were governed by unelected monarchies. Writer Jonathan Schell suggests, 'every political observer or political actor of vision has recognized that if life is to be fully human it must take cognizance of the dead' (121–2). But what is the proper way to remember the dead of a senseless world war? Should they be recruited, as the American Legion and others seem to think, to perpetuate patriotic, pro-militaristic narratives? The architectural folly that is the Waikīkī War Memorial and Natatorium should remind us that, instead of glorifying war, nationalism, and militarism, there is no better tribute to those fallen than to remember war's waste and futility.

# 3
# 'Unknown Soldiers': Remembering Hawai'i's Great War Dead

Hawai'i's Great War dead are among the forgotten casualties of the 1914–18 conflict. They have received almost no scholarly attention, and are missing from Hawai'i's history books, which tend to focus instead on World War Two rather than Hawai'i's much smaller role in the Great War. A memorial park and natatorium has been dedicated to them, but the swimming pool has long since fallen into disrepair and disuse. The memorial has been plagued with problems since its inauguration in 1927. Although popular with locals and tourists alike, problems with the natatorium's design meant that seawater would not flush away and be replaced as planned. Before long, swimmers could not see the bottom of the pool through the stagnant water. Concrete walkways soon began to peel and crack, the diving board became unsafe, and the stands began to crumble. Renovations in the 1940s could not solve the original design shortcomings and in the 1960s the pool was temporarily closed for health and safety reasons. In 1973 the City and County of Honolulu and the State of Hawai'i planned to demolish the Memorial. However, opposition to these plans came from patriotic organizations such as the American Legion, and ordinary citizens who formed a Natatorium Preservation Committee and in 1973 succeeded in getting the structure listed on the State Register of Historical Places.

The natatorium has been closed and fenced off since 1980, and in the years since then a lively and sometimes acrimonious debate has taken place over whether it should be refurbished, demolished, or perhaps transformed for other usage such as a beach volleyball court or car park. In 2001, the City and County of Honolulu decided, controversially, to refurbish the memorial at a cost of $10.8 million. The debate about that decision continues, but in all these discussions, there has been little mention of those the memorial commemorates.

Residents groups invoke their memory in their on-going attempts to persuade the State to return the memorial to its former glory. Aside from that, though, to most Hawaiians the dead are almost unknown. Democratic Senator Daniel Akaka stated: 'Today, few Americans recall the horrible events or heroes of World War I, with the exception of families, generations removed, who lost a loved one in that war over 80 years ago' (Kakesako).

Scant though it has been, the popular and official narrative of Hawai'i's role in World War One typically features recurring themes of honor, sacrifice, duty, and love of country. For example, on Memorial Day, 2002, Akaka dedicated a new marble headstone at the grave of Private John Rowe, who was killed in action in France on 31 July 1918. Akaka announced that Rowe had died 'in defense of freedom and democracy' and for the ideals of 'freedom, liberty, and peace' (Kakesako). [Fig. 3.1] Akaka tells a simple story, which is unambiguous and uncomplicated.

*Figure 3.1* Headstone of John Rowe. Photo by Brian Ireland.

However, the lives of these men were anything but simple. Hawai'i in the 1910s was a territory of the United States. Its population was diverse and included natives, Filipinos, Koreans, Portuguese, Japanese, Chinese and Americans. An ongoing campaign of '100% Americanism' gathered momentum with the outbreak of war against Germany. This campaign included a determined effort to close Japanese language schools and represented 'an integral part of the Americanization crusade that swept the nation during and after World War One' (Tamura 37). Under pressure from patriotic pressure groups such as the American Legion, school curriculum began to concentrate on American history and government, civic lessons, and daily nationalistic rituals such as flag raising (Tamura 37). The term 'slacker' was used to brand those who were thought to be avoiding military service and who were, by inference, unpatriotic. Vigilante groups sometimes punished the unpatriotic with more than harsh words: in 1917, the Bureau of Investigation, forerunner to the Federal Bureau of Investigation, set up the American Protective League, a vigilante-like organization, which consisted of 250,000 Americans who vowed to 'sp[y] on neighbors, fellow workers, office-mates, and suspicious characters of any type' (Kennedy 82).[1]

The Territory of Hawai'i played a minor role in the war effort. By the end of 1918, 9800 residents of Hawai'i were in American military service (Schmitt, 'Hawai'i's War') and approximately 200 in British or Commonwealth forces (Kuykendall, *Hawaii* 90). Only a small percentage of these men served in a war zone. In total, 101 died during or soon after the war. Seventy-nine of the dead were in the US Armed Forces and 22 in British Armed Forces. Of the 79, only eight were killed by enemy action. Seven died in France,[2] and one drowned when a German U-Boat torpedoed the troopship *Tuscania* off the coast of Great Britain. The cause of death of the other 71 servicemen is as follows: 36 died of flu and and/or pneumonia in the great epidemic that ravaged the world in 1918, five died in accidents, one of suicide, two of heart attacks, eight of unknown causes, and 19 of other natural causes. Only eight of the 71 non-combat-related deaths occurred in France. Of those, four died of flu, two in accidents, and two of unknown causes.

Hawai'i's Great War casualties have been mostly forgotten, which, it might be argued, befits their limited role in the conflict. As discussed in Chapter 2, the most significant site of remembrance for the Great War in the islands, the Waikīkī War Memorial Park and Natatorium, attempts to evoke feelings of patriotic duty and noble sacrifice. In that respect, it is typical of a wider American remembrance of the Great War, as G. Kurt Piehler explains: 'As portrayed in stone and in ceremony,

America's first European land war remained an idealistic struggle for liberty and democracy waged by a united people' (94). However, this simplistic, inchoate narrative of honor, sacrifice and devotion serves only to silence and erase counter narratives, while rendering aphonic those it is supposed to give a voice to. In its scale, which is arguably much out of proportion to the small role played by Hawai'i in the war, and by a process of careful omission in its inscription, the memorial provides only a monoglossic patriotic story, while omitting most of the mundane and perhaps more revealing aspects of the lives of the fallen. For example, the memorial infers that all of those it commemorates were killed in action in France. In fact, only 16 of the 79 who served in the US armed forces actually died in France, or on the way there, and only eight of those were killed by enemy action (Schmitt, 'Hawai'i's War'). This particular myth is persistent: in 2006, Linuce Pang, president of the Friends of the Natatorium local residents' group stated, 'These 101 men and women gave their lives to go clear over to Europe, all the way from Hawai'i. This [memorial] was to honor them' (Dingeman).

While the war was in progress, Hawai'i's newspapers assured readers that the war was a noble cause. After the war, when the nation began to reflect on the terrible loss and futility of the war, Hawai'i's press then assured islanders that the casualties were not in vain. According to the *Honolulu Star-Bulletin*, the soldiers' goal was to 'make the world free' ('Honor Roll'). The *Pacific Commercial Advertiser* insisted that men 'gave their lives that civilization might not be snuffed out and supplanted by "kultur"' ('Information'). The American Legion referred to the dead as 'our very own; flesh of our flesh, blood of our blood; stalwart sons of Hawaii-nei who laid down their lives that we might live to perpetuate the freedom for which they died. Crusaders for a noble faith ... [t]heir names are graven on our memorials and enshrined in our hearts as a Rosary of humility and gratitude' (Hill, Harold 50). This patriotic narrative has continued ever since.

The purpose of this chapter is, therefore, to explore journalist Michael Sledges's inquiry, 'To whom do the dead belong?' (178), not only by shedding light on these largely forgotten victims of the 'war to end wars,' but also by investigating the differences between private and 'official'[3] remembrance of these men, thus challenging the current single-narrative approach to the historical memory of Hawai'i's Great War dead. Sledge believes that a soldier's body 'is the physical representative, or envoy, of his nation and, as such, embodies its ideology, political beliefs, and culture' (26). Building on the work of cultural historian Elizabeth Hallam and sociologists Jennifer Lorna Hockey and Glennys

Howarth, Sledge argues that before death the physical self (what someone looks like) and the social self (how a person behaves, their belief system, and what they represent to others) are essentially the same. In general, a person's physical appearance cannot be disassociated from how they are perceived by those who know them. After death, however, the physical remains decay, and the social self becomes a disembodied idea, a memory of the individual rather than an ongoing relationship. In such circumstances, a new social self may be created by those left behind — relatives, friends, workmates, fraternal organizations, political groups, historians and also the state. This memory is open to interpretation or even manipulation, as the memory of the dead may not be a fair representation of what they stood for when they were alive. After death, many people become martyrs to causes they didn't necessarily believe in. In a similar way, soldiers may become martyrs to national causes they were ambivalent about, or even hostile to (Sledge 21–2).

In its scale, through its design, and in the noble words of the memorial plaque, the Waikīkī War Memorial Park and Natatorium proffers a sanctified and narrowly patriotic way of remembering the dead of the Great War. This single-narrative approach is replicated, to an extent, in military graveyards, for example at the Post Cemetery, Schofield Barracks, where 19 soldiers from the Great War are buried, and at the National Memorial Cemetery of the Pacific (also known as Punchbowl National Cemetery), where over 30,000 casualties and veterans of World War Two, the Korean, and Vietnam wars are buried (Carlson 8–12), as well as an unknown number of veterans of World War One.[4] Commemoration at civilian cemeteries, however, differs in revealing ways from remembrance in military gravesites. Scattered throughout the islands, the civilian graveyards in which most of the Great War dead are interred, offer a complicated and less ordered narrative than their military counterparts. For example, while religion may seem to be a common, unifying theme at all sites of remembrance, at military shrines such as Hawai'i's Great War memorial, where soldiers died 'for God and country,' religious devotion is inextricable linked to patriotic nationalism. However, in the denominational and nondenominational civilian graveyards in which most Hawai'i's Great War dead are buried, no such connection is made, unless relatives of the dead choose personally to do that through the inscriptions they place on headstones. These differences between what might be termed the 'public memory' of Hawai'i's role in the Great War — what historian John Bodnar refers to as 'a body of beliefs and ideas about the past that helps a public or society understand both its past, present, and by implication, its future' (*Remaking* 15) — and the 'private' or non-official memory can be profound: James Mayo's perceptive observation that 'a statue in a park represents patriotism, but a grave is a resounding reminder of the consequences of war' (*Landscape* 33), remind us that although warfare may occasionally embrace the high-minded and romantic ideals proposed in official ceremonies and symbols of remembrance, its inevitable consequences are also loss, grief, pain, and the silence of countless 'mute, inglorious Milton[s].'

## Hawai'i's war dead[5]

Of the 79 US servicemen named on the memorial, 21 were born outside the United States. Sixteen were born in the Philippines, three in Europe, one in Korea, and one in Canada. Only 34 then — less than half — were born in Hawai'i. Twenty-five of the 79 have surnames than can be identified as northern European in origin,[6] 23 of the names are Native Hawaiian,[7] ten are Portuguese,[8] four have Chinese surnames,[9] and one is Korean.[10] Only 16 — less than one-sixth — of the US deaths, combat-related or otherwise, actually occurred in a war zone. Of the remainder, 42 died in Hawai'i, 14 in the United States, two at sea, one in Canada, one in England, one in the Panama Canal Zone, and two in unknown locations. Fifty-three died in the time period in which the United States was involved in the war, that is, from 6 April 1917 to 11 November 1918. The remaining 26 died after the war ended of non-combat-related causes.

These statistics, which indicate the racial and national diversity of the fallen, show the folly of assigning a single patriotic motive to Hawai'i's war dead. Currently they are remembered as little more than ciphers in a militarized agenda. To illustrate the plurality of historical memory it is necessary, therefore, to explore the biographical detail of their lives. In so doing, their memory as individual human beings can be recovered. In addition, the stories of their lives and deaths can serve as a window into the racial and national landscape of Hawai'i at that time, which was so alarming to the advocates of '100% Americanism.'

The first enlistee from Hawai'i in 'Pershing's Army' (the American Expeditionary Force) to die in France was Private John R. Rowe. Rowe was killed by shellfire on 31 July 1918 in an advance on the Vesle River, and was buried near Chery Chartreuse. The *Star-Bulletin* states, 'he met his death in action and gave Hawaii a place on the honor roll of America' ('Hawaii Did Her Part'). While the first part of the statement may be an accurate factual account, the second part is an act of myth making. Rather than the high motives assigned by the *Star-Bulletin* to Rowe,

*Figure 3.2* Apau Kau, star of the Chinese baseball team, as depicted on a promotional poster of the era. Author's personal collection.

there is, in fact, nothing in the public record to indicate why Rowe enlisted. Before the war he went to Royal School and worked as an office boy at the *Advertiser*. He is described as having had 'a fine singing voice, and being part Hawaiian, he yearned for a musical career and went to the mainland, traveling with a company of Hawaiian singers.' This was the decade in which Americans discovered Hawaiian music

(Brown, DeSoto), and Rowe felt he had an opportunity to forge a musical career for himself outside of Hawai'i (Kakesako). According to the *Advertiser*, while on the mainland, he was given a Selective Service Questionnaire whereupon he then traveled from Texas to New York to enlist in the 39th Infantry on 2 February 1918. Rowe trained in North Carolina and was soon sent to France, arriving in May 1918, just two months before his death ('Hawaii's First').

In a letter written to his mother a few days before his death, Rowe stated, 'Don't worry, Mother dear. We have got to win this war. If I fail do not mourn for me as I will have done only my duty. All of us won't come back. I hope I shall. However, if I do not, always remember me as having done my full duty for my country' (Kuykendall, *Hawaii* xvi). Taken at face value, these words suggest that Rowe died for the reasons suggested by the memorial. However, Rowe may also have been trying to comfort his mother during a period of intense fighting. Paul Fussell notes, for example, the reticence of British troops, the 'refusal of the men to say anything in their letters home' (*Great War* 181). Fussell warns of the unreliability of using soldiers' letters as a historical source: 'Clearly, any historian would err badly who relied on letters for factual testimony about the war' (*Great War* 183).

Sergeant Apau Kau, also known as En Pau Kau (Char and Char 112), lived in Honolulu. He worked for Bishop & Co. and was manager and pitcher of the 'Chinese University' Baseball Team from Honolulu that toured the United States in 1915. [Fig. 3.2] Kau was, evidently, something of a minor sensation, as this *Waco Morning Star* game review notes:

> Apau Kau, of the Chinese University of Honolulu, yesterday afternoon pitched a perfect game against Baylor [Texas], allowing not a single hit, walking nobody, hitting not a man and allowing not a Bear to reach first base. Behind him his teammates played errorless ball, and put four runs across as a reward for his wonderful pitching. It sometimes happens that a pitcher will get through a game without allowing a hit, but the records are particularly short of perfect baseball, and that is what the clever young American citizen of Chinese descent played yesterday (*Our Letter*).

When the US Congress declared war on Germany on 6 April 1917, Kau was living in Pennsylvania and was a member of that state's National Guard (Purnell 131). He enlisted in the 315th Infantry in Philadelphia on 18 September 1917. According to *The Official History of the 315th Infantry*, the unit did its basic training and preparation for war at Camp Meade (now Fort Meade, Maryland). Kau, known as 'Sam' to his comrades, continued his interest in sport by joining his regiment's baseball and football teams. He was shipped to France in May 1918, on board the US transport ship *America*. The 315th Infantry spent a period of time training behind the lines, before being moved to the front in September. The unit was involved in heavy fighting in the Meuse-Argonne Offensive, and Kau was killed in action in Argonne on 4 November 1918, seven days before the Armistice.

Kau was born in Kohala, Hawai'i, the fourth of seven children. His parents, Kyau and Loy Sang Kau, of Kwangtung Province in China, came to Hawai'i to work as contract laborers (Purnell 131). They were among approximately 46,000 Chinese laborers drawn to Hawai'i prior to 1898 to work on sugar plantations. The Kau family had a farm in the Halawa Valley, Kohala. However, all seven children left the Big Island to seek opportunity elsewhere. During the Great War, Edward En Young Kai joined the US Army Medical Corps and another brother, En You, was a mess sergeant for the Hawaiian infantry at Schofield Barracks (Char and Char 111–12). There is no record of why Apau Kau joined the Pennsylvania National Guard or the regular US Army. He was, however, one of over a thousand Hawai'i-born Chinese to enlist in the US Armed Forces (Char 158). While his attitude towards the United States and assimilating American customs is unknown, American attitudes towards the Chinese in Hawai'i are well documented. For example, the Hawaiian Board of Immigration made the following remarks *circa* 1900 about Chinese immigrants to Hawai'i: 'A Chinaman is unprogressive. He remains a Chinaman as long as he lives, and wherever he lives; he retains his Chinese dress; his habits; his methods; his religion; his hopes; aspirations and desires. He looks upon foreign methods, appliances, and civilization with scorn as inferior to his own' (Fuchs 86). By 1920, however, in the view of Hawai'i's *haole* population, 'the Chinese had become "trustworthy, upright and honored ... law-abiding, law-respecting, thrifty, industrious, and respectable"' — at least, in contrast to the Japanese, whom the haoles saw as an increasing threat to social stability in Hawai'i (Daws 314).

Historian Lawrence Fuchs notes that by 1930, 'The Chinese, more than any other immigrant group, had already acquired those characteristics which foreign observers think of as "typically American." Among second-generation Chinese, the English language, Christian religion, and American business and political methods had been energetically adopted' (86). Was Kau one of these 'assimilated' Chinese? He was, after all, very interested in the American sport of baseball. During a game on the US mainland, Kau was heckled by one fan who shouted, 'You ... yellow men are good sports all right. We've taught you the great game of baseball, but you've turned 'round and beaten our sons in our own back yards. That's ingratitude' (Hoe 69). It is likely significant that Kau chose to enlist in Philadelphia knowing that, unlike most of those who enlisted in Hawai'i in the 1st or 2nd Hawaiian Infantry, there was a fair chance that he would be sent to France and would therefore see combat.

The attitude of haoles towards Hawai'i's Chinese residents during the Great War is, thus, hard to pin down. At different times, the Chinese were either despised as 'coolies' or compared favorably to the Japanese who were threateningly superior in numbers to both the Chinese and haoles. This ambiguity did not, however, affect newspapers of the period. The *Star-Bulletin* reported Kau's death in an article revealingly titled 'Hawaii Did Her Part on France's Blood-Red Fields: Manhood of Isles Sacrifice Life on Land and Sea in Cause of Liberty.' In death, Kau was included in the patriotic narrative of sacrifice for the national cause. Whatever Kau's motivations for joining the US military, the *Star-Bulletin* created its own war story, the sentiments of which would appear later on the memorial.

In the same article, the *Star-Bulletin* reported Private Louis J. Gaspar's death in a similar way to Kau's: 'Not alone were the Chinese, English and Hawaiian boys represented at the front for Hawaii, but a Portuguese boy, Louis Gaspar, fought the good fight for his country.' Gaspar was born in Honolulu in 1898, probably the son of one of the 114 Madeirans who arrived aboard the ship *Priscilla* in 1878, or the 800 Portuguese immigrants that arrived in Hawai'i in 1881 from Sao Miguel, or, in any event, one of the 12,000 Portuguese that arrived in Hawai'i between 1878 and 1887 (Fuchs 52). It is unlikely that his family were earlier settlers in Hawai'i since by the mid-nineteenth century there were less than a hundred Portuguese, or *Pokiki*, resident there ('History of Hawai'i'). Gaspar enlisted at Fort Shafter, on 1 April 1918, and was attached to the Hawaiian Infantry. He died, killed in action, in the Argonne region of France on 1 November 1918, just ten days before the Armistice.

The Portuguese in Hawai'i were viewed as not quite 'white' because of their swarthy skin and Southern European origins. They were, nevertheless 'white enough' to be viewed favorably by Hawai'i's haoles in comparison to the Islands' other ethnic groups. As Fuchs points out, Americans and northern Europeans were always positioned in high managerial or ownership roles, whereas Portuguese immigrants became the *luna* or supervisor class, and 'acted as day-to-day buffers between the haoles and Oriental laborers' (Fuchs 57). It is therefore possible that Gaspar joined the US Army not because he agreed with the war's larger aims but simply to gain acceptance into the otherwise exclusive *haole* social arena.

Private George B. Tom was born in Honolulu in 1898. He enlisted at Fort Shafter on 1 April 1918, and was attached to Company A, 6th Engineers. He died of pneumonia in France on 18 October 1918, less than four weeks before the war ended. The *Advertiser* reported he was 'a member of the famous "Aloha" contingent, composed entirely of men under or above the draft age, whose desire to serve their country manifested itself in a direct enlistment' ('Honolulu Will Pay'). The 98 men who comprised the 'Aloha' contingent had volunteered for the regular army knowing that they would probably be sent to the front at the earliest opportunity. They were so-named due to the manner of their send-off from the islands: 'Every youth resembled a human flower garden, so covered with leis as to be almost hidden. They responded to the cheers of friends by singing battle songs and the melodies of Hawaii nei' (Kuykendall, *Hawaii* 39). The *Advertiser's* account follows a familiar military recruitment narrative of young men from different ethnic groups putting aside their differences and sacrificing their lives for America. For example, the paper makes clear that Tom was a 'Honolulu Chinese boy,' and described his mother as 'of the old style of Chinese women.' The paper made much of the maternal affection shown by Mrs. Tom and noted that she was 'very motherly … as brave as any American mother. She cried a little, but smiled through her tears, just like many other mothers in Honolulu who received like sad news' ('Honolulu Will Pay'). Of course, the military and local elites did not 'put aside' racial differences, but instead sought to manage them. For example, the Hawaiian National Guard on O'ahu was segregated into Hawaiian, Filipino, Portuguese, Japanese and Anglo-Saxon companies (Kuykendall, *Hawaii* 41).

The *Advertiser*'s focus on Tom's mother predates America's post-war fixation with the sacrifice of those American mothers whose sons died in the war. These women were known as Gold Star Mothers, due to the practice of families of servicemen of flying a banner in the windows of their homes. This 'Service Flag' displayed a blue star for each member of the family serving in the US military. However, if a serviceman died in service, this was denoted by a gold star. In the aftermath of the Great War, Gold Star Mothers formed their own local and national organizations, and they quickly became a focus of remembrance. Throughout the 1920s, they lobbied the US government to fund a pilgrimage to

France, and in 1929, Congress passed legislation to this effect. A number of pilgrimages took place between 1930 and 1933. G. Kurt Piehler argues that America's focus on mothers, instead of, for example, fathers or wives, demonstrates how the nation tried to shape remembrance of the war in terms of maternal sacrifice for a noble cause (101–5). Whereas the *Advertiser* used Tom's death to further a patriotic agenda, Tom seems, however, to have had less lofty motives for going to war. The young soldier had married a young schoolteacher just before leaving for France, and when he volunteered in the Engineer Corps he told his parents only that, 'it was a good chance to learn all about autos and machinery' ('Honolulu Will Pay').

Perhaps the most controversial name on the Waikīkī War Memorial is that of Captain Francis J. Green. Born in New York City, in 1863, Green enlisted on 10 January 1918. His first appointment was as rank of major, but he was later called into service as a captain in the Infantry Reserve Corps. Green had alcohol problems but apparently had been sober for two years. Six months previous to his death, he had been given an appointment in charge of registration for the selective draft. However, when he went to Maui for draft registration purposes, he got drunk and put unexplained items on his expenses account. It appears that he was not short of money — he had never worked until his appointment in charge of registration and that alcohol was the sole cause of the error/misdeed. After he returned from Maui, his work deteriorated badly. He gave his resignation to the Governor on 10 January 1918 due to 'ill health.' However, he had met with the Governor and US District Attorney Huber and was told that he would have to answer charges of embezzlement. He was given time to make preparations and tell his wife. Instead, however, he told her he needed a rest and took the train to the Haleiwa hotel. Green told the hotel manager he was having chest pains but had ordered his car to be sent so he could drive to Honolulu the next morning. However, it turned out he had not ordered the car at all. He was found the next day, 11 January 1918, dead in his bed with his nightclothes on and a book under his arm. A federal warrant for misappropriating government funds of $29.00 was unknowingly issued several hours after he died. A preliminary doctor's report stated that there was 'nothing to indicate any possible cause of death but heart failure.' Some circumstances would, however, point towards suicide, for example, his trouble with the law, and lying to his wife and the hotel manager. Although a newspaper report mentions that his organs were sent for an autopsy, there is, however, no record of the results of this, and heart failure remains the official cause of death. His ashes were scattered in the ocean on 7 May 1918 ('Tragic Death').

Seaman 2nd Class Manuel Gouveia Jr. was born in Kealakekua, Hawai'i, in 1897. Described by the *Star-Bulletin* as a 'young Portuguese-American,' Gouveia enlisted in Honolulu on 28 April 1917 ('Hawaii Did Her Part') and served on two ships, the USS *Alert* and USS *Schurz*. The *Schurz* was originally a German ship called *Geier*, which was detained in Hawai'i and then incorporated into US Navy. It sank on 21 June 1918 after a collision with the oil tanker *SS Florida* in heavy fog off the coast of North Carolina, with the loss of one life — the unfortunate Gouveia. The ship drifted for about 12 miles after the collision and then went down in about 100 feet of water. Twelve other sailors were injured, and Gouveia's body was not recovered.[11]

Hawai'i's newspapers reported the deaths of soldiers in such a way as to invoke feelings of patriotism about the United States and maintain support for the war. For example, Private Henry J. Evans, who enlisted at Fort Shafter on December 17, 1917, and died of pneumonia at Fort Sill, Oklahoma on 5 February 1918, is described in a *Star-Bulletin* article as having expired 'before he attained his heart's desire of licking the Hun' ('Hawaii Did Her Part'). Private Gideon Potter enlisted in the Canadian forces in the 201st Seaforth Highlanders in August 1914, along with two life-long friends, Bill Lanquist and Frederick Gosling. He died of unknown causes in Belgium on 28 October 1917. Those are the bare facts. However, the *Star-Bulletin* transformed Potter's death into a 'sacrifice' for civilization: 'Potter occupies a grave in devastated Belgium where he fought to keep back the horde of Huns threatening the world' ('Hawaii Men'). The paper does not, however, dwell on the fate of Potter's friends. Lanquist was severely injured and had to undergo two years of operations to remove shrapnel from his body. Gosling was wounded three times, once by a sniper who put him in hospital for five months. Descriptions of wounds and long, lingering convalescence detract from the patriotic mono-narrative. So when Captain Clair B. Churchill, attached to Canadian forces serving with the British Army, died at Amiens in August 1918, the *Star-Bulletin* imagined his finals moments in terms that made war seem noble, and death purposeful: 'Honolulu knows he met death in battle with a smile' ('Hawaii Did Her Part').

The reality of war is, of course, somewhat different to newspaper reports or monument inscriptions. Private Manuel Rames[12] was from Paia, Maui. He was attached to US Army 20th Engineers, 6th Battalion, E Company, and died when the German submarine UB77 torpedoed

*Figure 3.3* Postcard depicting SS *Tuscania*. Author's personal collection.

the troopship *Tuscania* off the Northern Irish coast on 5 February 1918. [Fig. 3.3] Rames' death must have been particularly terrifying, as this survivor's account of the attack reveals:

> There was a loud report and a jar, which made the 15,000 hulk trembler. Immediately the ship was in complete darkness. There was frantic scramble for lifebelts. I would like to forget, (but I know I never shall,) the scenes that followed. The dreadful groping about in the dark of those who were trying to locate lifebelts and boats. The unsuccessful attempts to launch many of the lifeboats, the breaking of cables, which emptied scores of poor fellows into the bitter cold water, the frantic and futile shouts of men who struggled as the high seas choked and chilled them, and the slow but steady listing of the great ship ('Tuscania').

For many of those who did manage to escape in lifeboats, a cruel fate awaited. Some boats headed for the lights of Rathlin Island, unaware that the brightest light was that of Altacarry lighthouse warning them away from the jagged rocks of the island. The bodies of some soldiers who had jumped ship, or had been dumped into the water by toppling lifeboats, were washed up on the Mull of Kintyre. Ironically, British warships rescued most of those who stayed aboard the *Tuscania*. Rames'

*Figure 3.4* Graves of American sailors at Kilnaughton, Islay. Museum of Islay Life, Port Charlotte.

body was recovered and buried with 89 of his comrades at Kilnaughton on the island of Islay, Inner Hebrides, Scotland on 9 February 1918 (*Photographic Album*). [Fig. 3.4] In the summer of 1920, all of the bodies were exhumed from their graves at Islay and returned to the United States ('Returning'; Sledge 159), where Rames was subsequently reburied at Arlington National Cemetery. Rames is one of only three servicemen from Hawai'i to be commemorated on multiple World War One memorials: in 1920 the American National Red Cross erected a monument on the Mull of Oa, on Islay, to commemorate the dead from both the *Tuscania* and the *Otranto* (another US troopship that sank off Islay in 1918). The inscription on the memorial states, 'On Fame's eternal camping ground, their silent tents are spread, while glory keeps with solemn round, the bivouac of the dead.'[13]

No doubt, many of those who enlisted did so because they believed it was their patriotic duty. Edward Canfield Fuller was born in Hamilton, Virginia, on 4 September 1893, to Katharine Heaton Offley (daughter of Washington banker Holmes E. Offley) and Lieutenant Ben Hebard Fuller, a career military man who would, in later years, attain the rank of general, and serve as Commandant of the Marine Corps between 1930 and 1934. A graduate of the United States Naval Academy class of

*Figure 3.5* Edward Canfield Fuller (1916). US Naval Academy.

1916, Captain Fuller was attached to the United States Marines Corps when he was killed in action at Belleau Wood, France on 12 June 1918. [Fig. 3.5] Fuller was posthumously awarded both the Navy Cross and the Distinguished Service Cross. According to his citation for both medals, he was honored for 'extraordinary heroism while serving with the 6th Regiment (Marines), 2d Division, A.E.F. in action in the attack on Bois-de-Belleau, France, 12 June 1918. While fearlessly exposing himself in an artillery barrage for the purpose of getting his men into a position of security in the attack on Bois-de-Belleau, Captain Fuller was killed and thereby gave his life in an effort to protect his men' (*Military Times*). Fuller is buried at Section 3, Lot 369 B, of the United States Naval Academy Cemetery, Annapolis. His father, who had 'never recovered from the sad loss of his son,' was buried alongside him in 1937 (Millet and Shulimson 233).

The *Star-Bulletin's* published a soporific obituary of Captain Fuller in 1919: 'Chateau Thierry: Who can ever forget that wonderful time when America's brave marines turned the tide of battle in favor of the allies? Asleep on that battlefield lies Captain Edward Fuller of Honolulu who, commanding a company of U.S. marines, laid down his life in the struggle to turn aside the Hunnish horde' ('Hawaii Did Her Part'). The Fuller family's connection with Hawai'i was rather brief, though: Ben Hebard Fuller served at the Naval Station, Honolulu from 1904 to 1906 (*Who's Who*). By that time, he was in his 30s, and had attained the rank of major. Presumably his young wife and family moved to the islands with him (his daughter Dorothy Nelson Fuller would have been approximately eight years old in 1904 and Edward Fuller 11 years old). However, in September 1906, Major Fuller left the Islands to take command of the School of Application in Annapolis, and no future assignment took him back to Hawai'i (Millett and Shulimson 226). Of course, this does not detract in any way from Captain Edward Fuller's service to his country and it is, in fact, surprising that this Navy Cross and Distinguished Service Cross winner is largely unknown in Hawai'i, aside from the brief inscription on the Waikīkī War Memorial. It is, nonetheless, an overstatement to describe him as one of 'Hawaii's own,' given his limited connection with the islands.

Lieutenant Henry Henley Chapman was a career soldier. He was a cadet at the US Military Academy from 14 June 1913 to 20 April 1917, and accepted an appointment on 20 April 1917 as 2nd Lieutenant of Infantry at Catasauqua Pennsylvania. He served with the 120th Infantry from 10 May 1918 until his death in France on 29 September 1918 of unknown causes ('Hawaii Did Her Part'). Private George K. Dwight enlisted at Fort Shafter and was attached to the Gas and Flame Corps 30th Engineers. He died at Annapolis, Maryland on 27 January 1918 of lobar pneumonia. In letters home to his mother he talked of enjoying training and not being bothered by the bitter East Coast winter weather ('Hawaii Did Her Part'; 'Service Flag'). As stated previously, letters home cannot be taken at face value. However, there is here some indication that, like the 'Aloha' volunteers, Dwight enlisted in an army unit that he knew had a fair chance of seeing battle.

Ivan Montrose Graham was born in Honolulu in 1895. He went to Punahou Academy and worked for the Advertiser as school correspondent and as a member of the editorial staff. He enlisted in Honolulu on June 13, 1911, and graduated from the US Naval Academy, Annapolis,

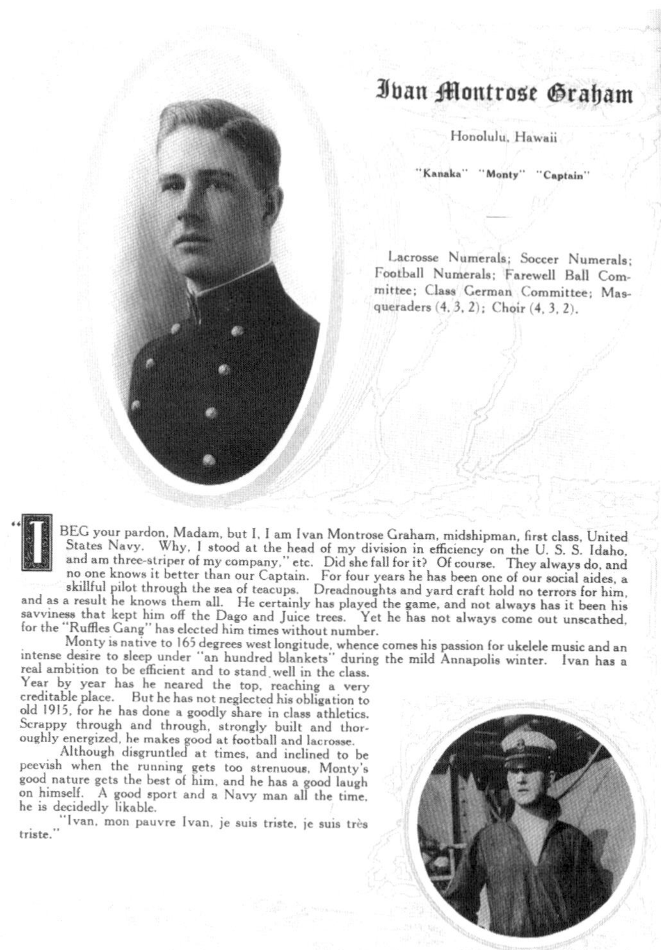

## Ivan Montrose Graham

Honolulu, Hawaii

"Kanaka" "Monty" "Captain"

Lacrosse Numerals; Soccer Numerals; Football Numerals; Farewell Ball Committee; Class German Committee; Masqueraders (4, 3, 2); Choir (4, 3, 2).

"I BEG your pardon, Madam, but I, I am Ivan Montrose Graham, midshipman, first class, United States Navy. Why, I stood at the head of my division in efficiency on the U. S. S. Idaho, and am three-striper of my company," etc. Did she fall for it? Of course. They always do, and no one knows it better than our Captain. For four years he has been one of our social aides, a skillful pilot through the sea of teacups. Dreadnoughts and yard craft hold no terrors for him, and as a result he knows them all. He certainly has played the game, and not always has it been his savviness that kept him off the Dago and Juice trees. Yet he has not always come out unscathed, for the "Ruffles Gang" has elected him times without number.

Monty is native to 165 degrees west longitude, whence comes his passion for ukelele music and an intense desire to sleep under "an hundred blankets" during the mild Annapolis winter. Ivan has a real ambition to be efficient and to stand well in the class. Year by year has he neared the top, reaching a very creditable place. But he has not neglected his obligation to old 1915, for he has done a goodly share in class athletics. Scrappy through and through, strongly built and thoroughly energized, he makes good at football and lacrosse.

Although disgruntled at times, and inclined to be peevish when the running gets too strenuous, Monty's good nature gets the best of him, and he has a good laugh on himself. A good sport and a Navy man all the time, he is decidedly likable.

"Ivan, mon pauvre Ivan, je suis triste, je suis très triste."

86

*Figure 3.6* Yearbook entry for Ivan Montrose Graham (1915). US Naval Academy.

in 1915. He was due to take up his post at Destroyer Force, Queenstown Ireland, but was taken ill at his point of embarkation, the Canadian port of the St. Lawrence. Lieutenant Graham died of pneumonia in hospital in Quebec, Canada on Sept 21, 1918. He had been married less than two years, and had an infant child. He also had a brother at the US Naval Academy ('Hawaii Men'). Although there is nothing in the historical record to suggest why Graham joined the US Navy, it seems clear he was an eager and willing enlistee. [Fig. 3.6]

Captain Philip Overton Mills also appears to be a willing volunteer. Born at Fortress Monroe, Virginia in 1882, his father was General Samuel Meyers Mills, Chief of Artillery of the US Army, and his brother Captain Paul Deuckla Mills was a liaison officer attached to the Fourth French Army. A former pupil of St. Paul's school in Concord, New Hampshire, and a Harvard graduate (Class of 1905), Mills had something of a privileged life: he played for three years on the Harvard football team, was a member of a number of exclusive clubs, such as the Racquet and Tennis Club in St. Davids, Pennsyvania, and the Tuxedo, Philadelphia and Harvard clubs in Concord, Pennsylvania ('Harvard Athlete'). It was perhaps the memory of his French mother that motivated him to volunteer, in 1916, for the Norton-Harjes Ambulance Corps, an American volunteer unit attached to the French Army.[14] Mills served for seven months and then gave some consideration to joining the Foreign Legion. However, when the US declared war, he returned to America to enlist. From 12 May 1917 to 14 August 1917, he attended the First Plattsburg Training Camp, and he accepted his appointment as captain on 15 August 1917 at Plattsburg Barracks, New York. Attached to the G Company, 308th Infantry, he was shipped to France aboard the SS *Cretic*. According to L. Wardlaw Miles, author of *A History of the 308th Infantry, 1917–1919,* Mills passed the time by entertaining his comrades: 'Captain Mills unearthed a badly mutilated piano from the depths of the hold and with it did much to relieve the monotony. The sight of this handsome officer in hip boots flushing the decks with a hose will never be forgotten by his devoted men' (Miles Chapter 2, p. 2). Mills served overseas from 6 April 1918 until 26 July 1918, when he was killed at Ker Avor, a French rest camp. He had been training troops how to use a French rifle grenade when it exploded prematurely, injuring two soldiers and killing Mills (Gaff 78; Miles Chapter 4, p. 7). Miles eulogizes Captain Mills as 'powerful of frame and deep of voice, full of jest, the very figure of an ideal soldier' (Chapter 1, p. 5) who was 'unsurpassed' as a 'leader of men' (Chapter 4, pp. 6–7). [Fig. 3.7]

Mills' father was in charge of a battalion of the Sixth United States Artillery, which was sent to Hawaii in 1899 ('Assignments'). It is unclear if his son traveled with him, as at this time Philip Mills was a pupil at St. Paul's School in Concord, New Hampshire. After graduating from St. Paul's, he enrolled at Harvard University, receiving his degree in 1905. It is likely, therefore, that Philip Mills lived in Hawai'i at some point or points between 1905 and 1916, whereafter he joined the

*Figure 3.7* Philip Overton Mills. Radnor Historical Society Collection.

Norton-Harjes Ambulance Corps. As well as being commemorated on the plaque at the Waikīkī War Memorial, Mills is also commemorated at Harvard, where his name is carved in stone on walls of the Memorial Room in the Memorial Church, on the St. Paul's war memorial in Concord, New Hampshire, and at the Radnor War Memorial in Wayne,

*Figure 3.8* War memorial at St. Paul's School in Concord, New Hampshire. Photo by Lisa Laughy.

Pennsylvania. [Fig. 3.8] The inscription at Harvard reads: 'While a bright future beckoned they freely gave their lives and fondest hopes for us and our allies that we might learn from them courage in peace to spend our lives making a better world for others' (*Memorial Church*). The inscription on the memorial at St. Paul's reads: 'In memory of the boys of St. Paul's School who gave their lives in the Great War 1914–1918' (Laughy). The inscription at the war memorial in Radnor reads: 'To the men and women of Radnor township who served in the World War and to those who gave their lives' (Patterson). [Fig. 3.9] [Fig. 3.10] Given the facts of Mills' life, it is hard to come to any other conclusion other than, until

*Figure 3.9* War memorial at Radnor, PA. 1922. Radnor Historical Society Collection.

his death, he remained, as Miles says, '[t]rue to the ideals of his soldier father,' and that he willingly 'laid down his life for his own country and for the beloved France of his mother' (Chapter 4, p. 7).

Second Lieutenant John Stephen O'Dowda was born on O'ahu, and lived in Ewa. O'Dowda went to St. Louis High School, was a graduate of Punahou Academy (1914) and was formerly an assistant sports writer

*Figure 3.10* War memorial plaque at Radnor, PA. Radnor Historical Society Collection.

for the *Advertiser*. He moved to the mainland in 1916 to go to college in Reno. However, when war broke out, he enlisted on 10 August 1917 and entered an officer training camp. He joined the aviation section of the University of California, and within three months was sent to Garden City, New York to await shipment across the Atlantic. His orders changed, however, and he instead went to Gerstner Field, Louisiana to continue training. In July 1918 in Dallas, Texas, he married a girl he met at university in Reno. O'Dowda, it seems, had options other than

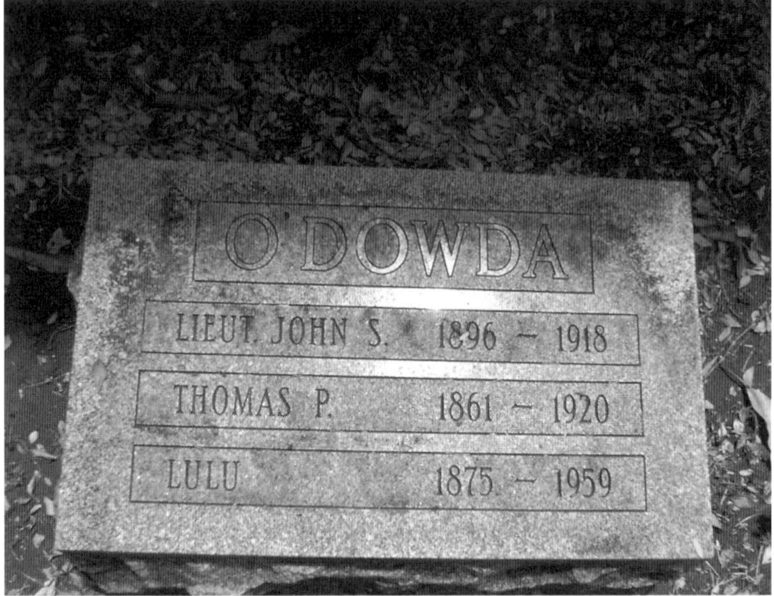


*Figure 3.11* Headstone of John Stephen O'Dowda. Photo by Brian Ireland.

military service. Even if he did feel any pressure to enlist, it seems probable he could have avoided action had he wanted to do so. He served with the Air Service from 10 August 1917 until his death on 13 November 1918 in an airplane accident. The *Star-Bulletin* described him as 'one of that daredevil crew of Uncle Sam's, a soldier of the air force' ('Hawaii Did Her Part'). [Fig. 3.11]

Another serviceman perhaps deserves more attention than history has so far given. Lieutenant James Henry R. Bryant was born on 15 September 1898 in Hana, Maui, Bryant went to school in California from 1912–15, and from 1915–17 he went to Hitchcock Military Academy in San Rafael. After graduation he returned to Kailua, Hawai'i for a short time, but left for Canada in August 1917. The next month he enlisted in the Royal Flying Corps. He arrived in London in March 1918 and was then sent to Italy, arriving on 10 June 1918 to join up with 28th Squadron Royal Air Force. His time spent in the war zone was short — he was, in fact, killed in action less than four months later, on 4 October 1918 after his Sopwith Camel crashed during a bombing attack on Austrian forces at the Campoformido aerodrome in north east Italy. According to a doctor who treated Bryant in an Austrian Military Hospital, after the crash the airman shot five Austrian troops before collapsing. He would later die of wounds received in the crash. Although he was buried with full Austrian military honors on 7 October 1918 in the hospital cemetery, his body was disinterred after the war and reburied at an English cemetery at Tezza, Italy ('Hawaii Boy'). Bryant's story has all the hallmarks of a 'Boy's Own' style action adventure. In some US states, individuals who exhibited fighting qualities like Bryant's have been commemorated with an individual, rather than, or as well as, a group memorial. It seems odd, therefore, that this particular American has not been singled out for any special memorializing, and that his acts of valor have largely been forgotten. It could be, though, that as Bryant fought for the British, his biography is less useful for maintaining the dominant Americanizing narrative. Its performative power requires an unambiguous and simplistic story of dedication and sacrifice for the United States, not for the imperial power of Great Britain.

## Public and private memory

Militaristic narratives rely on a hierarchic, ordered system of control that is not replicated in civil society and so needs to be repeatedly supported by way of memorials, commemorations, and displays. Writer Ian Lind notes, 'militarization is a dynamic and continuing process [that] must be continually reinforced and recreated, its rewards reasserted, rituals reenacted' (41). In the aftermath of World War One, the US government insisted that its buried servicemen would remain in France. However, many relatives of the slain wanted their men returned to the United States for private burial and mourning. The War Department distributed 75,000 questionnaires to the families of the dead. Of the approximately 50,000 that were returned, 71 percent responded that they would prefer the repatriation of the dead ('Objection'). The government's policy was based partly on practical issues, such as the sanitary condition of the corpses, or the estimated $8,000,000 cost of disinterring, transporting, and reburying perhaps as many as 50,000 bodies. Both the War Department and the US Army were in favor of disinterring the dead from scattered battlefields and reburying them in new memorial cemeteries in France and England. For patriotic groups such as the American Legion and the American Field of Honor organization, however, the compelling reason against repatriating bodies to the United States was more political than practical. At the Legion national convention in Minneapolis, a resolution was passed opposing the return of bodies from France, favoring instead reinterment in war cemeteries in France, Belgium and Britain. In this way, the Legion said, the graves of those who made the 'supreme sacrifice' would act as 'permanent memorials of America's unselfish service to humanity' ('Objection'). Republican representative from Ohio, Simeon Davison Fess, whose son Lowell Thomas Fess helped found the American Legion in Paris, argued that thousands of individual burials scattered across the United States would not have the lasting impact of a small number of war cemeteries in France. He stated, 'if the bodies were to be delivered at their former homes then without a great assemblage of graves in one place, a lesson to posterity, of the sacrifice made, will be lacking' ('Objection').

What was at stake here was how the war would be remembered: would it be recalled as a unified and noble national sacrifice, as symbolized by white-marble war cemeteries, funded and supervised by government agencies, or would the narrative be fragmented by the scattered *lieux de mémoire,* and the distinctly individual losses symbolized by family funerals and graveyards? Eventually, a compromise solution was reached: the government would honor the wishes of those families who wanted their loved ones returned, and for those who did not, where possible, their relatives would be reburied in war cemeteries in Europe. Although, according to Kennedy, most relatives 'eventually consented to leave the dead where they lay' (367), many relatives from Hawai'i did, however, ask that their relations be returned to the Islands.[15] Among those returned were four out of the eight soldiers who were killed in action (Apau Kau, Antone Mattos, John Rowe and Henry K. Unuivi)[16] and five out of the eight who died in France of non-combat-related causes (Richard Belmont Catton, Daniel K. Io(e)pa, George B. Tom, John Stephen O'Dowda and Clarence J. Watson). In total, at least nine out of the 16 who died in France were returned for burial in Hawai'i, a higher percentage than the overall American repatriation and reburial figures, and, perhaps an indication that the families' attitude to the war was less enthusiastic than the memorial conveys.

For relatives of the dead, a memorial may serve as 'substitute grave' (Moriarty, 'Material' 653), especially if the remains of their loved ones have never been recovered. However, when both a grave and a memorial exist, relatives may view the memorial as irrelevant or superfluous. Alternatively, a war memorial may offer some consolation that their relative's death was either not in vain, or was for a higher purpose. Art historian Catherine Moriarty argues that relatives who were unable to visit battlefield graveyards 'needed, in the absence of a body, some readily available focus for their grief. They ... needed to stage symbolic honoring, in the absence of a corpse' ('Absent' 12). Cultural historian

Alex King notes that memorials are places where mourners are 'encouraged to moderate or escape from grief by cultivating positive emotions towards the deaths of their friends and relatives' (173). However, a war memorial, or indeed a war cemetery, functions in this way only when it generates positive communal memory. Sociologist Bernard Barber asserts, for example, that such shared memory 'both confirms the legitimacy of the sentiments expressed and reinforces their strength in those who gather together to express them' (65). At the graveside, however, for mourning relatives the experience is likely to be personal and individual. For some, then, if a war memorial is not irrelevant, it is, at best, a secondary site of remembrance. For others, though, it serves as the primary site where the death of their loved ones is given meaning. Clearly then, different sites offer multiple kinds of mourning and remembrance, and therefore, the possibility of deviance or dissent from official types of remembrance.

The resting places of the 79 listed on the memorial as US servicemen are widespread and varied. Nineteen are buried at Schofield Barracks; two are buried at Puea Cemetery in the Kapalama district of Honolulu; 13 at O'ahu Cemetery; four at Kawaiahao Church Cemetery in Honolulu; three at other O'ahu graveyards; 13 on other Hawaiian islands apart from O'ahu; one was cremated; five are buried in the United States; two are buried in the United Kingdom; and one was lost at sea. The remaining resting places are unknown. The appearance of these graveyards varies a great deal: some are dignified and well kept, others dilapidated and over grown. Apart from those buried at Schofield, all gravesites are on civilian-owned and civilian-used property.

Military cemeteries and civilian cemeteries differ in their approach to interring and remembering the dead. Whereas military cemeteries are dominated by themes of order and control, the civilian cemeteries in which most of Hawai'i's Great War dead are buried are often cluttered and messy, thereby encouraging a different type of remembrance. They reveal what Ferguson and Turnbull call, 'a certain acceptance of jumble, of differences in the size, scale, inscription, and tilt of headstones, the placement of trees, the arrangement of flowers' (109). In contrast, at the National Memorial Cemetery of the Pacific — the largest and most-visited military cemetery in Hawai'i — uniformity is the order of the day. Located in Pūowaina Crater, an extinct volcano locals call 'Punchbowl' because of its distinctive shape, the huge cemetery overlooks downtown Honolulu and is, therefore, a significant reminder to the civilian populace of American military sacrifice, and of dues owed. [Fig. 3.12] Although the cemetery is, in the main, a product of World

*Figure 3.12* National Memorial Cemetery of the Pacific at Punchbowl. Photo by Kathie Fry.

War Two, the idea of a cemetery at Punchbowl first arose in the late 1890s. Honolulu was, at that point, a rapidly growing city, and cemetery space was in short supply. Punchbowl seemed an obvious choice for a new graveyard location, given that it was, supposedly, an ancient sacrificial site. However, opponents of the proposal feared that new burials would contaminate the city's water supply. Furthermore, some objected to the symbolism of a 'city of the dead' overlooking the new residential homes being built for some of Honolulu's richest citizens. The cemetery was not built and these concerns would again be raised when the idea was revisited in the 1940s (Carlson 23–7). Those who died in the Pacific Theater were, at first, interred in temporary graveyards throughout the Pacific. Pearl Harbor victims were buried, hastily, at sites throughout O'ahu, on military bases such as the Kaneohe Marine Corps base, at Schofield Barracks, and at a new navy cemetery at Halawa (Carlson 31). However, in 1948, the US Congress responded to pressure from veterans' groups and the families of the dead for a single, dedicated site, by appropriating funds for the construction of a national cemetery at Pūowaina Crater. Concerns about contamination of Honolulu's water supply were allayed when the Territorial Board of Health reported that the natural geography of the crater was not conducive to pollution from human remains (Carlson 33). Work began in

*Figure 3.13* Honolulu Memorial at the National Memorial Cemetery of the Pacific. Photo by Brian Ireland.

August 1948, and the first interments were made on 19 July 1949. Eventually, nearly 13,000 World War Two dead were interred in the cemetery (Carlson 10; *National Memorial*).

In 1964, the American Battle Monuments Commission erected the Honolulu Memorial, which consists of a 70-step ceremonial staircase, flanked on each side by 'Courts of the Missing' — tablets, on which are engraved the names of over 28,000 men whose bodies were either never recovered, or who were buried at sea (*Honolulu Memorial* 5). [Fig. 3.13] At the top of the staircase, a dedication stone leads to a reflecting pool, in which stands a central tower, decorated with a 30-foot female figure of Columbia standing on the prow of a US Navy aircraft carrier. [Fig. 3.14] A 'Court of Honor,' in the style of a Roman tomb, extends from each side of the central tower. It contains a small chapel and two map galleries, which tell the story of the progress and triumphant conclusions of the Pacific and European campaigns in World War Two, as well as the Korean conflict which, the gallery claims, was 'brought to a successful conclusion' with the Armistice of 1953. It is significant that, although two half-tablets dedicated to the Vietnam War dead were added to the Courts of the Missing in 1980,

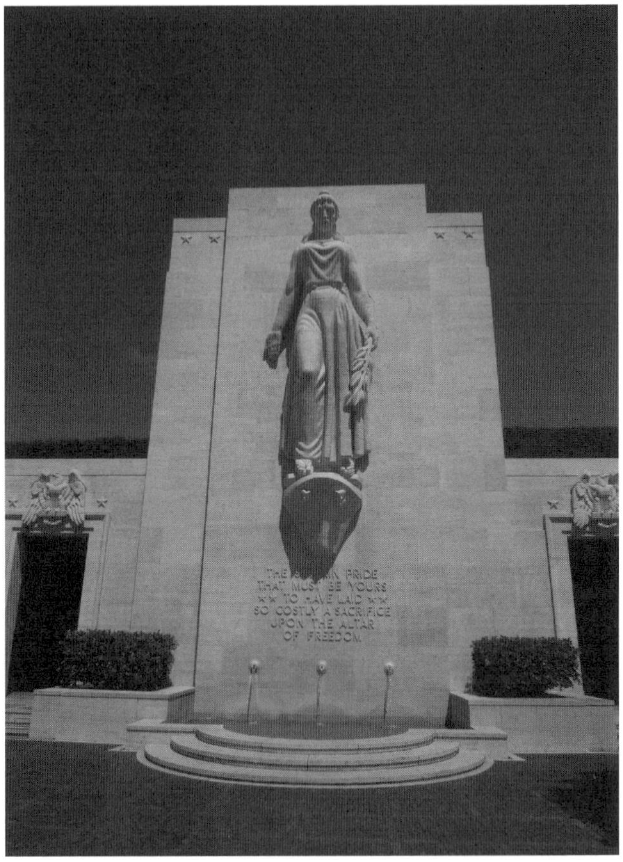


*Figure 3.14* Statue of 'Columbia,' Honolulu Memorial at the National Memorial Cemetery of the Pacific. Photo by Brian Ireland.

the map galleries make no reference to the US defeat in Vietnam. This suggests that, like the Waikīkī War Memorial Park and Natatorium, the cemetery is dedicated not only to remembrance of the dead, but also to national victory.[17]

It is not difficult to determine the sentiment of the Honolulu Memorial. Visitors are invited to identify with the victorious American forces by generous use of the first-person, plural personal pronoun 'we.' Altogether, 'we,' 'our' and 'us' are inscribed or written 26 times on the memorial and galleries. The war is described in a sanitized and simplified manner, which champions devotion and sacrifice for the nation state as a man's highest achievement and greatest honor bestowed. For example, the words 'sacrifice,' 'gave their lives' or 'laid down their lives' are mentioned eight times; 'honor' is mentioned twice; 'service,' five times; 'God' or 'Lord' five times (not including inscriptions in the chapel); and 'free,' 'freedom' or 'liberation,' seven times. In the map galleries, variations of the word 'defense' are used ten times. This narrative reflects traditional American attitudes about the purpose and conduct of American wars, and also how Americans view their role in world affairs. For example, military historian Brian Holden Reid has identified a number of themes likely to reoccur in the discourse of American warfare, such as the tendency to exaggerate American vulnerability, the belief that the United States is an 'underdog,' the assumption that the United States acts only defensively, not aggressively, and the belief than anything less than total victory is, somehow, a defeat. These assumptions underpin the sentiments expressed by the Honolulu Memorial. For example, mention of Pearl Harbor will undoubtedly invite visitors to reflect on America's supposed lack of preparedness for the attack. It was America's insistence on Japan's unconditional surrender that led to the atomic bombings of Hiroshima and Nagasaki (described rather coyly in the galleries as 'the devastation from the air'). The historical narrative presented in the galleries also reflects the supposed American national characteristic of being 'slow to anger, but furious when aroused' (318). It takes the form of an arc, beginning with the 'surprise attack' at Pearl Harbor, the steady build-up of American forces in the Pacific, the concentration of overwhelming American military might, culminating in the atomic destruction of two cities, ending the war. The Honolulu Memorial is, therefore, not only a conduit for one version of 'what happened,' it also reflects how Americans view themselves, as citizens of a country that is essential peaceful, but often provoked into war.

In pre-Cook times, Pūowaina, or 'hill of sacrifice,' was an important religious site for Hawaiians. Like many other Hawaiian place names, Westerners renamed Pūowaina as 'Punchbowl,' in part, because the Hawaiian language was difficult for them to master, and additionally because the process of naming connotes who is in charge. As Western influence increased in the islands, the naming and renaming of geographical features by Westerners was part of an ongoing process of power transference from native to non-native. That the crater was once used for human sacrifice seems to adumbrate the latest incarnation of sacrifice, this time for the nation state. However, Westerners have always regarded the practice of human sacrifice as barbaric, so while the continuance of that *topoi* and *mythoi* may add ritualistic meaning and depth to the processes of remembrance now occurring at the cemetery, it is also a signifier of the supposed 'civilizing process.' To Western eyes, these ancient practices were culturally opaque, and because they were carried out by brown-skinned, non-Christian natives, they judged them as primitive and savage. When the crater was surveyed, restructured, and an orderly environment imposed, ancient meaning was thus overlaid with modern, 'civilized' burial and commemorative practices. At Pūowaina/Punchbowl, then, a comparison is offered between the old and the new, but in the design of the cemetery and words of the inscriptions, a verdict has already been reached.

The imposition of Western order is never more prominent than when the military is involved. In the cemetery, warning signs notify visitors of forbidden behavior and prohibited items, such as jogging, picnicking, dog walking, smoking, or consuming food and beverages (the last of which is a particularly ill-thought-out restriction, given the cemetery's location in an arid, volcanic crater). A tourist brochure instructs visitors of appropriate conduct at the cemetery:

- The Cemetery will not be used as picnic grounds.
- All graves will be decorated during the 24-hour period preceding Memorial Day with small United States flags which will be removed immediately after Memorial Day. Flags are not permitted on graves at any other time.
- Plantings are not permitted on graves at any time.
- Potted plants will be permitted on graves ONLY [sic] during the 10-day period before and after Christmas and Easter.
- Statues, vigil lights, glass objects of any nature or any other type of commemorative items are not permitted.
- Installation of one permanent floral container is authorized on each grave (Singletary 4–5).

In contrast to most non-military cemeteries, visitors and relatives of the dead at Punchbowl must therefore meet fairly strict conditions of entrance. There are, of course, 'social expectations about personal behavior in a sacred place' (Mayo, 'Memory' 63) and this applies to both military and non-military cemeteries. In addition, Punchbowl is a major tourist attraction, which draws visitors on a much larger scale than any community cemetery has to contend with. Nevertheless, the scope and extent of Punchbowl's rules mark it as a specifically militarized *lieu de mémoire*.

Non-military cemeteries tend to be more welcoming than this, and also more likely to allow relatives the freedom to remember their dead as they see fit. This is illustrated in the divergence in the practice of grave marking at military and non-military sites. The granite headstones at Punchbowl are arranged in symmetrical, evenly-spaced lines and are horizontal, rather than vertically placed. The types of headstones, and the inscriptions upon them, are strictly regimented. This rule was, however, tested when controversy erupted soon after the cemetery was opened to the general public on 19 July 1949. It was Department of the Army practice to use flat grave markers at national cemeteries. However, in preparation for the public opening of the cemetery, temporary grave markers were erected. The markers took the form of the Christian cross and the Jewish Star of David. They were colored white and placed vertically at the head of each grave. In 1951, however, when the Army announced that it would replace the erect grave markers with flat stones, local and national veterans' associations made public their objections. Some complained that this was a cost-cutting exercise and that the memory of the fallen was being disrespected. Others raised aesthetic issues: for example, one opponent compared the newly-designed cemetery to a 'vacant lot' (Carlson 43). However, flat headstones were the norm for national cemeteries in the United States, and the Army was determined not to make Punchbowl an exception to that rule. Soon after all the grave markers were replaced, the controversy died down. This was, after all, a minor skirmish among similarly-minded people, who had already won the main battle in the creation of a national cemetery at Punchbowl. Nevertheless, this incident illustrates that the scope, scale and nature of remembrance of the dead — particularly those who die in conflict — are often contested, and this may even take the form of internecine battles between various military interests. In this instance, the power of the Army and federal government was enough to win the argument against various veterans' groups and politicians.

The Department of Veterans Affairs currently has an obligation to supply a free headstone or marker for the unmarked grave of a qualified veteran in any burial ground in the world. Relatives can choose one of 29 symbols from an approved list to put on the headstone. The inscription on the headstone may only contain the name of the soldier, the branch of service, highest military rank achieved, any war service, any civilian or veteran affiliations, a personal message or appropriate terms of endearment, any medals received, the date of death, and the deceased's hometown or state. There are both ritualistic and practical motives for the military's systematic, uniform approach to burial and remembrance. In civilian cemeteries, affluent relatives can afford costly grave markers, which contrast with the humble markers of the less prosperous. In American military cemeteries, however, the grave markers of officers and enlisted men are of the same design. This suggests an equality of sacrifice in which rank and social standing are irrelevant. This policy was adopted from a similar British practice of marking the graves of the Great War dead. The impetus of the Imperial War Graves Commission was that 'those who have given their lives are members of one family, and children of one mother who owes to all an equal tribute of gratitude and affection, and that, in death, all, from General to Private, of whatever race and creed, should receive equal honour' (Gaffney 25; Fussell, *Great* 197). Although the Hawaiian National Guard was segregated by race, no such separation was allowed in any of Hawai'i's military or civilian cemeteries.

Schofield Barracks has been a US military base since December 1908, when engineer Captain Joseph C. Castner began construction of the base's first temporary buildings. Conditions at first were grim: the base was situated on the Leilehua Plain, a barren stretch of land in the centre of O'ahu, and in the first few years water was in short supply. Until the 1930s, when permanent barracks were built, soldiers lived in shacks and tents, with earth floors (Linn 71–2; *Historic Guide*). A shortage of sewers, together with harsh climate conditions and the normal exertions of military life, meant that the post cemetery was in constant use. The cemetery was established in 1912, and it contains the remains of almost all of the servicemen listed on the Waikīkī War Memorial who have not been buried privately. The eligibility criteria for burial in a post cemetery is different to that of a national cemetery. For example, at the National Memorial Cemetery of the Pacific in Honolulu, the basic criteria is that veterans, Reservists and National Guard members with 20 years qualifying service are eligible for burial in the cemetery. In addition, veterans with discharges other than dishonorable, their spouses and dependent children may be eligible, as well as those who die on active duty (*Burials and Memorials*). In contrast, Schofield Post Cemetery is intended solely for active and retired military members and their dependants. [Fig. 3.15]

Unlike Punchbowl, Schofield Post Cemetery is not a tourist attraction. Its location, well away from popular tourist areas, means it attracts only those absolutely determined to visit. There is limited access by public transport, and the cemetery is not particularly well signposted. After having identification papers checked at one of the base's official entry points, civilian visitors must find their own way to the cemetery. One of the stone columns supporting the cemetery's wrought-iron gates is decorated with a Department of the Army crest, designating this space

*Figure 3.15* Schofield Post Cemetery. Photo by Brian Ireland.

as a military *lieu de mémoire*. Inside, a small wooden rotunda contains a map of the cemetery and an index of the dead. A central path leads to a large flagpole, which is flanked by small decorative cannons, two Grecian urns, and a few unadorned stone benches. The limited extent of the decorative and commemorative structures at Schofield Post Cemetery invites comparison with the more ornate Punchbowl Cemetery. At just over six acres, Schofield Post Cemetery is significantly smaller than the sprawling 112-acre site at Punchbowl. In addition, there are only around 2700 gravesites at Schofield, far short of the 34,000 at Punchbowl. Although both cemeteries were built to hold the remains of US military personnel and their families, Schofield is also the burial place of four Italian Prisoners of War from World War Two, seven American soldiers executed for capital crimes, and hundreds of foetal remains dating from 1956 to 1988 (*Historic Guide*). By interring enemy casualties — usually not present in American national cemeteries (Arlington being a notable exception to that rule), criminals who did not sacrifice themselves for America but instead had their lives taken away by the state, and the tragic but decidedly non-military remains of what were, presumably, miscarriages, abortions and stillbirths, Schofield Post Cemetery presents multiple stories of the past.

This is also reflected in the wide variety of headstones and grave markers permitted, most of which are — in contrast to Punchbowl — placed upright rather than flat. Some headstones have ornate decorations; one inscription is written almost entirely in Korean; an occasional marker has a design which denotes membership of a private organization, such as the Freemasons; in addition, some grave markers are either damaged, with large chips missing, or so badly weathered that the inscriptions cannot be fully read. This contrasts with the neat and orderly grave markers at Punchbowl, many of which appear 'as new' (it is possible that the upright grave markers at Schofield cemetery are more difficult for grass cutters to negotiate than the flat stones at Punchbowl, thus making damage more likely). All of these elements create room for multiple meanings and interpretations: unlike Punchbowl, there is no central memorial at Schofield, no insistence on identical grave markers, and therefore no all-encompassing effort to tell visitors how or why those interred have died.

Although the Post Cemetery is a somewhat more relaxed space than Punchbowl Cemetery, it is, however, not devoid of regulations and rituals designating it as a militarized space. For example, a memorandum posted in the rotunda from Leslie W. Stewart Jr., Chief, Casualty/Mortuary Affairs dated 10 May 2006, lists a number of cemetery rules, and also details what the public can and cannot do. For example, visitors are informed that floral arrangements will be removed on the 14th day of each month, and that no artificial flowers are permitted. In addition, all temporary vases and containers are removed on that date. No personal items are to be placed on, or attached to the headstone. Two items are mentioned specifically — beer cans and soda cans. While this seems a little random, it is possible that this specific instruction is a product of the American visitor experience at one of America's more famous memorials and tourist attractions, the Vietnam Veteran's Memorial in Washington D.C. It is common practice there for visitors, especially those who are related to, or who personally know someone listed on the memorial, to leave personal items at the wall. In the past, these have included beer cans, and a variety of other seemingly inappropriate items (Sturken, *Tangled* 78–80).

Just as some visitors to the Vietnam Veterans' Memorial enact their own personal rites of remembrance, and this often involves behavior that is normally not tolerated at sites of national commemoration, visitors to Schofield Post Cemetery sometimes break the rules. For example, a large sign at the center of the cemetery lists the following floral regulations:

- Fresh cut flowers & temporary flower containers are permitted & should be removed when not in use.

- Floral items and other types of decorations will not be secured to headstones or markers.
- Floral items will be removed when they become faded [or] unsightly.
- Statues, vigil lights, glass objects of any nature, & other types of commemorative items are not permitted on the grave at any time.
- All floral items will be removed on the 1st & the 15th of each month, or when the flowers become unsightly.
- Plantings will not be permitted on the graves.
- Only one permanent flower vase will be permitted on the graves.

The purpose of these regulations is, of course, to maintain an appearance of uniformity, and to prevent the display of any commemorative objects that may be considered disrespectful or out-of-place. Nevertheless, even a cursory survey of grave markers reveals that relatives and friends of the deceased have been breaking these rules. When I visited the cemetery in April 2009, I noticed a shell necklace draped over one headstone, and a stone statue of the Virgin Mary placed in front of another. A 'Happy Easter' balloon flew from one grave, while a flower *lei* was attached to the headstone of another. Other graves had a soda can, a soda bottle and a grapefruit placed (not littered) on them. One headstone had a Christmas decoration placed upon it. These items suggest relatives of the dead have rebelled, gently, against the rules imposed upon them by the military, but also that military authorities have turned a blind eye to these poignant intrusions of private grief.

Nineteen soldiers from the Great War are buried in the post cemetery.[18] They were interred at various dates from August 1918 to August 1919, and their headstones are all located in section two, rows S18 to S27 and T18 to T26. [Fig. 3.16] Situating the graves in such a close grouping suggests that the soldiers died together for a common cause. This may be misleading, however. The remains of many World War Two casualties were disinterred in the late 1940s for eventual reburial at Punchbowl. As a result, other graves were resituated and concentrated within the Post Cemetery (Steere and Boardman 527). It may be it was only at this stage that the dead from the Great War were grouped together for reburial. That being said, the suggestion of a patriotic common purpose is compelling, and is enhanced by the lack of detail on the headstones, which provide only the deceased's name, the unit he was attached to, and the inscription 'USA.' The only deviation to this pattern is that on the two grave markers belonging to the only non-commissioned officers in the group, their ranks are indicated. This minimalist approach leads to (at least) two competing interpretations. On the one hand, it could

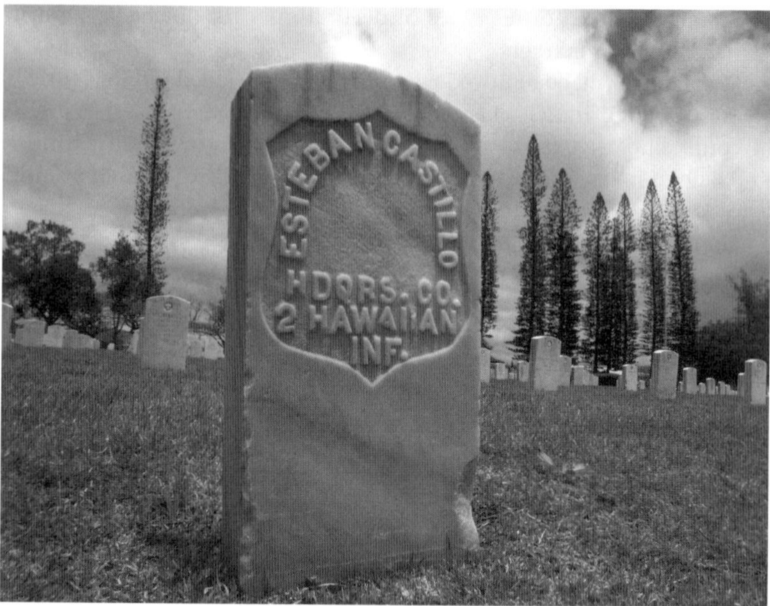


*Figure 3.16* World War One headstones at Schofield Post Cemetery. Photo by Brian Ireland.

suggest an equality in death that perhaps the soldiers may never have experienced in life. All soldiers, regardless of age, rank, race, and social status are deemed to have sacrificed themselves equally for the state. On the other hand, by providing only the barest of details, the grave markers create lacunae, which visitors must fill by contemplating the circumstances of the soldiers' deaths. These reflections are, of course, guided by the patriotic context in which they occur: the sacred, patriotic spaces where soldiers are buried do not encourage much contemplation beyond the familiar narrative of honor, duty, and service to one's country. The concentration of graves, and the minimalist approach to providing information about the fallen, therefore offers multiple interpretations of meaning and effect.

In contrast to the regimented and formal spaces of military cemeteries, community gravesites of Hawai'i's war dead offer a more individual and less ordered remembrance of military sacrifice than the traditional monoglossic narrative. These cemeteries are usually situated amongst the local population: for example the Catholic Cemetery in King Street, where Private John Kuulei Kaea was buried, or the Kawaiahao Church cemetery at

Punchbowl Street, where Private Edward N. Kahokuoluna is interred, are both situated between the tourist Mecca of Waikīkīand the busy downtown commercial district. In contrast, Punchbowl National Cemetery is situated aloof from the metropolis, like a shining 'city upon a hill' (Winthrop 282, 294–5), and Schofield Post Cemetery is situated on a military base far away from areas where tourists tend to congregate. Community cemeteries tend to be welcoming public spaces that invite entrance. As they are less proscriptive than military cemeteries about the types of remembrance they allow, community cemeteries are protean spaces which allow 'memory to grow' (Ferguson and Turnbull 109). However, even when military personnel are buried in civilian cemeteries, the nature of their interment often depends on whether the ceremony is organized by the family or by patriotic groups such as the American Legion. For example, a number of Great War dead were buried under the auspices of the Legion. These burial ceremonies followed military procedures, and featured military symbolism such as flag bearing and gun salutes. In the years following the Great War, veterans' groups revisited gravesites to hold ceremonies of remembrance. However, these recurring rituals also act as a reminder to civilians of military sacrifice and continuing devotion to the state.

Michael Sledge states: 'it has been clearly established that the military can exercise its authority, at least to a large degree, over its soldiers even after they are killed' (172). Although Sledge's observation refers mainly to the physical remains of the soldiers, such military jurisdiction is often exercised over the hows, whys and lessons to be learned from the soldiers' deaths. For the dead, service to country sometimes often does not end, even in the graveyard. O'ahu Cemetery was founded in 1844 as a site for the graves of Hawai'i's burgeoning foreign population. It contains the graves of, and memorials to, many of Hawai'i's most prominent citizens. Taking their place alongside casualties of the US Civil War, and World War Two, are 14 Great War victims, two of whom (Sergeant Apau Kau, and Private John Rupert Rowe) were killed in action.[19] Kau died on 5 November 1918, and was originally buried on the battlefield in the Ravine de Molleville, France. His body was, however, disinterred and brought home on the transport ship *Logan* on 15 March 1922. Kau was reburied at O'ahu Cemetery in a military funeral with firing squad. Members of the American Legion and Veterans of Foreign Wars were present, together with members of the Chinese baseball team he was once a member of ('Back Home'). His headstone is of simple construction, consisting of: a rectangular block of white marble approximately four feet tall, on a solid square base.

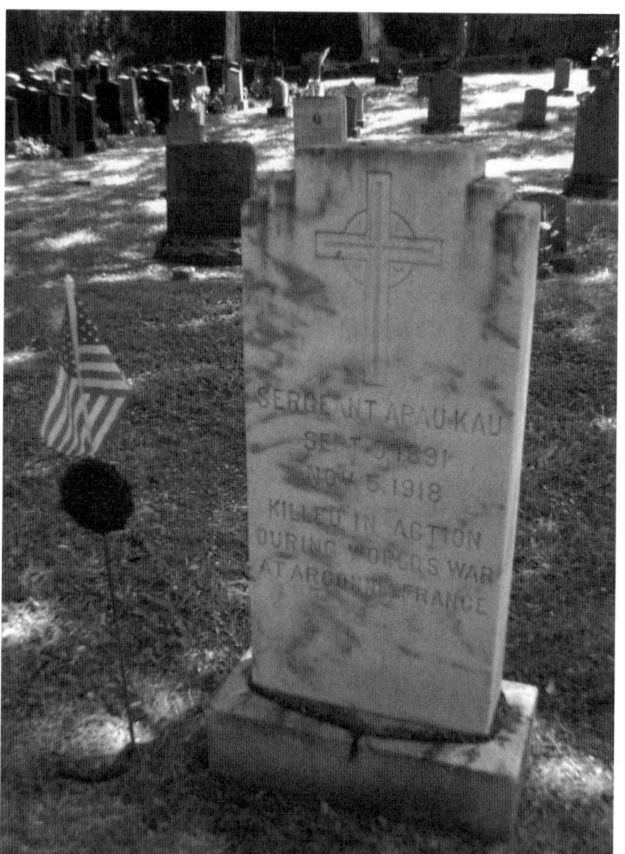

*Figure 3.17* Headstone of Apau Kau. Photo by Brian Ireland.

The inscription on the headstone states, 'Sergeant Apau Kau, killed in action during world's war at Argonne, France.' Kau's grave is directly behind John Rowe's, and behind and slightly to the side of George Tom's. Tom and Rowe were buried together on 15 September 1921 in a ceremony organized by the American Legion. The ceremony featured a double firing squad, provided by the US Army ('Honolulu Will Pay'). [Fig. 3.17]

John Rowe died on 31 July 1918. His body was disinterred after the war, at his family's request, and was shipped home to Honolulu on 10 September 1921 on the transport ship *Buford*. He was reburied at O'ahu Cemetery on 15 September 1921. Originally, his grave marker stated only Rowe's name, rank and unit. However, in 2002, Rowe's descendants erected a new headstone, which is rectangular in shape, about three feet in height and 14 inches in diameter. Near the top of the stone is a circle containing a cross, and below a new inscription stating, 'First WW I combat casualty from Hawaii.' On the rear of the marker is an inscription paraphrasing Rowe's last letter home to his mother. It states, 'I have done my duty for my country.' Due of its modern construction and erection, the marker is clean and less weathered than the markers of Kau and Tom. Apart from the new inscriptions, the stone is not much different from the previous marker, except that it offers more historical detail about Rowe's military career.

His descendants wanted the change as they believed Rowe had not received the recognition he deserved (Kakesako). This is curious, as Rowe is listed on the Waikīkī memorial, and American Legion Post 17 is named after him. However, Rowe's status as 'Hawaii's first son to lose his life in defense of the United States during the First World War' (Akaka) is incorrect, given that a number of Hawai'i residents enlisted with British forces long before the United States entered the war, and 22 of those who died in service are listed on the Waikīkī memorial. In addition, Rowe was not the first person from Hawai'i enlisted in American forces to die in service: that was Frank P. Dolin, an aviator who died of pneumonia at the Post Hospital, Jefferson Barracks, St. Louis, Missouri on January 6th, 1918. Rowe was, however, the first enlistee in American forces from Hawai'i to die in France. This was recognized by the *Star-Bulletin* in 1919, when the paper printed an honor roll which distinguished clearly between those 'killed in action' and those who 'died in service' ('Hawaii Did Her Part'). In seeking recognition for Rowe's status as the first 'KIA' from Hawai'i, Senator Akaka and the American Legion are tacitly acknowledging that the inclusion of over 60 names on the Waikīkī memorial who died in service of various non-combat related causes, artificially inflates Hawai'i's roll in the war, and deflects attention away from those like Rowe, Tom, and the others who were actually killed in action.

Private George B. Tom died of pneumonia in France on 18 October 1918. His body was disinterred after the war at his family's request, and he was buried with Private Rowe, under the auspices of the American Legion in O'ahu Cemetery on 15 September 1921. His headstone is a simple affair, approximately three feet high and one foot across. On top is a crucifix, and on the main body of the stone a simple inscription reads: 'George B Tom, Co A 6TH ENGS AEF, DIED IN FRANCE, 1893–1918.' Tom's headstone is weathered and shows signs of natural aging. In other circumstances it would be just another marker in the corner of a rural cemetery. However, in 1928 Chinese veterans set up the Kau-Tom American Legion Post 11, and its members hold yearly remembrance services (Purnell 131). In doing so, they exercise and retain a measure of control, even in a civilian cemetery, over how and why Hawai'i's war dead are remembered.

John O'Dowda died in an airplane accident in France on 13 November 1918. Like Rowe and Tom, his body was disinterred at his family's request and returned to Hawai'i for reburial on 8 August 1921 at O'ahu Cemetery in an elaborate military ceremony. The American Legion, Spanish War Veterans, British War Veterans, and the St. Louis College Alumni Association attended this service ('Lieut. O'Dowda'; 'Funeral Services'; 'Many Honor'). Although buried by the military, the extant headstone is not military issue (*History of Government*). It is placed flat to the ground, and sits on a rough stone base. At approximately 23 inches across by 12 inches in length and eight inches in height, the marker is of non-military design and dimension. Its inscription reads: 'O' DOWDA, LIEUT. JOHN S 1896–1918, THOMAS P 1861–1920, LULU 1875–1959.' One can assume that this is a family plot and O'Dowda is buried beside his father and mother. The plot is well-kept and tidy, and unlike the graves of Rowe, Kau, and Tom, there are no military trappings (such as American Legion markers). Given that O'Dowda was buried by the military, it is likely that he had a standard headstone, but when his parents died in later years, family members replaced the military headstone with a collective family marker. The extant marker offers a different way to remember O'Dowda than triumphant newspaper reports, or the conformity of a military grave marker. Second Lieutenant John Stephen O'Dowda was only 22 when he died an accidental death in France just a few days after the Armistice. His father outlived him by two years and his mother by 41 years. This very personal tragedy contrasts with previously mentioned victorious narratives of sacrifice, honor, and patriotism.

There is no comfortable way to remember the death of Yeoman 1st class Frederick Char. Born Waipahu, Hawai'i in 1895, Char lived in Honolulu until his enlistment at Pearl Harbor on 20 April 1917. He served on the USS *Navajo* until his death at Pearl Harbor on 31 October 1918. His cause of death is listed only as amputation of legs, arms, and a fractured skull. It seems likely, therefore, that he was involved in an accident with some type of heavy machinery that would cause such horrendous injuries. Char is buried at O'ahu Cemetery, among the graves of sailors and marines from other conflicts. However, the type of marker

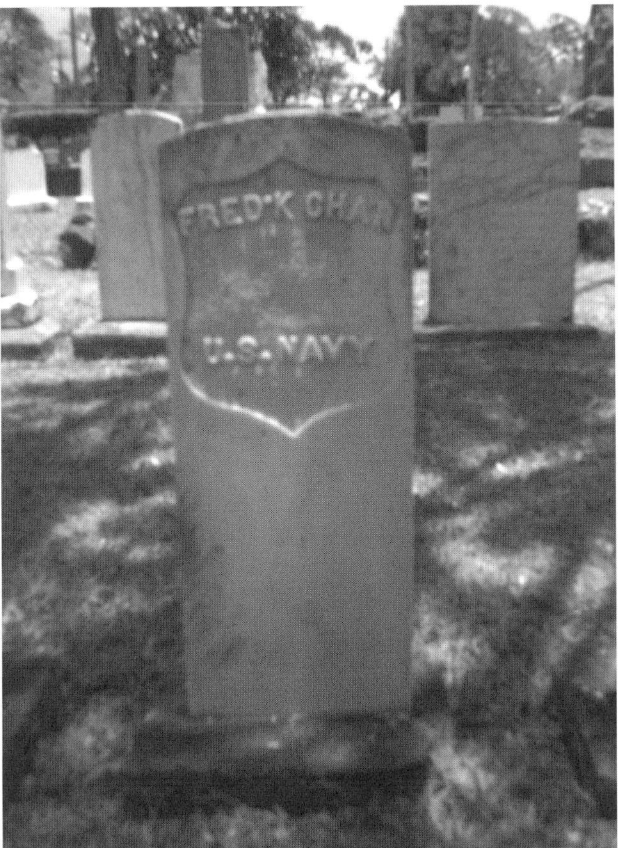


*Figure 3.18* Headstone of Frederick K. Char. Photo by Brian Ireland.

used for Char is unusual in that it is modeled on, but not exactly the same as, the authorized US Civil War marker intended only for members of the Union Army. It is a slab design, approximately 30 inches in height (about twice that of standard Civil War markers). The top of the marker is slightly curved, and on its face is a sunken shield in which the bare inscription, 'FRED K CHAR, U.S. NAVY' appears in *bas-relief*. This minimalist, even secretive, mode of inscription is unusual even for military grave markers of this time period, but is perhaps unavoidable given the gruesome nature of Char's death. [Fig. 3.18]

In general, military modes of remembrance do not focus on the chaotic nature of war and death, nor do they focus on its bloody realities. From this perspective, Char's accidental death serves no purpose, as only death in sacrifice to the state can offer patriotic lessons for today's generation. Until Punchbowl National Cemetery opened in 1949, this section of the graveyard was used for US Navy burials. There is evidence of military remembrance here, not just in the conformity of the headstones, or their minimalist, secretive inscriptions, but also in their layout in straight rows — unlike the disordered civilian graves around them. Although they died in different time periods, in different wars, and also in times of peace, this layout suggests a unity of purpose in the deaths of these men. The only thing connecting them in life and death is a monoglossic mode of remembrance, which furthers narratives of order and shared sacrifice. As if to illustrate this point, a tall, white flagpole has been erected in this section of the cemetery as if to remind the dead they still owe an allegiance to the flag.

Carel Justus De Roo was born in Holland, in either 1846 or 1847. He lived in Honolulu, and enlisted on 2 January 1918. He was attached to the Quarter Master Corps in the rank of Field Clerk until his death by cancer at Honolulu on 25 May 1918. De Roo is buried in a plot of land reserved for Freemasons. His headstone is one of many in that area which are decorated either with the symbol of a square and compass enclosing a letter 'G,' or a similar symbol indicating a Masonic affiliation. His low key inscription reads: 'CAREL JUSTUS DE ROO, NOV 6 1846, MAY 25 1918.' Again, there is little room here for narratives of glory or victory. De Roo was, after all, in his early 70s when he died — hardly the image of a youthful 'son' of Hawai'i or of the United States required for patriotic sacrifice. Furthermore, De Roo died of natural causes in Hawai'i. Lastly, he was a 'paper pusher' and not a combat soldier, a role that by its very nature lacks the danger and glory required for sacrifice. [Figure 3.19]

Patriotic organizations tend to remember and publicize only those individuals whose deaths further familiar themes of order, duty, and sacrifice. They retain control over the memories of the deceased as long as those memories remain useful to that end. In those cases where the deceased do not fit into the military narrative, such as De Roo's death of cancer, or Char's gruesome accident, it appears that little or no effort is made to remember these men, or make rituals from their deaths to instruct present and future generations about military or patriotic duty. Some of those buried at O'ahu Cemetery, whose causes of death do not serve to foster devotion to the military or the state, have been neglected entirely. According to the map located in the cemetery's main office, Herman Kaaukea is buried in the same section as Kau,

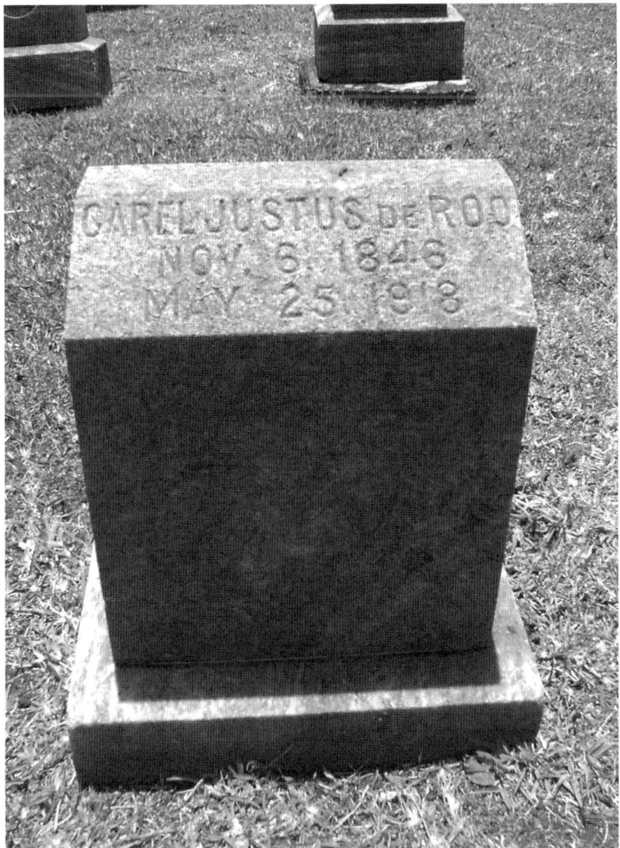


*Figure 3.19* Headstone of Carel Justus De Roo. Photo by Brian Ireland.

Tom and Rowe. However, there is no extant marker for his grave. No trace could be found either of the markers for five other soldiers supposedly buried in the cemetery.[20] It appears these men, whose deaths were, perhaps not coincidentally, of flu, lobar pneumonia, pneumonia, and intestinal instruction (in other words, all non-heroic, 'ordinary' deaths), have now finally been discharged from military duty.

With no military cemetery in which to bury its Great War casualties, O'ahu Cemetery's tranquil, orderly setting must have seemed an appropriate site. Because of its rural location, it was considered more dignified than, for example, Kawaiahao Cemetery, in Honolulu. Although the coralstone built Kawaiahao Church was at one time known as 'the church of the alii, or royalty,' the cemetery attached to the church was also the final resting place of many 'common' Native Hawaiians, who were buried in both marked and unmarked graves (Damon 99). It is ironic, however, that Native Hawaiians considered Kawaiahao a very dignified final resting place and thus many non-native sailors, whalers, and other fortune seekers were denied burial there. Cemetery historian Nanette Napoleon Purnell notes, for example, that the church 'only allowed members of "good faith" to be buried there, effectively excluding many of the foreign population' (15).

Although four of the servicemen named on the memorial are buried at Kawaiahao, none of those burials was organized by the Legion.[21] Only one headstone still stands, that of Edward N. Kahokuoluna. [Fig. 3.20] This is perhaps the most poignant of all the burial sites discussed, not only because to its setting and history, but also due to the design of Kahokuoluna's grave marker. Although the inscription itself is a fairly basic three-line dedication, stating 'EDWARD N. KAHOKUOLUNA, 1895–1918, REST IN PEACE,' a small black and white photograph has been lovingly

*Figure 3.20* Headstone of Edward N. Kahokuoluna. Photo by Brian Ireland.

added just below the deceased's name. This is not a military headstone, as it does not match the design or dimensions of any of those authorized. Furthermore, the photograph is a family preference that would be in violation of approved military designs. Whereas anonymous names promote the idea of a common cause and mask individual pain and suffering, the effect of seeing Kahokuoluna's faces stirs the opposite emotion.

Unlike the Waikīkī War Memorial, which, because of its scale, asks viewers to step backwards and away to get a better view, this grave marker has a haptic quality that draws one towards it. Although the marker is weathered, it is still in fairly good condition. There is no trace of the grave markers of the other three soldiers buried here, however. Although this suggests that Kahokuoluna may have had family members attending his grave until relatively recently and the others did not, it may also simply be that Kawaiahao graveyard is a disorganized civilian site that also has to compete with the demands of a modern city. For example, some headstones were lost when Queen Street was laid. In any event, the Legion and the military play no role in remembering any of these casualties, partly because the causes of their deaths are not amenable to the promotion of militarism and patriotism, but also because Kahokuoluna's family asserted control over his memory, thus offering a very different narrative to that of either the military or the memorial.

This point is further illustrated when one considers those soldiers buried in Puea Cemetery, a compact graveyard on the corner of School and Kapalama streets, close to the Bishop Museum. Puea is one of four cemeteries on O'ahu owned by the State of Hawai'i. It is in a residential neighborhood and although unfenced, is enclosed on all sides by roads and houses. It is divided into three sections, one owned by the state, one by the City and County of Honolulu, and one by the Kaahumanu Society (*Hawaii State* 8). The two parts run by the State and the City and County are overcrowded and dilapidated: many headstones are broken or have fallen over, and the site lacks grass cover due to poor watering. The State's portion is the larger of the two, and it is there that two of Hawai'i's Great War dead are buried — Adam Young Aki, and Frank K. Aki Jr. The section owned by the City and County of Honolulu predates the Territory of Hawai'i as an 'old native burying ground [in which] the only way to locate graves in the old portion is to find sunken spots' (*Hawaii State* 31). In contrast, the section of cemetery run by the Kaahumanu Society is clean, neat, and well looked after. Its green grass offers a remarkable contrast to brown earth that marks the rest of Puea.

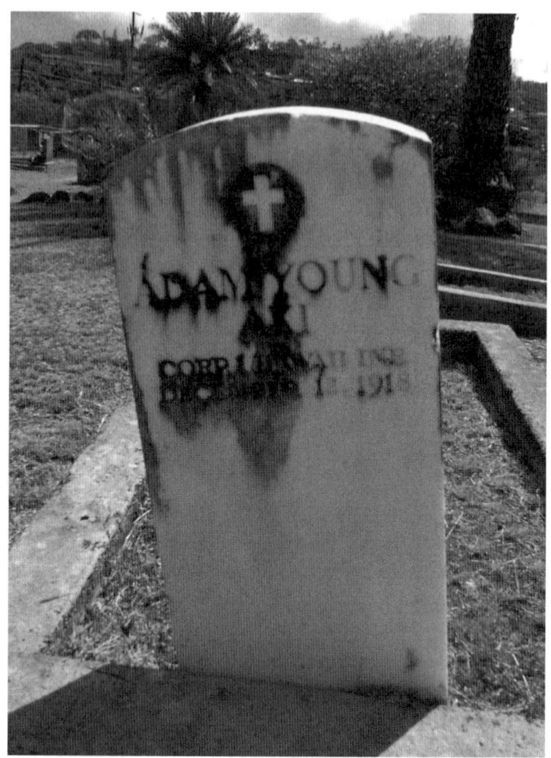

*Figure 3.21* Headstone of Adam Young Aki. Photo by Brian Ireland.

Private Adam Aki was born on Kona, Hawai'i in 1896. He lived on O'ahu, however, until his enlistment in Honolulu on 12 July 1918. While attached to the 1st Hawaiian Infantry he fell ill and died of peritonitis and appendicitis at the US Naval Hospital, Pearl Harbor on December 12, 1918. [Fig. 3.21] Aki's gravesite is surrounded by a 6-inch concrete border, which seems to have protected it over the years from the worst effects of weather and neglect. His headstone is a standard government issue — a white marble slab, approximately 28 inches in height and 12 inches across. A Christian cross is engraved near the top of the stone, and below that a faded inscription reads, 'ADAM YOUNG AKI, CORP 1 HAWAII INF, DECEMBER 12, 1918.' The marker is chipped, weathered, and has begun to list. There are no indications of anyone visiting the grave site in the recent past. It seems likely that the headstone will eventually fall over or fracture, like many of those around it. Private Frank K. Aki, Jr. was born in Honolulu in 1895. He lived in Hilo, and enlisted there on

18 July 1918. Although he was attached to 2nd Hawaiian Infantry, Frank Aki was only in the military for 12 days: he died of pneumonia at Schofield Barracks on 30 July 1918. Although it appears from the map and guide in *Hawaii State Cemeteries* that, as late as 1987, Frank Aki's grave was marked with a headstone and wire border, there is no trace of it today.

Adam Aki was only 22 when he died and Frank Aki, 23. In all likelihood, both were conscripts. As there is no glory in these deaths, there is no need for the military or veterans' groups to maintain control over these men's memories. In fact, Puea Cemetery contains many military headstones, most of which are in a poor state of repair. Like most civilian cemeteries, there is little order here. The graves are not laid out in rows, borders are either unmarked, or delineated with a variety of materials including stones, wooden or plastic fences, and cinder blocks. Puea is an ethnically diverse cemetery and space abounds for many types of remembrance. The overall atmosphere of Puea is, however, neglect. Instead of serving as a space for remembrance or contemplation, in reality, Puea promotes an absence of memory. Any attempt at military remembrance here, any attempt to impose order, is destined to be defeated by disorder and disarray.

King Street Catholic cemetery is the final resting place of Private Kuulei John Kaea. Born in Honolulu in 1892, Kaea enlisted in Honolulu on 7 July 1918. While attached to the 1st Hawaiian Infantry, Kaea caught pneumonia and died at Fort Shafter Hospital on 16 March 1919. One hot Saturday afternoon, in the summer of 2003, I set out to look for Kaea's grave. I spent a few hours searching among the headstones and grave markers, retracing my steps occasionally to ensure I had not missed a marker. However, all trace of Kaea's physical remains is gone. His name is preserved only on casualty lists and as an inscription on the Waikīkī War Memorial. Like most of those named on the memorial, he never saw combat, and never left Hawai'i's shores. His death of natural causes occurred four months after the war was over. These bare facts sit uncomfortably with Hawai'i's popular memory of its Great War dead.

## Conclusion

There is common acceptance now among historians that if we are to do justice to the past, we must encourage a 'plurality of memory' (Moriarty, 'Material' 661). In this chapter I have endeavored to show that remembrance of Hawai'i's Great War dead has, to this point, been restricted to the officially sanctioned, state-endorsed, and military-approved story of duty, honor, and sacrifice for the nation. This mono-memory silences and erases other narratives, and fails to tell the full story of Hawai'i's war dead. The final resting places of many of these men in community graveyards offers, however, a different, less ordered, more personal, and more complete story of those soldiers who died 90 years ago in the Great War.

# 4
# Hooray for Haolewood? Hawai'i on Film

Western explorers and adventurers such as Captain James Cook, William Ellis, and Charles Stewart, returned from the Pacific with exciting 'South Seas' tales of Eden-like islands, idol-worshipping natives, man-eating cannibals, lost treasure, and beautiful, available native women. Novelists such as Herman Melville, Mark Twain, Robert Louis Stevenson, and Henry de Vere Stacpoole would later add elements to the mythology in their semi-fictional tales. By the time Hollywood started making movies about the South Seas in the early years of the twentieth century, there was already familiar, exotic imagery to draw upon — recurring plot devices that were evident in the stories of earlier adventurers and novelists, with themes of mystery, romance, danger, adventure, opportunity, and utopianism. As recent scholarship has shown, Westerners have created, in all of these mediums, semi-mythical places, whose inhabitants reflect Western desires and prejudices:

> Western intrusions into Hawai'i — from early explorers, traders, and missionaries, to planters, diplomats, and military leaders, to travel agents, airline companies, and foreign visitors — have seen Hawai'i as a welcoming feminine place, waiting with open arms to embrace those who come to penetrate, protect, mold, and develop, while simultaneously lacking that which would make it fully realized (and which the intruders conveniently believe themselves to possess). Maps of Hawai'i from Captain James Cook's expeditions represent Hawai'i with soft, curved, breast-like mountains and mysterious coves and bays ... Missionary accounts of 'the natives' emphasize their darkness; naked, unashamed, promiscuous (Ferguson and Turnbull 6).

In contrast to these exotic images, the Japanese attack on Pearl Harbor probably accounts for the other major impact Hawai'i's has on the

American consciousness. The attack caused over 2400 military and civilian deaths, and was a catalyst for American entry into World War Two. It also gave the US military an opportunity to fulfil its long-standing ambition of installing a military government in the islands. Shortly after the attack, General Walter Short asked Hawaii Governor Joseph Poindexter to transfer power to the US military, and thus began period of military rule, which lasted until October 1944 (Anthony 8). The US Navy, in particular, had always wanted more authority in the islands. For years, it assumed that war with Japan was inevitable, and that Hawai'i's Japanese residents would act against American interests. For example, in his 1939 autobiography, *Sea Duty*, Admiral Yates Stirling, the senior officer at Pearl Harbor from 1930–33, repeated his view that 'the Territory should be in the hands of the national government, that suffrage for the local population should be limited, and that on the ruling Cabinet of the Islands there should be a considerable proportion of high-ranking Army and Navy officers' (Packer and Thomas 31–2). According to journalist John Gregory Dunne, Stirling's autobiography was 'almost a bible of Navy attitudes' at this time' (50). Furthermore, Pearl Harbor gave the military the opportunity for a massive land grab: as Kyle Kajihiro reveals, 'Large tracts of land were seized through presidential executive orders, swelling military land holdings to its peak of 600,000 acres (242,806.8 hectares) in 1944' ('Brief Overview' 2).

As well as being a fully-functioning military base, Pearl Harbor is, today, one of O'ahu's major tourist attractions. The USS *Arizona* Memorial attracts up to 4000 visitors a day (White 510), and since 1999, the USS *Missouri*, moored on 'Battleship Row,' has functioned as a popular floating museum. Tourism is Hawai'i's largest industry, followed closely by US Defense Department spending, and the 'mili-tourism' (Imada 330) on display at sites such as Pearl Harbor plays a significant role in both spheres. Although there are a number of crossover points in tourism and military narratives, there is also, however, much liminal space between these two contrasting images of Hawai'i. While scholars have examined both areas individually, no attempt has yet been made to join the two parts together — to use a cohesive, holistic, approach to examine, for example, exactly what part Hawai'i plays in the American national consciousness. Is Hawai'i a 'paradise of the Pacific,' a militarized 'Gibraltar of the Pacific,' or some combination of both? How did the Pearl Harbor attack affect America's view of Hawai'i, and what part did Hollywood play in shaping their views? University of Hawai'i professor Floyd Matson states, 'To people who live anywhere else, as we know, Hawai'i is a state of mind. But it is not always the same state of mind ... [T]here is doubtless a kind of "monomyth" at the heart of the matter-one which has much to do with islands but little to do with *these* islands' (40). As Matson notes, the reality of Hawai'i, and the Hawai'i that exists in the American mind, are two separate entities.

## The war story

There is no other medium that best illustrates America's imaginary Hawai'i than Hollywood movies. Houston Wood argues, 'most of what Euroamericans today know about Hawai'i they have learned from movies and television' (103). Hawai'i and Hawaiians have been shaped and reshaped by Hollywood to meet the needs and expectations of a mainland American audience, just as the New World and Native Americans were invented then reinvented by European colonizers to meet their needs. Tom Engelhardt refers to this 'invented' aspect of the conquest of America as the 'American war story,' a narrative that acts as a 'builder of national consciousness' (5). Engelhardt's analysis of this 'war story,' using a wide range of historical and cultural artefacts and productions, offers a useful framework for analyzing Hawai'i's role in the war story and in the American national consciousness. It is particularly valuable for examining movies, since his analysis deals with the link between political decision-making and the stories we tell about the past and about other peoples, which influence those decisions.[1]

Engelhardt argues that war and remembrance of war, more than any other single factor, shapes America's foreign and domestic policies. He states:

> From its origins, the war story was essentially defensive in nature, and the justness of American acts was certified not only by how many of *them* died, but by how few of *us* there were to begin with. The band of brothers, the small patrol, or, classically, the lone white frontiersman gained the right to destroy through a sacramental rite of initiation in the wilderness. In this trial by nature, it was the Indians who, by the ambush, the atrocity, and the capture of the white women ... became the aggressors, and so sealed their own fate (5).

Engelhardt traces the war story back to frontier times when captivity narratives depicted settlers victims and Indians intruders in their own land. 'Massacre' stories — the wagon train in a circle, the homestead being attacked — reverse the roles of invader and invaded. Historian

Patricia Limerick notes a similar pattern of inversion in modern times:

> Ranchers ... fac[ing] pressures from urban and recreational developers and from expanding coal companies ... cast themselves as the natives resisting invasion. 'I have become, for all practical purposes, an Indian,' said one white Montana rancher. 'Like the Indian, I am standing in the way of progress because I live and work above part of the world's largest known reserves of fossil fuel.' Ranchers, he argued, 'are the new vanishing race' (158).

In cinema, Mike Wallace traces this narrative back to D.W. Griffith's influential *The Birth of a Nation*. He states,

> A central mythic image was the wagon train drawn up in a defensive circle against hordes of screaming redskins until rescued by the Seventh Cavalry. This iconography (borrowed from D.W. Griffith's *The Birth of a Nation*, which depicted a band of whites holed up in a cabin and surrounded by hordes of screaming blacks until rescued by the Ku Klux Klan) not only inverted the reality of the historical and moral relations between whites and Indians, but once it was widely accepted, it provided a latent set of images and values that could be detached from their original context and deployed to lend an aura of self-righteousness to other foreign policies. The most notorious case in our lifetime was Vietnam (262).

Such has been the enduring quality of this mythology that it has been repeated endlessly in high school history textbooks, continuing for present and future generations comforting, self-righteous war stories that Americans like to tell about themselves. James Loewen points out, for example, that textbooks 'give readers no clue as to what the zone of contact was like from the Native side [and] invert the terms, picturing white aggressors as "settlers" and often showing Native settlers as aggressors' (*Lies My* 115).

In the traditional frontier war story, the outnumbered settlers are destined for slaughter, which makes the inevitable retribution against savages all the more sweet. Engelhardt argues that these early tales of slaughter and revenge act as paradigms for how Americans write their history and how they are expected to respond. The story of the besieged Alamo, for example, reverses the roles of invader and invaded and led to military retribution against Mexico complete with its own catch-phrase, 'Remember the Alamo!' Similarly 'Remember Custer' became the excuse for the 1890 massacre of Sioux at Wounded Knee, 'Remember the *Lusitania*' an excuse for American involvement in World War One, nuclear retribution against Japan was accompanied by the slogan 'Remember Pearl Harbor,' 'Remember Tonkin' became the justification for the Vietnam War, and 'Remember 9–11' the battle cry for the 'war against terror.'

When viewed from the standpoint of a descendant of the original inhabitants, however, a different side of the 'war story' is revealed:

> Their [American] illegal invasion [of Texas] forced Mexico to fight a war to keep its Texas territory. The Battle of the Alamo, in which the Mexican forces vanquished the whites, became, for the whites, the symbol for the cowardly and villainous character of the Mexicans. It became (and still is) a symbol that legitimized the white imperialist takeover. With the capture of Santa Anna later in 1836, Texas became a republic. Tejanos [native Texans of Mexican descent] lost their land and, overnight, became the foreigners (Anzaldúa 6).

Engelhardt argues that the American national narrative is based on war stories about savage, uncivilized 'Indians' and peaceful, civilized settlers. These stories offer a comfortable historical narrative that is free from unsettling themes such as genocide, colonialism, and imperialism. Media analyst Michael Parenti claims that in television and movies, 'The homeland, the safe place, is American White Anglo-Protestant, or at least White. It is inhabited by people who are sane and care about life. The enemies are maniacal and careless with lives, including their own' (14). In cowboy films, for example, the intruder changes places with the intruded upon when Indians are shown attacking forts, wagon trains, and homes. Seldom do these movies portray Westerners attacking Indian homes and villages because, as is evident in atypical genre movies like *Little Big Man* (1970) and *Soldier Blue* (1970), such images remind viewers that they are the descendants of intruders and invaders.

Hollywood portrayals of Hawai'i have changed throughout the twentieth century to meet the requirements of American movie audiences. Although some stereotypes and themes are present throughout, three distinct phases can be detected. Before World War Two, Hawai'i and its people were portrayed as exotically different to America; after World War Two, Hollywood movies still portrayed Hawai'i as exotic, but in various ways Hawai'i is made to seem similar to, or connected to the rest of the United States; and from the mid-1950s through the 1960s,

'American Hawai'i' was displayed as a racial paradigm, an example the troubled mainland ought to follow. In each distinct period, Hawai'i is shaped according to the desires of the mainland American audience. In each phase, Hollywood found the Hawai'i it needed, the perpetually available 'other' place that could be, in turns, the primitive Pacific, the brave site of attack on 'American soil,' or the enticing model of racial harmony. A close analysis of these phases of film making will illustrate how Hollywood helped create images of the islands that situate Hawai'i in the triumphal 'war story' which, Englehardt argues, has become America's prevailing image of itself.

## Hawai'i as the exotic other

Pre-World War Two Hawai'i movie titles emphasize difference, such as non-American exotic locations, animals, phrases or practices. Some examples of this are *The Shark God* (1913), *Martin Eden* (1914), *Aloha Oe* (1915), *Kaolulolani* (1916), *The Island of Desire* (1917), *The Bottle Imp* (1917), *The Hidden Pearls* (1918), *A Fallen Idol* (1919), *Passion Fruit* (1921), *Hula* (1927), *The Chinese Parrot* (1927), *The Kamaaina* (1929), *Aloha* (1931), *Bird of Paradise* (1932), *China Clipper* (1936), *Trade Winds* (1939), *Karayo* (1940), and *South of Pago Pago* (1940). In contrast, post-Pearl Harbor movies that feature Hawai'i have non-exotic names that are often connected to the US military, such as *Air Force* (1943), *Million Dollar Weekend* (1948), *Miss Tatlock's Millions* (1948), *The Big Lift* (1950), *Go For Broke* (1951), *Sailor Beware* (1952), *Big Jim McLain* (1952), *From Here to Eternity* (1953), *Miss Sadie Thompson* (1954), *Beachhead* (1954), *Hell's Half Acre* (1954), *The High and the Mighty* (1954), *Mister Roberts* (1955), and *The Revolt of Mamie Stover* (1956).

Pre-Pearl Harbor movies also tend to have specific Hawai'i or Hawaiian place names in their titles. In the pre-war years, such titles evoked images of an idyllic island paradise that mainland Americans could escape to for the price of a ticket at their local cinema. Examples includes *Hawaiian Love* (1913), *It Happened To Honolulu* (1916), *Happy Hawaii* (1928), *Waikiki Wedding* (1937), *Wings Over Honolulu* (1937), *Hawaii Calls* (1938), *Hawaiian Buckaroo* (1938), *Charlie Chan in Honolulu* (1938), *Honolulu* (1939), *Hawaiian Nights* (1939), *Moonlight in Hawaii* (1941), and *Honolulu Lu* (1941). In contrast, between 1942 and 1956 only one movie — *Ma and Pa Kettle in Waikiki* — has a Hawai'i place name in its title. This may reflect a change in how mainland Americans thought about Hawai'i. In the post-Pearl Harbor years, Americans no longer considered Hawai'i as a place apart from the rest of the country. While it was still a distant territory, geographically and politically, the Japanese attack had foregrounded Hawai'i in America's national consciousness.

Americans have traditionally imagined Hawai'i and other 'South Seas' islands as places of restful relaxation away from the rigors of life on the mainland United States. These islands are places where the 'normal' rules of behavior do not apply. Hollywood movies have played a large role in creating this enduring myth of an uninhibited island paradise and the conventions of the genre rarely reflect the reality of Hawai'i and its people. For example, *Bird of Paradise* (1951) was filmed in Hawai'i and features Hawaiian language and the Hawaiian god, Pele (Wood 11). Its plot is sensationalist and derivative: Frenchman Andre (Louis Jourdan) is shocked and disgusted when his otherwise demure Polynesian girlfriend Kalua (Debra Paget) throws herself into a volcano as a sacrifice to a pagan god (Reyes and Rampell 65). In movies such as *The Idol Dancer* (1920) and *Mutiny on the Bounty* (1962) lascivious native women are willing to share their bodies with white explorers or seamen. Audiences are often told, in 'South Seas' movies, that natives consider European explorers as 'gods,' and what primitive woman would not want to please her god?

Haunani-Kay Trask insists that for Americans, Hawai'i is '[m]ostly a state of mind ... [t]his fictional Hawai'i comes out of the depths of Western sexual sickness that demands a dark, sin-free native for instant gratification.' The image and attraction of Hawai'i, Trask believes, comes in part from 'slick Hollywood movies' (*Native* 136–7). In the early years of film, Hawai'i was depicted as being different to, or 'other' than the United States. Hawai'i was exotic, primitive, and dangerous. Common themes that emphasize these differences include plots about volcanoes, savage and perhaps man-eating natives, sexually available native women, explicit displays of licentiousness, strange social customs, and pagan religious practices. In movies such as *Aloha Oe* (1915) and *A Fallen Idol* (1919), the leading native ladies are royals (Wood 113), a reminder that Hawai'i was different, feudal, and anachronistic. In as much as their budget would allow it, many of these movies linger on the beautiful, exotic landscapes of Hawai'i and other Pacific islands, another factor that emphasizes difference from America. Historian Robert Schmitt reveals, for example, 'At least 11 of the pictures made in or about Hawai'i featured volcanoes, either real ... or fictional. Most of these volcanoes were filmed in fiery eruption ... threatening either to claim the heroine, overrun a village, or even blow up an entire island. One Hawai'i-made movie, *South of Pago Pago,* contained a smoking volcano that did not erupt, to the astonishment of several reviewers'

(*Hawai'i in the Movies* 5). Schmitt's study of Hawai'i movies that were released between 1898 and 1959 illustrates that 10 out of 11 'volcano movies' were made before Pearl Harbor, out of a total of 75 movies made between 1898 and 1941 inclusively. In contrast, after Pearl Harbor only one was released (*Bird of Paradise*).

Like the tourist literature of the period, Hawai'i was deliberately marketed as a place where the sexual rules of American society were either relaxed or completely absent. Hollywood relied on blatant sexual stereotyping of native women to emphasize this difference. Westerners directly associated the physical racial characteristics of native women with this supposed sexual wantonness. Even today, as University of Iowa professor Jane Desmond notes, tourists expect hula dancers to be young, slender, attractive, dark-skinned, longhaired brunettes. This look, Desmond affirms, 'communicate[s] the notion of "Hawai'i" as different from the United States' (135). Native women are, according to these movie scripts, unlike the supposedly chaste and 'civilized' American women of the time. In contrast to these reserved females, native women are alluring and sexually available. The occasional filmmaker who threatened this stereotype was met with industry and audience disapproval. For example, when Robert Flaherty was tasked by Paramount to go to Samoa to make a similar documentary to his successful *Nanook of the North* (1922), his resulting work, *Moana* (1926), proved to be a disappointment to the studio, as it portrayed none of the stereotypical images that American audiences had come to expect. As film critics Thomas and Vivian Sobchack point out, 'In commercial desperation, Paramount misguidedly advertised the film as "the love life of a South Sea siren" and the film, not delivering what it promised, proved to be a box office flop' (344).

Hollywood perpetuated the image of Hawai'i in particular as a peaceful, romantic paradise. In *Honolulu*, for example, actor Robert Young states, 'I'd like to go to Hawai'i. It's quiet and peaceful there.' His co-star, actress Gracie Allen, sings, 'I know it's gonna be, a great big blow to me, unless I find romance in Honolulu.' The 1927 film *Hula* features Clara Bow as an 'unconquered island girl who comes face to face with love!' (Schmitt, *Hawai'i in the Movies*, 29). In *Tin Pan Alley* (1940), actresses Alice Faye and Betty Grable sing, 'Hawai'i, a lovely Hawai'i. It's like Heaven on the blue Pacific shore. Oh won't you let me go-a, to the land of sweet aloha, won't you let me linger there forever more.'

To a large extent, American audiences of that time period simply imposed mainland racial attitudes onto Hawaiian society. Yet, the idea that Hawai'i was poly-racial also served to remind those mainland audiences how different Hawai'i really was. For example, *Bird of Paradise* (1932) is based on a 1912 Broadway musical by Richard W. Tully, which historian DeSoto Brown describes as 'deeply offensive racism.' For example, one white character states that he 'kept his soul, his white soul, pure from contamination with the brown race.' The musical also features 'the phony concept of human sacrifices leaping into hot lava in Hawai'i' (6). *Bird of Paradise* begins with a dramatic scene in which a native girl (Dolores Del Rio) saves a white sailor from a predatory shark. Immediately the stereotypical images of both the danger and romance of 'The Islands' are shown. Like the 1952 remake, this version of *Bird of Paradise* features a ludicrous volcano sacrifice scene that reminds viewers of the primitive, barbaric and thoroughly *un-American* nature of the natives.

*Flirtation Walk* (1934) stars actors Dick Powell and Ruby Keeler. In one scene the couple encounter, first, some Native Hawaiian fishermen, and then a native *luau*. These scenes serve to remind the audience that Hawaiian customs are different to American. The fishermen, for example, are 'torch fishing,' described by Powell thus: 'the fish see the torch, they come to the surface, the fishermen spear them.' The *luau* is composed of 'a chorus line of 100 Hawaiian dancers' (Schmitt, *Hawai'i in the Movies* 40) who form two concentric rings, the men kneeling on the outside ring, and a troupe of exotically dressed women facing a lone dancer in the center of the circle. Keeler asks Powell, 'What do they do at a love feast?' and Powell replies, coyly, 'Oh they just eat and, uh, stuff and things.' When, after a suitable period of condescending anthropological study, the natives are allowed to notice the *haole* couple, the natives giggle and squeal in childlike fashion, and invite the duo into their circle. Powell sings a (surprisingly good) version of a traditional Hawaiian song *in Hawaiian*, which is at the same time both impressive and slightly unsettling. One wonders why a native Hawaiian is not shown singing in his/her own language. The answer is, of course, that *Flirtation Walk* is not about Hawai'i or the Hawaiians, who serve only as a backdrop to the affairs of Westerners. They provide 'color,' but because they are 'colored,' they cannot take center stage.

By appropriating Hawaiian culture in this unapologetic way, Hollywood contributed to Hawai'i's ongoing cultural colonization. For example, as Wood recounts, 'Powell explains to newcomer Keeler that the *luau* is a feast "in honor of love." He further suggests, in the highly censored language of the time, it is a place for ravenous lovemaking' (105). In this particular scene the *haole* couple are not part of the action. Instead, they view the Hawaiians' performance from a safe distance, as if viewing wildlife. They, like the movie audience, retain their power as voyeurs of 'safe savagery' (Wood 115). This scene suggests that because Hawaiians are supposedly closer to nature and more primitive than Americans, one is likely to see in Hawai'i the kind of hinted-at group sexual encounters that would be unthinkable on the mainland. Made with the full cooperation of the US Army (*New York Times*), the movie's military propaganda value was evident straight away. A *Variety* review noted, for example, the plot's 'Background of West Point [that] allows the army to cop nice publicity and the picture to possess some snappy drill and brass button stuff.' At a screening reviewed by the *New York Times*, an American Legion band played 'a stirring military air,' which, the *Times* claimed, served as a 'rousing recruitment poster' and 'had a packed and ululant house howling with patriotic fervor.'

*Waikiki Wedding* (1937) stars Bing Crosby and features similar elaborate Hollywood-style *hula* dancing set to slack key guitar and orchestral music. Crosby's version of 'Sweet Leilani,' sung in Hawaiian, instantly became a big hit and the song won 'Best Song of 1937' at Hollywood's Oscar ceremony. The story behind the song offers insight on the parasitical workings of the Hollywood studios:

> Paramount studios, like all movie companies, preferred to have the music in its films written by staff employees to keep the royalties in house. Thus they resisted putting 'Sweet Leilani,' a song by Harry Owens, bandleader at the Royal Hawaiian Hotel and not in their employ, in the film. But Bing Crosby, star of the film and the most popular singer in the country, insisted (Brown, DeSoto 7).

The main plot of *Waikiki Wedding*, however, features a romantic adventure tale with all the ingredients that made Hawai'i in this period exotic and different to mainland American audiences. Where in America would one find, for example, 'mass native hula dances and one striking thigh-grinding sequence by a mixed team on gigantic tom-toms' (*Variety*) or Bing Crosby 'in a welter of grass skirts, tropical sunsets … and a razor-back pig'? (*New York Times*). The plot is a mixture of crime, adventure, and romance. A gang of Native Hawaiian men kidnaps actress Shirley Ross. Although she is rescued by Crosby, a bizarre and unbelievable plot twist that entails Ross having to throw a pearl into a volcano, leads to Ross being held captive by a Hawaiian priest. Again, Crosby comes to the rescue and the couple makes their escape as the volcano erupts in the background. *Waikiki Wedding* features many of the familiar plot themes of the early Hawai'i or South Seas movies, including volcanoes, threatening natives, pearls and adventure.

Although these are, for the most part, artistically inconsequential movies, visual images conveyed to large groups of viewers can create powerful and enduring mythologies. Both *Flirtation Walk* (1934) and *Waikiki Wedding* were released in the aftermath of infamous and racially inflammatory crime cases. In 1928, for example, Myles Fukunaga, a 19-year-old Japanese hotel worker, abducted and murdered a 10-year-old *haole* boy called Gill Jamieson, a crime for which he was subsequently executed. Furthermore, in 1931, Navy wife Thalia Massie accused five local men of raping her. The subsequent trial sparked a racial controversy and eventually led to the kidnapping and murder of one of the five accused by Massie's husband, mother, and a US Naval seaman. While audiences today may laugh at such portrayals of gangs of threatening Hawaiians in vintage movies, in the late 1930s these scenes would have resonated strongly with mainland audiences, reminding them of the supposedly dangerous and primitive circumstances that white settlers faced living amongst 'natives.'

*Hawaii Calls* begins in San Francisco, with shots of passengers boarding a cruise ship, and the ship sailing out under Golden Gate Bridge. The effect of this is to remind viewers that to get to Hawai'i one must first leave America and then travel by ship for days to reach this foreign destination. As one character states, their destination is more a state of mind than an actual place: 'Honolulu, Waikiki, bananas, pineapple, hula dancers [and] sunshine.' This exotic imagery is reinforced when the ship arrives in Honolulu and dozens of native boys swim alongside waiting for passengers to throw money overboard. Two young stowaways, *haole* Billy Coulter (Bobby Breen) and Native Hawaiian Pua (Pua Lani), dive into the water to join the other boys. Billy is, in effect, 'going native' in emulating his friend's athletic feat. On the run from the ship's captain and the law, the two boys are taken in by a Native Hawaiian lady named Hina (Mamo Clark). Again, to emphasize cultural difference, every native speaks Hawaiian when they are with their own cultural group whereas haoles speak only English.

The plot of *Hawaii Calls*, such as it is, centers on a plot to steal US Navy Commander Milburn's secret plans, which are 'valuable to the safety of the Hawaiian Islands.' A German spy named Muller recruits local criminal elements like Julius, a Japanese driver and servant for Milburn's fiancé's family. This plotline has all the military excuses for American involvement in Hawai'i, namely the internal and external threat of disloyal Japanese and a concerted effort on behalf of 'foreign' Axis powers to obtain plans for the defense of Hawai'i. When Julius, a long-time servant to the Millburns, 'betrays' his colonial masters by stealing the secret plans, the movie asks the audience to gaze not in the direction of the obviously incompetent Milburn or at the wisdom of sending supposedly top secret plans with a lone naval officer on a civilian cruise ship, but instead at the disloyalty and treachery of the previously trusted Japanese man — a metaphor for the overall situation of the Japanese in Hawai'i and their relationship with America. The end of the movie relieves the audience however: with the help of Billy, the conspirators are discovered and shot to death by police.

A sub-theme of *Hawaii Calls* is concern by the Americans for the welfare of Billy in Hawai'i. He is, as the audience has been reminded on a number of occasions, a white boy who is in danger of going native. Billy himself is aware of this fact, in that he asks Milburn if he is 'disappointed' in his behavior. Milburn tells him, 'Captain O'Hare says he wouldn't be surprised if you went back [to the United States] of your own accord.' The movie's message is that Hawai'i is a good place for a vacation, is strategically significant and therefore needs the 'protection' of the United States military, but is also filled with dangerous foreigners and criminal elements. Although he is an orphan, Billy is still cultured: he sings beautiful songs throughout and is mindful of his manners. In contrast, Pua lives with an extended Hawaiian family and yet is almost feral in nature. Obviously, therefore, Hawai'i is no place for a Caucasian boy. As he leaves the islands on O'Hare's ship, Billy, now dressed in a miniature navy uniform, sings 'Aloha Oe.' Ashore, Pua and Hina bid him a tearful farewell as he heads home to America, the homeland, the place *Hawaii Calls* tells us, where he really belongs.

*Honolulu* (1939) is about a mainland movie star called Brooks Mason (Robert Young), who trades identities with his double, George Smith (Robert Young), a plantation owner in O'ahu, so that he can go on vacation. Mason tells Smith, 'All I know about Hawai'i is pineapples and ukeleles.' As if to emphasize the racial otherness of the Hawaiian Islands, on the outward boat journey a bandleader introduces Dorothy March (Eleanor Powell), in blackface, who performs 'a tribute to the islands' as 'a natural drum dance, of *hula* and her version of a native dance, "done with taps."' Powell proceeds to tap dance through a bizarre Hollywood interpretation of Hawaiian dance and music that *Variety* describes as 'combining Hawaiian drum dance, a hula, and tap version of native dance.' When the ship arrives in Honolulu a montage of images including Diamond Head, surfers, palm trees, beaches and local fishermen set the scene and remind the viewer that this is, indeed, a foreign paradise.

*Honolulu* features a Chinese man in a prominent role, Smith's servant, Wong (Willie Fung). According to *Variety*, however, Wong provides only 'brief but hilarious contributions' in a stereotypical role where the audience is asked to laugh at the 'foreigner' who speaks such broken English as 'Me know, me know.' *Honolulu* makes full use of the image of Hawai'i as a paradise by showing many 'outdoor' scenes, even if they were shot on a soundstage. For example, one scene features a waterfall, at the base of which is a *luau* (feast) with a circle of Hawaiian and *haole* diners. Native Hawaiian dancers, singers, and musicians entertain this group. The scenes remind viewers that Hawai'i contains people, customs, and scenery that are not American. *Honolulu* is so bad, according to the *New York Times*, 'if things are the way the picture makes out [Hawai'i] should be freed before the Philippines' (1580–1). A comment such as this would be near impossible in the post-Pearl Harbor world.

## Americanizing Hawai'i after Pearl Harbor

Before World War Two Hawai'i was a marginal part of the United States. Leila Reiplinger, a Hawaiian hula dancer who travelled to New York in 1940, recalls, for example, a history teacher who thought, 'we were still the Sandwich Islands' (Desmond 108). In contrast, a post-Pearl Harbor 1942 article in *Asia Magazine* referred to the Hawai'i as 'American Hawaii' (Desmond 119). Authors Beth Bailey and David Farber assert: 'Hawaii is about as far from "representative" as one can get in 1940s America. Hawaii was at the margin of American life as well as of the war' (19). No single incident would change the course of American history in the twentieth century more than the Japanese attack on Pearl Harbor on 7 December 1941. Almost 2500 US servicemen and civilians were killed and a severe blow dealt to US military and national prestige. The attack would have wide-reaching effects on life in Hawai'i, but it would also effect change in Hollywood and the 'South Seas' genre of film.

After the attack on Pearl Harbor, many Hollywood movies about Hawai'i served to further this aim of Americanization. They did this by eliminating Native Hawaiians from the screen, replacing them with an almost all-white cast, and emphasizing the normality of everyday American life in the islands. Even the titles of movies about Hawai'i changed: before the war many movies had titles with colors in them, perhaps to emphasize racial differences between white and black, and to suggest the possibility of forbidden inter-racial liaisons. Jane Desmond notes that between 1920 and 1939, 'more than fifty feature films were made in or about Hawai'i. A genre of South Seas island romance was particularly popular, often featuring interracial romance between native women and Caucasian men (businessmen, shipwreck victims) visiting the islands' (109). Some examples of movies with color-laden titles are *The Black Lili* (1921), *The White Flower* (1923), *Beware of Blondes* (1928), *The Black Camel* (1931), *The Blonde Captive* (1931), *White Heat* (1934), and *Mutiny on the Blackhawk* (1939). In contrast, not one movie listed in Robert Schmitt's *Hawai'i in the Movies* that was made after Pearl Harbor, has a color in the title.

The exotic locales of pre-war movies were replaced, for a time, in post-Pearl Harbor movies with backdrops of military bases, built-up urban areas, factories, shipyards, yacht clubs, city scenes, and modern technology. For example, the 1956 movie *The Revolt of Mamie Stover* does not focus on palm trees, beaches, or the scenic majestic of Diamond Head. Instead, it tells the seedy story of a Honolulu prostitute. Most of the action in that movie takes place indoors, at a nightclub, a residential home, or in restaurants or hotels. One scene is set on a golf course and country club. Similarly, *From Here to Eternity* chooses, with one notable

*Figure 4.1* Postcard depicting beach scene from *From Here To Eternity* (1953). Author's personal collection.

exception, not to feature exotic locales and instead focuses on indoor scenes at Schofield Barracks or at River Street brothels. [Fig. 4.1]

Pre-Pearl Harbor movies emphasize how different the United States was to the supposedly exotic, primitive, and dangerous Hawaiian Islands. They achieve this by frequent use of recurring thematic elements and visual reminders, including an emphasis on nature, wildlife and landscape, plots about volcanoes, savage natives, cannibalism, sexual obtainable native women, explicit displays of nudity and passion, odd social customs, and pagan religious rites. In the years after Pearl Harbor, however, Hollywood movies served to remind mainland Americans that Hawai'i was part of the United States, as American as apple pie and baseball. Hollywood may have been responding to changing audience expectations — assuaging the American 'feel good' factor. For example, the Japanese attack on Pearl Harbor led to such vicious retaliation by the United States that many commentators and historians view the war in the Pacific as being essentially different to the war in Europe. John Dower points to the racial nature of propaganda and newspaper coverage as evidence that Americans viewed the Japanese as vicious, subhuman savages, and that the Pearl Harbor attack released 'emotions forgotten since our most savage Indian wars were awakened by the ferocities of the Japanese commanders' (33). American audiences needed to feel that such ferocity was justified: no one wants to be seen as a racist, after all, and no one wanted to be reminded of the American colonization of Hawai'i. Therefore, if Americans convinced themselves that they were the innocent party, that *they* were attacked at Pearl Harbor, and that the attack was more perfidious in nature than simply two colonial armies tussling over their governments' colonial possessions in the Pacific, then attention could be drawn away from the racist nature of the retaliation and from the fact that the Japanese attacked only military targets on the 'American Gibraltar.'

In Hollywood movies, Hawai'i's Americanization was achieved through subtle changes in recurring themes and imagery, and also by omission. Pre-war movies usually featured native village activities such as feasts, ceremonies, religious practices etc. These social customs emphasized how different native society was compared to Western. However, as Houston Wood notes, at the beginning of World War Two, 'Native village life all but disappear[s], a tropological development that reaches its contemporary form in the Elvis films of the 1960s' (117). Whereas exotic and sometimes threatening native men, dressed usually in native attire, played major roles in early Hawai'i films, in post-Pearl Harbor movies such masculine native exoticism disappears from the screen.

There is no post-Pearl Harbor equivalent of Duke Kahanamoku, for example, who features in many early Hollywood films and television shows (Brennan).[2] In most of these movies Hawaiians are either entirely absent, or they play small roles as waiters, barmen, or musicians. In *From Here to Eternity*, for example, the only Hawaiians on view are servants, waiters, and entertainers, all of who are dressed in non-native apparel or non-threatening aloha shirts.

Americanization in Hollywood movies also operates by focusing less on nature and landscapes and more on urban and industrial Hawai'i, or on the US military. For example, ten Pre-Pearl Harbor movies about Hawai'i had military themes — *Excuse Me* (1925), *The Non-Stop Flight* (1926), *The Flying Fleet* (1929), *Leathernecking* (1930), *Flirtation Walk* (1934), *Navy Wife* (1935), *Wings Over Honolulu* (1937), *Dive Bomber* (1941), *Navy Blues* (1941) and *In the Navy* (1941). In contrast, and for obvious reasons, many post-Pearl Harbor movies feature war or military themes. These include *Submarine Raider* (1942), *Air Force* (1943), *December 7* (1943), *On an Island with You* (1948), *Task Force* (1949), *Sands of Iwo Jima* (1949), *The Big Lift* (1950) *Operation Pacific* (1951), *Go For Broke!* (1951), *Sailor Beware* (1952), *From Here to Eternity* (1953), *The Caine Mutiny* (1954), *The Revolt of Mamie Stover* (1956), *The Lieutenant Wore Skirts* (1956), *Away All Boats* (1956), *Jungle Heat* (1957), *Torpedo Run* (1958), *The Gallant Hours* (1960), *In Harm's Way* (1965), *Tora! Tora! Tora!* (1970), *Midway* (1976), and *Pearl Harbor* (2001) (Schmitt, *Hawai'i in the Movies*; Reyes and Rampell).

Not only do these movies focus on Americans and American culture and divest Hawai'i of Native Hawaiians and their culture, many of them also perpetuate myths about the Japanese attack on Pearl Harbor that serve to make the Japanese look savage, devious and barbaric. Engelhardt states, 'At the heart of the war story lay the ambush, extraordinary evidence of the enemy's treacherous behavior. While all ambushes involved deceit, none was more heinous than the "sneak attack," that surprise assault on a peaceful, unsuspecting people' (39). [Fig. 4.2] Such 'sneak attacks' occur in movies such as *Submarine Raider, December 7, The Final Countdown* (1980) and *Pearl Harbor,* where civilians are attacked as well as military targets. In fact, much if not all of the damage caused to the city of Honolulu was a result of spent US Navy shells that had been fired into the air and had then fallen on civilian areas. For example, an explosion at the Governor's Mansion that killed one civilian was actually caused by a Navy five-inch anti-aircraft shell (Editors 101).

In the movies, however, showing historically incorrect attacks on US civilians perpetuates the image of the Japanese as devious and savage.

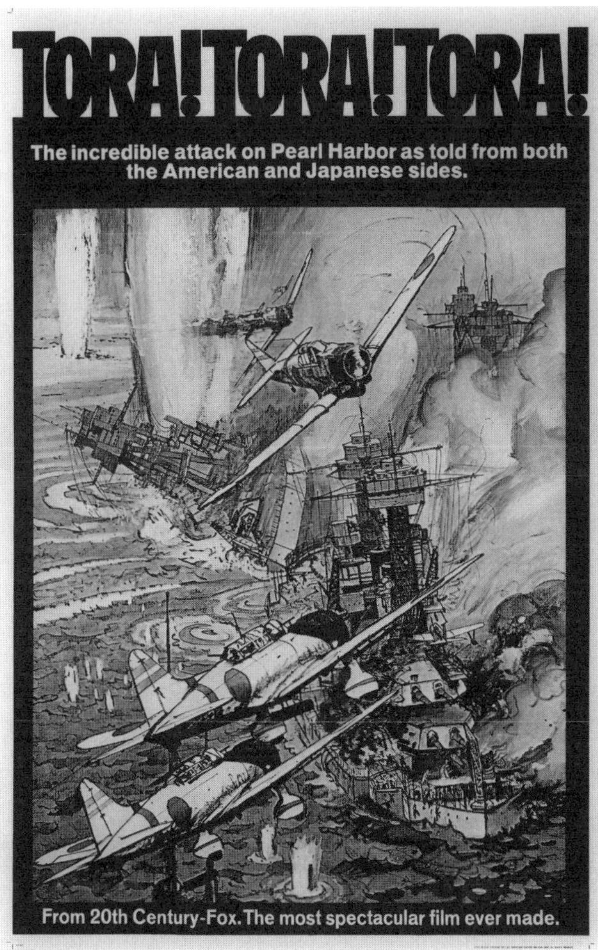


*Figure 4.2* 'Sneak Attack' depicted in promotional poster for *Tora! Tora! Tora!* (1970). Author's personal collection.

In *Submarine Raider*, for example, an American woman 'survives the shelling of her luxury yacht in Hawaiian waters by a Japanese aircraft carrier,' and a Federal agent fights 'suspected spies and saboteurs in the Islands' (Reyes and Rampell 15). In *Task Force*, Japanese warplanes attack three American women playing tennis. *In Harm's Way* contains a scene in which a Japanese plane attacks a civilian couple on a beach. In *Pearl Harbor*, a Japanese pilot attacks a civilian convertible car. In John Ford's documentary *December 7*, Japanese citizens in Hawai'i spy on the US Fleet and report back to the Japanese Embassy. When the Japanese finally attack in *December 7*, warplanes attack civilian targets as well as military. The movie *Air Force* 'claims there were Japanese snipers on Maui and that Japanese vegetable trucks from Honolulu smashed into the planes at Hickam Field' (Reyes and Rampell 11). The plot of *Jungle Heat* involves labor disputes and Japanese spies on Kauai, where, according to Schmitt, 'war veterans' groups strongly objected to its portrayal of disloyalty among Japanese residents' (*Hawai'i in the Movies* 71).

These movies dehumanize the Japanese and paint them as totally immoral, deviant, underhanded, and barbaric. Engelhardt states, 'The Japanese attack on Pearl Harbor fit the lineaments of this [war] story well. At the country's periphery, a savage, nonwhite enemy had launched a barbaric attack on Americans going about their lives early one Sunday morning' (5). Clearly Hollywood was determined to play its part in forming this narrative and it is now clear in hindsight that such misinformation and propaganda had the desired effect: the *New York Times* notes, for example, that a 1942 theater audience for *Submarine Raider* 'was in fine hissing form' at the movie's 'scrupulously fair ... portrayal of the enemy' (1874).

Engelhardt notes in the war story that when a savage enemy massacres Americans, rumors often spread that either traitorous Americans were involved, or perhaps, the savage enemy was part European in heritage. After all, what else could explain how and why savages could defeat a civilized people? Thus, when Custer's Indian killers were defeated in 1876, rumor spread that white men dressed as Indians were leading the attack, or that Sitting Bull was a 'half-breed' Frenchman. Engelhardt notes that when General Douglas MacArthur heard the news that his air force in the Philippines had been destroyed from the air, he 'refused to believe that the pilots could've been Japanese. He insisted they must have been white mercenaries' (39). Fussell points out that in any war, 'one's defeats and disasters are caused by treasonous traffic with the enemy rather than by one's own blundering amateurism is always a popular idea' (*Wartime* 39–40). Of the Pearl Harbor attack, Fussell notes, 'it was believed that Japanese working on Oahu had cut big arrows in the fields to guide Japanese planes toward their target.' In the aftermath of the battle, 'a dog barking on the beach at Oahu was said to be barking in Morse, conveying treasonous messages to a Japanese submarine listening offshore' (*Wartime* 40). Movies such as *Submarine Raider* and *Air Force* perpetuate the myth of treasonous Americans of Japanese descent helping the enemy. The documentary *December 7* goes even further in depicting a German intelligence officer helping to coordinate spying operations with Japanese Embassy staff in Honolulu.

*December 7* is, perhaps, the best example of Hollywood's attempts to portray pre-Pearl Harbor Hawai'i as dissimilar to the United States. In the film's narrative, Hawai'i was once primitive but has now been 'civilized' by American influence. The narrator 'Uncle Sam' states, for example, 'Where once was a village of grass huts, a modern American city now stands.' The 'Big Five,' mostly American and *haole* business interests are described as the 'backbone, big brain, and nerve center' of the Territory. Uncle Sam states, however, 'My islands are of many races, many colors,' thus introducing viewers to the racial make-up of the islands, and the 'problem' of the Japanese. The Japanese had their own 'Big Five' in the Islands, and the Japanese population outnumbered Americans in Hawai'i by two to one — a demographical factor important in perpetuating the war story. As Engelhardt notes, 'inferior American numbers were invariably translated into a numerology of [enemy] destruction' (5). So too was the 'sneak' attack on outnumbered Americans in Fort Hawai'i translated into a numerology of Japanese destruction. *December 7* portrays Hawai'i as a tourist paradise with its guard down: 'On a hilltop Uncle Sam lay fast asleep,' it states, thus perpetuating the 'sneak attack' narrative that Engelhardt posits as an essential part of the 'war story.' Engelhardt adjudges, for example, that Ford 'drew on last-stand imagery to display a fleet (and a nation) caught in the oceanic equivalent of a box canyon and nearly wiped out' (47).

However, where the movie most emphasizes how dissimilar Hawai'i was to the United States is in its depiction of the Japanese. In *War Without Mercy*, John Dower illustrates how Americans reduced the Japanese to a status of subhuman in order to make their destruction easier and more palatable. They were racially different — 'yellow' not white, and more akin to animals than humans. Thus, American newspapers began referring to the Japanese in simile and metaphor as monkeys, baboons, gorillas, dogs (or mad dogs), mice, rats, vipers, rattlesnakes, and cockroaches. They had no mind of their own and were, instead, herd-like, resembling sheep or cattle (77–93). As subhuman 'yellow dwarf slaves' (84) or 'robots' (86), the Japanese were dehumanized and therefore made suitable for slaughter. Illustrations of hybrid insect-like Japanese in *Leatherneck* magazine were accompanied by such genocidal commentary as, 'the breeding grounds around the Tokyo area must be completely annihilated' (91).

In *December 7*, by careful framing, editing, and special effects, director John Ford creates images of the Japanese in Hawai'i as insect-like hordes threatening to overrun the outnumbered American population. For example, he uses montage, quick editing and fast-paced music to suggest the ant-like Japanese are overwhelming whites. Furthermore, Ford uses frequent close-ups of Japanese as a reminder of physical racial otherness. A Japanese official is shown as a bowing, grinning fool, for example. Also, Japanese kids are shown singing 'God Bless America,' but the narrator says theirs is 'a hyphenated loyalty.' The first 83-minute length version of *December 7* was banned by the War Department because, in the commonly-accepted version of events, the US military objected to portrayals of its ineptitude. However, an Oscar-winning 30-minute version of the documentary, without references to racial differences and Japanese espionage, was eventually released in 1943. It is possible that it was the original version of *December 7*'s portrayal of Hawai'i as a unique place, quite unlike the United States, that US authorities objected to. Such a depiction would have reminded wartime American audiences that Hawai'i was, in essence, a US colony, and may have called into question the scope and extent of American retaliation.

Recurring thematic elements and visual images of early Hollywood movies about Hawai'i or the South Seas emphasize the exotic and primitive otherness of islands. In contrast, films such as *From Here to Eternity*, *The Revolt of Mamie Stover* and *Big Jim McLain* de-emphasized such otherness by ignoring familiar plot devices about volcanoes, savage natives, and cannibalism. Furthermore, post-Pearl Harbor movies tend to show urban rather than rural life, in contrast to earlier movies that focus on themes of nature, wildlife and landscape. Gone too were Hawaiians with their 'odd' social customs, strange language and pagan religious rites. Instead we have plots that focus on Americans and the Americanization of Hawai'i in areas such as technology, politics, culture, and the military.

Like no other movie, *Big Jim McLain*, starring John Wayne, attempts to 'Americanize' Hawai'i. Wayne is more than a bit-part player in Engelhardt's war story, as cultural historian Gary Wills tangentially notes:

> John Ford had come out of World War II in love with the Navy, with military units in general, and with America's new imperial role in the world as the asserter of freedom everywhere. The three 'Seventh Cavalry' films he made with Wayne from 1948 to 1950 reflect this attitude, and put Wayne at the center of Cold War sensibility striving for social discipline in time of trial. In 1949, the Soviets exploded their first atom bomb and Communists won their war for China. In 1950, President Truman escalated the nuclear competition by deciding to create the hydrogen bomb. The image of cavalry units surrounded by

hostile Indians echoed the fears of Americans trying to remain steady as peril increased. Wayne became the cool but determined model for Americans living with continual danger (147).

*Big Jim McLain* is a documentary-style work of anti-communist propaganda in the same vein as other 'anti-Red' movies as *The Red Menace* (1949), *I Married a Communist* (1950), and *I Was a Communist for the FBI* (1951). This documentary technique adds weight to a flimsy script and authority to otherwise laughable portrayals of supposed communists who, Wills notes, 'abjure smiles [and] cannot speak without sneering' (184). Wayne (whose character shares initials with Senator Joseph McCarthy) is an investigator for the House Committee on Un-American Activities who is sent to Hawai'i to find communist agitators. A younger, impetuous sidekick called Mal Baxter (James Arness) accompanies him. The film has a see-through plot, cardboard characters, and poor acting. However, it is notable for the way in which it transforms earlier movie images of Hawai'i as different and exotic into a Hawai'i that is loyally American.

Wayne's villains are untypical of earlier Hawai'i movies. In those early movies, criminals and rogues are typically either natives or of mixed race. In *Big Jim McLain*, however, the villains are mostly Caucasians. In other words, they are un-American because they are communists, not because of their skin color or racial origin. This reflected a new Cold War trend in film making that played off fears of 'reds under the bed,' the McCarthy hearings, blacklists, and paranoia about foreigners. These villains are involved in a plot to disrupt shipping and stop supplies to US troops fighting the Korean War. Their methods are both modern and devious: they plan not only to instigate and exploit labor disputes, but also to use bacteriological warfare, spreading diseases using rats as plague carriers. Such imagery could only serve to remind the viewing audience of earlier dehumanizing propaganda about the Japanese. The plot utilized irrational fears about labor unions, such as the International Longshoremen's and Warehousemen's Union, and economic strikes such as the sugar workers' strike of 1946, a pineapple workers' strike of 1947, and an ILWU strike of 1949.[3] Wayne's mission was to find who or what was un-American, and to eliminate it, thus drawing Hawai'i even closer into the American fold.

The movie opposes earlier stereotypes about Hawai'i as backward and rural. For example, unlike previous movies in which travellers arrive on ships and alight at the Aloha Tower dock, Wayne travels in a state of the art commercial jet and arrives at the newly built Honolulu International

Airport. There are no native urchins on view begging for coins as in *Hawaii Calls*. Instead there are carefully orchestrated hula girls to welcome tourists with *leis*. When Wayne and Baxter arrive at their duplex, Baxter displays more modern technology when he sets up a listening device to spy on the occupants of the next apartment. That the occupants are honeymooners adds to the well-worn theme of titillation and male-gaze voyeurism of this genre of movies. However, Wayne's comment to Baxter, 'Who do you think we're working for — Dr. Kinsey,' adds to the modern 'cutting edge' feel of the movie. Later we are told that the contents of a suspect's luggage are 'microscopically photographed,' and that 'security agencies have been listening to some very interesting conversations.' This information not only conveys that the security services are on top of the communist problem, but also illustrates that all the modern technological resources of America in the 1950s are also available in Hawai'i.

Unlike earlier films, evident in *Big Jim McLain* are a contemporary, tiled hospital, a psychiatric hospital, a modern doctor's office, and the clean, tourist-filled Royal Hawaiian Hotel. Instead of the native outrigger canoes of *Mutiny on the Bounty* and many other early movies, in *Big Jim McLain* we have scenes set at the Outrigger Canoe Club, where modern American yachts predominate. Furthermore, in mentioning that she 'attends a course of lectures at the university on Saturdays,' Wayne's love interest, Nancy Olson (actress Nancy Vallon) subtly reminds the audience that Hawai'i is no longer the culturally 'backward' island of earlier movies and is now a modern, sophisticated state like any other.

Like no other film before or since, *Big Jim McLain* reverses the role of invader and invader, or colonist and native. A prime example of this is the movie's portrayal of the Honolulu Police Department, which is very different to how the HPD was viewed before World War Two. For example, in the 1930s during the infamous Massie rape case, island haoles, the military, and mainland newspaper and political interests criticized the Honolulu Police Department as corrupt and prejudiced against Caucasians (Wright; Packer and Thomas; Stannard, *Honor*). Just two decades later, however, Wayne assures the audience that the Honolulu Police Department 'rates A1 on an FBI list of municipal police departments.' This image is reinforced by actor Dan Liu's competent and assured performance as the Chief of Police who, at the end of the movie, rescues Wayne from a beating and probably death at the hands of a communist gang. [Fig. 4.3]

As for the native population of Hawai'i, gone are earlier images of bare-breasted warriors as in *South of Pago Pago*, topless hula-dancers like

*Figure 4.3* Lobby card showing actor John Wayne attacked by communists in *Big Jim McLain* (1952). Author's personal collection.

Delores Del Rio in *Bird of Paradise*, or the more modest but still sexy Clara Bow, showing her navel, in *Hula*. [Fig. 4.4] Instead we have native men in Aloha shirts, long pants or a suit and tie, and female hula dancers dressed conservatively with their midriffs covered. All of the natives have a *hapa-haole* (half white) look, and there are no really dark-skinned actors on display. There are no inter-racial romances for the lead characters, and only one example of this in the whole film — a minor character *haole* married to a briefly glimpsed Japanese woman. Indeed, the color white dominates in this movie, whether it is the white of sailors' uniforms, the 'whiter-than-white' motives of Wayne and Baxter, or the Caucasian actors who play virtually all of the lead character roles. For example, Madge (Veda Ann Borg), a loud *haole* woman tells Wayne, 'I wanna show you how we *kamaainas* live' as she takes him to both the Royal Hawaiian Hotel and a restaurant whose patrons are predominantly *haole* also. Madge's contention that she is a *kamaaina*, a 'child of the land,' reverses the role of native and interloper, and is a common appropriation of both Hawaiian culture and political rights.

"SOUTH OF PAGO PAGO"
with VICTOR McLAGLEN and JON HALL


*Figure 4.4* Lobby card, *South of Pago Pago* (1940). Author's personal collection.

Even the Japanese are recruited into this reversal: while many suspects in the 'sneak attack' murder of Baxter are Japanese, it is clear in the movie that the Japanese community has already been recruited as an American ally in the Cold War. Engelhardt states, 'With remarkable speed in the immediate postwar years, three enemy nations, Germany, Japan, and Italy, became "Free World" allies,' more like 'us' and less like 'them' (58). For example, when a communist complains that Wayne attacked him without provocation, Police Chief Dan Liu states, 'We all have provocation to attack you, [we're] all Americans.' Similarly, the Japanese wife of communist spy Willie Namaka is portrayed sympathetically and now works as a nurse on a leper colony to atone for her earlier communist leanings. Like the old Japanese priest at a Shinto temple, Mrs. Namaka volunteers information willingly, as in the film's narrative all loyal 'Americans' should. Just eight years earlier in *December 7*, John Ford was using these very same images to suggest the foreign, un-American nature of the Japanese in Hawai'i. In a final bizarre twist, a Polish immigrant who has immigrated to the islands tells Wayne, 'I came *here* to the West Coast,' thus moving Hawai'i thousands of miles east, and closer to America.

*From Here to Eternity* is based on James Jones' controversial novel of the same name. The novel was, in fact, too controversial to be translated directly to screen and a toned-down screenplay by Daniel Taradash was used instead. The movie starred Burt Lancaster as first Sergeant Milton Warden, Ernest Borgnine as 'Fatso' Judson, Montgomery Clift as Private Robert E. Lee Prewitt, Frank Sinatra as Private Angelo Maggio, Donna Reed as Lorene, Deborah Kerr as Karen Holmes, and Philip Ober as Captain Dana Holmes. Directed by Fred Zinnemann, *From Here to Eternity* was nominated for 13 Academy Awards of which it won eight.

Set in Schofield Barracks just before the attack on Pearl Harbor, *From Here to Eternity* examines the relationships of two soldiers and their women. Sergeant Warden pursues a dangerous relationship with his Commanding Officer's wife Karen Holmes risking court martial, and Private Robert E. Lee Prewitt (or 'Prew') falls in love with Lorene, a 'hostess' in a Honolulu private club called the New Congress Club. Obviously the inference here is that Lorene is a prostitute and the club a brothel. However, this type of explicit subject matter was considered too risqué for inclusion in a movie in 1953 and the roles were, consequently, toned down.

Neither of these relationships are the typical clean-cut affairs that one might expect, however. There are some subdued gray areas regarding prostitution, adultery, abuse, and drunkenness — not what audiences had come to expect from Hollywood's mythical Hawai'i. The Apollo [Movie] Guide states 'While it's set on the eve of the Pearl Harbor invasion, *From Here to Eternity* has less to do with the Second World War than it does with the stress of social change — something that was jump-started by the onset of war.' Social change in *America*, that is. The movie is not about Hawai'i as such. It is, instead, a conservative film, which values traditional social structures within the US military and in America as a whole. Critic Brandon French states, 'In Zinnemann's movie, American society, the capitalist economy, and various social institutions — such as marriage, motherhood, and the Army — are taken off the hook. There may be a bad marriage, or a corrupt officer or two, but the basic structures are sound' (56). *From Here to Eternity* thus serves to reinforce traditional American values using Hawai'i as a backdrop and Pearl Harbor as a rallying call for Americans (and Hawaiians) to forget their personal problems and rally behind the flag.

*From Here to Eternity* leaves out the racial issues present both in James Jones' novel and in the military itself. For example, in the novel Prew says to Violet, 'Why in hell would I marry you? Have a raft of snot-nosed nigger brats? Be a goddam squawman and work in the goddam pineapple fields for the rest of my life? Or drive a Schofield taxi? Why the hell do you think I got in the Army? Because I didn't want to sweat my heart and pride out in a goddam coalmine all my life and have a raft of snot-nosed brats who look like niggers in the coaldirt' (112). Prew's reluctance to marry a non-Caucasian was also fueled by examples of disastrous inter-racial match-ups. For example, Jones describes Prew's views on 'Dhom, the G Company duty sergeant, bald and massive and harassed, crossed his eyes, trailed by his fat sloppy Filipino wife and seven half-caste brats; no wonder Dhom was a bully, condemned to spend his life in foreign service like an exile because he had a Filipino wife' (111). These scenes and viewpoints are entirely omitted from the movie, as are virtually all references to race and racism in the military or in Hawai'i. *Variety* states, 'The bawdy vulgarity and the outhouse vocabulary, the pros and non-pros among its easy ladies, and the slambang indictment of Army brass have not been emasculated in the transfer to the screen, but are certainly shown in much better taste for consumption by a broader audience.' *The New York Times* also praises the movie's 'job of editing, emending, re-arranging and purifying a volume bristling with brutality and obscenities' (2715).

These racial and sexual omissions make *From Here to Eternity* distinct from earlier movies that focus on these very themes to attract viewers. The movie elides racial difference and smoothes over Honolulu's sex industry and the military's role in it. The Hawaiian sex trade, that so attracted early moviemakers and, in World War Two, was officially sanctioned by the US military, marked Hawai'i as different. To sailors, soldiers, airmen, and tourists, Hawai'i represented a place other than America, a place where sex was readily available and inter-racial sex possible. As *From Here to Eternity* sanitizes or omits altogether these facts, it makes Hawai'i less out of the ordinary and unusual, and instead transforms it into just another American community with everyday American problems. The movie focuses not on the exoticism of Hawai'i or Hawaiians but instead on issues that a mainland audience could identify with, particularly class differences between military ranks — 'the GI anger against the army "brass",' which was a major theme of post-war literature (Zinn 418).

Like Prewitt, Maggio's role in the film is to demonstrate the injustice of life in the Army. He is forced to do guard duty when he should have been on a weekend pass. He goes AWOL and states, 'Can't a man put his lousy hands in his lousy pockets in the street? I ain't no criminal. I ain't no coward.' Even pragmatist and career soldier Warden recognizes the injustice of the system. He tells Prewitt, 'Life's crummy. Miserable.' He warns him also not to be a loner as, 'maybe back in the days of the pioneers a man could go his own way but today you gotta play ball.'

Just as the Office of War Information asked Americans to come together for the war effort, Warden reminds potential loners that the days of the rugged individual are over and that everyone must now pull together for America. Eventually the appeal to patriotism leads Prewitt to forget about past injustices and to contemplate his return from being AWOL. When Lorene asks him why, he replies, 'What do I want to go back into the Army for? I'm a soldier.' Despite everything, he believes that the Army will take care of him. Besides, there's a war to fight with the Japs. He states, 'They're pickin' trouble with the best Army in the world.'

*From Here to Eternity* has been praised for how successfully it evokes the sense of Hawai'i in pre-war days. Such praise is deserved to the extent that the military scenes ring true. However, despite references to Kaneohe, the Kalakaua Inn, the Royal Hawaiian Hotel, and Kuhio Beach Park, and apart from the occasional Hawaiian or Chinaman appearing as a waitress or passer-by, it is difficult to tell whether this is Hawai'i or California. There is the occasional glimpse of Hawai'i, such as a Hawaiian band playing in a restaurant, but even with the film's music the predominant song played throughout is 'Re-enlistment Blues,' sung by an American soldier. The movie also lacks the exotic scenery, which was a feature of earlier movies in the genre. Most of the action takes place inside Schofield Barracks or in Honolulu. Only one scene — Lancaster and Kerr's memorable romp at Kuhio Beach Park — reminds viewers that this is Hawai'i. This particular scene cannot, however, deflect attention away from the general *mis en screen,* which is anything but exotic.

## Hawai'i as multicultural model

The year 1955 seems to be somewhat of a turning point in the South Seas film genre. Combined, of course, with other media, political policies and social factors — not the least of which was a political push for Statehood — 14 years of Hollywood movies emphasizing Hawai'i's Americanness seemed to have had the desired effect. With the 'war story' embedded in the American consciousness, perhaps now the image of a thoroughly American Hawai'i might be used in a different way. The year 1954 saw the momentous Supreme Court Case *Brown versus Board of Education.* Its outcome threatened to undermine America's whole social structure. Perhaps then Hawai'i could be utilized as a successful example of the melting pot, of different races living together in harmony. From 1955 onwards, many Hollywood movies about Hawai'i deal with issues of inter-racial relationships and racial intolerance albeit, for the most part in a deliberately frothy and lightweight way. This reverses a recognized Cold War trend in Hollywood movie making of relegating social issues to the sidelines. As author Dennis McNally notes, 'Raging anti-Communism clawed at American culture and disembowelled, among other things, American films; nearly one third of them had dealt with serious social themes in 1947, but in 1952 it was one eleventh' (108).

Many films in the 'South Seas' genre reverse this Hollywood trend of demoting social issues. For example, *South Pacific* (1958) features an inter-racial relationship between a young American officer and a native girl. *Blue Hawaii* (1961) has *haole* Chad Gates (Elvis Presley) marrying a half-Hawaiian half-French girl named Maile Duvall. *Diamond Head* (1963) features an oppressive American rancher named Richard Howland (Charlton Heston), who tries to stop his sister Sloan (Yvette Mimieux) from marrying Native Hawaiian, Paul Kahana (James Darren). At the same time, as film critics Luis Reyes and Ed Rampell point out, Howland is 'Blind to hypocrisy and disclaiming racial discrimination' as he 'carries on a clandestine love affair with the lovely Chinese Mei-Chen, who is to bear his son' (128). *Midway* features a sub-plot about race and prejudice concerning an American pilot and his Japanese-American fiancée. Of course, inter-racial relationships feature also in pre-World War Two movies about Hawai'i, but there is a different dynamic at work. Rarely do relationships between dark-skinned men and white women occur in these movies, such was the racial climate of the time. Houston Wood identifies only one movie, *White Heat* (1934), in which a Caucasian woman is attracted to a native man.

In these Hollywood movies, Hawai'i acted as a role model for the turbulent mainland society of the late 1950s and onwards. Racial strife and civil unrest can be overcome, these movies suggest, if Hawai'i acts as a paradigm for the way Americans handle racial issues. The enduring image of Hawai'i and other South Sea Islands of a welcoming romantic paradise, with sexually available natives, still remained. In *Ma and Pa Kettle in Waikiki* (1955), for example, one character states, 'Hawai'i, Waikīkī, palms swaying in the moonlight. Oh it's just too romantic and wonderful.' If it was an overstatement that 'everybody wants to go to Hawai'i,' as actor James Darren states in *Gidget Goes Hawaiian* (1961), Hollywood movies were certainly ensuring, with their images both of half-dressed natives and under-dressed Americans, that Hawai'i was the place to be for those Americans interested in forbidden or illicit inter-racial sex.

In the late 1950s and 1960s the image of Hawai'i as warm, feminized, and welcoming, and of its native people as sexually available, served as background for the type of inter-racial romances that had disappeared from this genre of movies decades before. In the early era of cinema, many films about Hawai'i or the South Seas featured inter-racial romances. As Houston Wood notes, many of these movies include female Hawaiians of Royal ancestry who fall in love with the flotsam and jetsam of Westerners who wash up on Hawai'i's shores: 'The films suggest that Hawaiian women of such esteemed blood are worthy of the average American Davids and Keiths who pursue them. The dangers inherent in racial mixing are at the heart of these films, but they include acknowledgement of the possibility that these dangers can be surmounted if the Native is royal' (113). Wood observes that by the 1930s, 'racial mixing had become unequivocally unacceptable. When the racially tolerant *Aloha Oe* was remade as *Aloha* in 1931, the notion of a successful racial intermarriage was no longer offered in the final reel' (113).

This trend was reinforced by the Pearl Harbor attack, as it seemed that proof now existed that those deemed 'foreign' (the Japanese), or 'different' (brown-skinned Hawaiians), were as dangerous and devious as we had always been led to believe. In the movies, the disappearance of inter-racial romance continued throughout the 1940s and into the mid-1950s. However, as the *Brown* Supreme Court judgment gradually effected changes in American society in the late 1950s and, more extensively in the 1960s, the theme of interracial romance again began to permeate Hollywood's South Seas movies. While Caucasian characters remain foregrounded in these movies, and familiar stereotypes remain in portrayals of non-whites, the dramas and melodramas of inter-racial relationships began to reappear.

In *Enchanted Island* (1958), based loosely on Herman Melville's novel *Typee*, the crew of a whaling ship land in the Marquesas Islands, where they are greeted by beautiful, scantily clad native women. When their puritanical Captain orders them back to the ship, sailor Abner Bedford (Dana Andrews) refuses. A fight ensues and Bedford and another sailor, Tom (Don Dubbins), run off into the undergrowth. Abner then begins a passionate relationship with voluptuous native girl, Fayaway, played by American actress Jane Powell. Soon, however, the sailors begin to suspect that the natives are cannibals. When Tom disappears, and natives are seen wearing items of his clothing, Bedford turns away from Fayaway in disgust, believing her to have concealed Tom's grisly death. However, he overcomes these feelings, realizing that he should not judge the natives' customs, although he considers them abhorrent. Eventually, however, Abner and Fayaway flee from the village. This is, after all, no place for a white man or semi-civilized woman. Fayaway pays the price for her interracial romance when she is murdered by the tribe's medicine man. Abner, however, returns to the ship from which he fled and is, for some unexplained reason, promoted to first officer.

The novelty of interracial romance in *Enchanted Island* is lessened somewhat by this genre's traditional custom of employing a non-native actress in the role of a native. One critic called Powell 'the most unlikely blue-eyed Polynesian yet, with her maidenform bra always clearly visible beneath her ... sarong' (Reyes and Rampell 298). As in earlier movies, the audience is more accepting of miscegenation if the native does not display the physical characteristics of the supposedly inferior race. Nevertheless, unlike most movies about Hawai'i or the South Seas made between 1941 and the mid-1950s, an interracial romance does, at least, take place. It may well be that in the racially aware atmosphere of the post-*Brown* era, Warner Brothers chose for that reason to release a movie based on a book that is considered to be sympathetic to natives and non-judgmental about inter racial romance.

In *Mutiny on the Bounty* (1962), a Tahitian native girl called Maimiti (actress Taritatumi Teriipaia) falls in love with a British Naval officer, Fletcher Christian (Marlon Brando). That Maimiti is played by a real-life Polynesian woman is a significant change in direction for Hollywood. Luis Reyes states, 'The producers felt from the start that a pure Polynesian should be selected to portray Maimiti' (Reyes and Rampell 214). In countless previous movies, native girls that have sexual or romantic relationships with Western men are played by non-native substitutes. Sometimes these actresses are obviously Caucasian, such as Dorothy Lamour in *Aloma of the South Seas* (1941), and sometimes they have the *hapa-haole* (part Caucasian, part Hawaiian) look and are played by Central or South American actresses such as Raquel Torres in *White Shadows in the South Seas* and Rita Moreno in *Pagan Love Song* (1950). [Fig. 4.5] It is perhaps because of the changing racial climate of the United States in the late 1950s and early 1960s that *Mutiny on the Bounty*'s promoters made such efforts to cast a genuine, dark-skinned native to play the role of an indigenous person.

That *Enchanted Island* and *Mutiny on the Bounty* are set in the historical past is perhaps a sign that Hollywood was still, however, treading carefully in the area of inter-racial romance. These movies did not cause race riots, or upset the social order, a fact that seems to have emboldened filmmakers. Most movies from this point on feature contemporary Hawai'i, instead of historical Hawai'i, and persist with the theme of inter-racial relationships. For example, *Gidget Goes Hawaiian* is a contemporary movie and an advertisement for Hawai'i's tourist

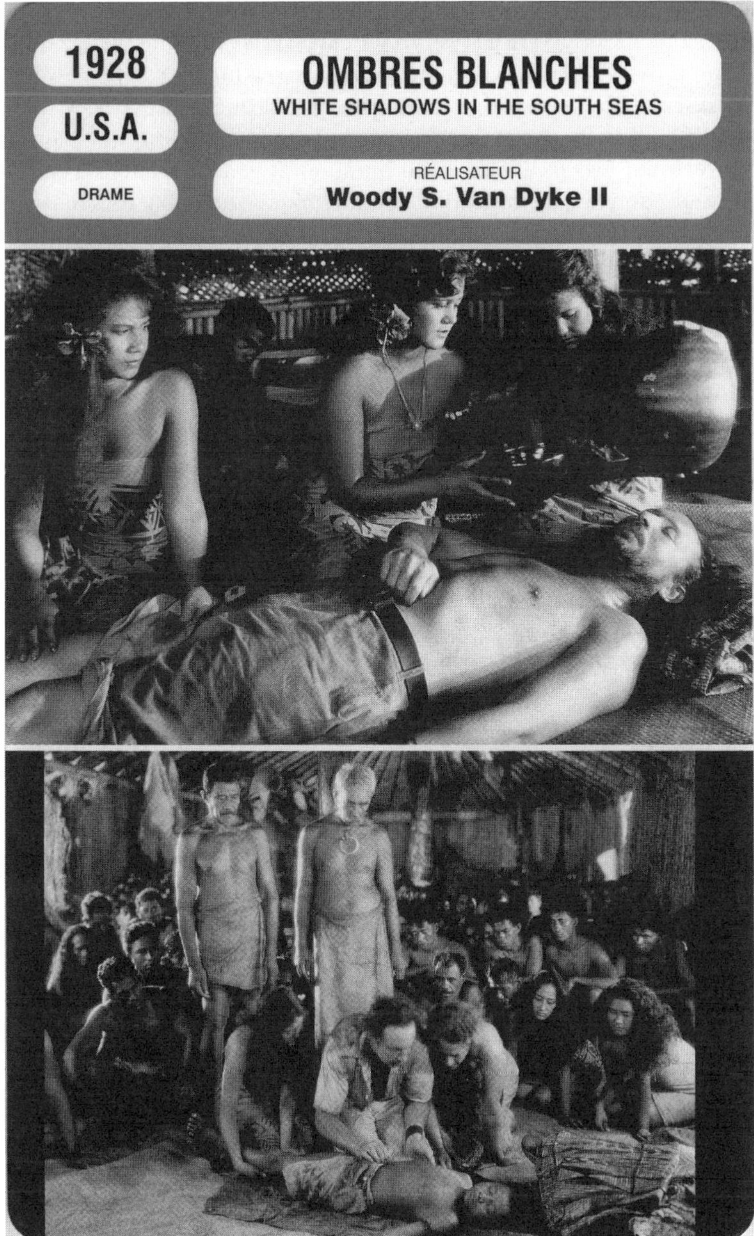


*Figure 4.5* *White Shadows in the South Seas* (1928). Author's personal collection.

industry in 1961. While the movie is primarily about the romantic antics of a group of Caucasian American tourists, in one scene Gidget (Deborah Valley) surfs with a muscular, dark-skinned Native Hawaiian man. There is a sexual edge to their frolics: at one point Gidget kneels on all fours at the front of a surfboard as the Hawaiian puts his head between her legs to lift her onto his shoulders. This scene is a carbon copy of the real-life frolics of some female Caucasian tourists with native beach boys in the 1930s. One Waikiki beachboy recalled a conversation with an American tourist in which she said, 'When I was nineteen, you took me in tandem. Can you imagine what it was like for me, going to a Catholic school on the mainland, to have a man take me surfing? To sit on top of me, on the back of my legs. The thrill I had. Skin to skin' (Desmond 126). That night, Gidget's boyfriend Moondoggie (James Darren) sings a song that seems to be an ode to inter-racial romance:

> You hear the native boys all sighing, down on Mauna Loa Bay
> Cause when the Gidget goes Hawaiian, she goes Hawaiian all the way.
> Now there's a rumor on the island, she flirts with every passer-by,
> Cause when the Gidget goes Hawaiian, she catches each Hawaiians eye.

A trio of Elvis Presley movies — *Blue Hawaii, Girls, Girls, Girls!* (1962), and *Paradise Hawaiian Style* (1966) — is also set in contemporary Hawai'i. *Blue Hawaii* features Presley as *haole* Chad Gates. Like the character White Almond Flower in *The Idol Dancer* who had 'the blood of vivacious France, inscrutable Java and languorous Samoa' running through her veins, Presley's girlfriend Maile Duvall (Joan Blackman) is half-Hawaiian and half-French. However, when she states, 'My French blood tells me to argue with you and my Hawaiian blood tells me not to. They're really battling it out inside me,' she is reversing the stereotype of early movies in the genre. For example, in *The Idol Dancer* it is White Almond Flower's French blood that makes her 'civilized' and keeps her base 'native' desires under control. In *Blue Hawaii*, however, Duvall's French side is problematic, while her Hawaiian blood supposedly gives her the welcoming, friendly characteristics that make her a personification of a contemporary, tourist-friendly Hawai'i.

According to Floyd Matson, *Blue Hawaii* 'trotted out nearly every confused stereotype of "island" life and culture that had accumulated through the career of the South Sea syndrome' (40). However, the movie's racial themes are worthy of note: the inter-racial romance in

*Blue Hawaii* was an early 'first step' for Hollywood in the 1960s, that would lead eventually to the first inter-racial kiss between a European-American and an African-American on American television, between Captain James Kirk (William Shatner) and Uhura (Nichelle Nichols) in a 1968 episode of *Star Trek* entitled 'Plato's Stepchildren.'

*Midway* is an account of the 1942 battle that turned the tide of the war in the Pacific in America's favor. The movie mixes actual war footage with staged battles, and also 'borrows' scenes from another war movie entitled *Tora! Tora! Tora! Midway* is male-dominated and action-driven. [Fig. 4.6] Some of the most well-known male actors of the 'Greatest Generation' star, including Charlton Heston, Henry Fonda, Glenn Ford, James Coburn and Robert Mitchum. To balance this over-abundance of testosterone, a subplot has Heston's son Ensign Tom Garth (Edward Albert) engaged to a Japanese-American girl called Haruko Sakura (Christina Kokubo). To add to the melodrama, Kokubo is a suspected spy and her parents are soon to be shipped to an internment camp on the United States mainland. Heston wrestles with his conscience about whether to help his possible future daughter-in-law. Eventually he decides to call in favors with military intelligence and she is released.

*Figure 4.6* *Midway* (1976). Author's personal collection.

Although *Variety* calls this a 'phony subplot,' this is more than a simple plot diversion. The context of this movie, made 25 years after the Pearl Harbor attack, was both ongoing Cold War animosities and a triumphant reminder of the values of America in the post-Vietnam War era. Like its predecessor *Tora! Tora! Tora!* (1970), *Midway* allots significant portions of the movie to show the Japanese side of the battle. Neither do these movies feature racially demeaning stereotypes of the Japanese, as had many previous Pacific war movies. This is laudable, of course. However, both of these movies focus only on battle, and neglect to provide any social, political or historical context. There is no discussion in either movie of, for example, the prelude to war or of the subsequent American response that ended at Hiroshima and Nagasaki. In fact, *Midway* reminds its audience that the atomic bombings were justified and that Hiroshima was a legitimate military target. On three separate occasions, for instance, the film connects the Japanese military to Hiroshima by use of subtitles. Not only is it where Admiral Yamamoto resides, the movie narrates, the Japanese Navy also leaves from Hiroshima Bay to attack Midway Island.

By focusing only on displays of military hardware, battle and heroism, these movies tell a depoliticized, deracialized version of the war. For example, when a Japanese Admiral empathizes with a destroyed squadron of American planes and their 'fourteen brave crews' who died like 'our Samurai,' the very real racial hatred felt by both sides in the conflict is erased from history. In fact, no one hates anyone in this movie, and war is portrayed as a passionless exercise conducted by masculine men just 'doing their jobs.' This movie is, therefore, very much a product of its time. In the post-World War Two years Japan was an ally of the United States: cinematic reminders of Japanese military barbarity would have been an unwelcome distraction from the Manichean Cold War narratives of good/bad, communist/democratic, red/red, white and blue that the US government encouraged in the cinema and media. In these films it was now acceptable to show the Japanese military as professional and brave. David Desser notes:

> It was not until after the war that the United States could undertake a reconsideration of its opponents. Thus we find, years later, films that attempt to separate the Wehrmacht officer from his Nazi superiors, with such figures as Erwin Rommel emerging as ambiguously tragic heroes. And although it is significant in terms of how racism found its way into the Vietnam era, and into Vietnam War films, that we find more portrayals, more personifications, of our European former antagonists than our Asian enemies, we can still point to such films as *Hell*

> *in the Pacific* (1968), *Tora! Tora! Tora!* (1970), *Midway* (1976), and even the more recent *Farewell to the King* (1989) as endowing some human subjectivity to the Asian objects of America's aggression and bloodlust (87).

The inter-racial love affair in *Midway* needs to be seen in the context of the Cold War zeitgeist. Americans and the Japanese were allied against the Soviet Union and *Midway* therefore whitewashes and sanitizes issues such as the internment of over a thousand Japanese-Americans in Hawai'i. Indeed, the internment camp in the movie looks more like a community center than a prison, and Kokubo's parents are docile and respectful towards Americans. Kokubo has the only raised voice of resistance and anger. She states, 'Damn it, I'm an American! What makes us different from Italian-Americans or German-Americans?' The most obvious answer is, of course, her race. However, Heston replies, 'Pearl Harbor, I suppose,' thus excusing Americans from blame for internment by making it seem a 'natural' reaction. *Midway*'s American audience had been preconditioned to accept such a sleight-of-hand by years of exposure to 'sneak attack' narratives about Pearl Harbor. In the post-Vietnam era, the theme of reconciliation — healing a divided nation — was prevalent in all aspects of American life.[4] The inter-racial relationship in *Midway* also serves as a healing act. While America waged war on an Asian people in Vietnam, *Midway* reminds its audience of the compassionate nature of Americans. For instance, Heston calls in favors and puts his career on the line to free Kokubo. The internment of Japanese is portrayed as, at worst, an understandable precaution, and compassionate Americans in authority like Heston allow the love affair between Kokubo and Albert to blossom, thus healing the wounds caused by war.

## Conclusion

Cinema, like all other forms of media in a modern society, acts on a number of different levels. It is an information provider, an art form, a vehicle for mindless escapism, but also a medium for the propagation of society's dominant values. Sociologist Jacques Ellul argues that Americans are particularly vulnerable such influences because of their reliance on, and constant exposure to, the mass media. He states:

> all modern mass propaganda profits from the structure of the mass, but exploits the individual's need for self-affirmation; and the two actions must be conducted jointly, simultaneously. Of course this

> operation is greatly facilitated by the existence of the modern mass media of communication, which has precisely this remarkable effect of reaching the whole crowd all at once, and yet reaching each one in that crowd (8).[5]

Cinema offers an ideal opportunity for the propagandist to ply his trade because, Ellul contends, the individual is alone in a crowd, vulnerable, with his defenses lowered. He states:

> The movie spectator also is alone; although elbow to elbow with his neighbors, he still is, because of the darkness and the hypnotic attraction of the screen, perfectly alone. This is the situation of the 'lonely crowd,' or of isolation in the mass, which is a natural product of present-day society and which is both used and deepened by the mass media. The most favorable moment to seize a man and influence him is when he is alone in the mass: it is at this point that propaganda can be most effective (8–9).

The United States also has such inequality of wealth that those without political or financial power, such as Native Hawaiians, are particularly vulnerable to unfair or demeaning cinematic portrayals. Hollywood is, of course, not solely responsible for creating stereotypes of Polynesians or of the Hawaiian Islands. Throughout the twentieth century, however, Hollywood movies played a role both in the transfer of power from natives to colonizers, and the maintenance of the new power relationships. For example, cinema helped paint the portrait of the Japanese as sneaky, foreign, inscrutable, and suspicious aliens, and this helped lay the groundwork for internment of the Japanese in Hawai'i in the aftermath of the attack on Pearl Harbor. Furthermore, the misleading cinematic representation of Hawai'i and its people (and of Polynesians in general) contribute to the current image of Hawai'i as a feminized, sexually-vulnerable paradise populated by exotic and compliant natives.

Assigning motives to a broad range of films released over a number of decades is a risky and imprecise venture. Noting that much of the Hawai'i and 'South Seas' genre fits neatly into Engelhardt's 'war story' does not imply a structured plan or design by filmmakers. Instead, these themes illustrate how Hawai'i has been imagined throughout the years and how it has been reshaped to fit the requirements of the American public. Sometimes, however, filmmakers misjudge those requirements. For example, it could be argued that the 'lesson' Hawai'i movies offered in interracial harmony in the late 1950s and 1960s went generally unheeded by

Americans. Movie images of a racial paradise may have caused many Caucasian Americans to visit Hawai'i to *escape* from racial tension on the mainland. Hawai'i became the personification of an idealized, Arcadian America, sufficiently different from the mainland so that Americans could leave behind their everyday worries, but also sufficiently 'American' as to be familiar and non-threatening. Desmond notes, for example, Hawai'i gave American tourists a 'sense of escape from domestic U.S. tensions [and] a feeling of still being in the United States (English predominates, no passport required for U.S. citizens, U.S. currency, U.S. brand names in hotels and products, etc.), and Hawai'i provides a truly safe exoticism for white mainlanders. This experience reinforces their sense of still being the "core" of the American nation' (Desmond 140).

Cinematic depictions of Hawai'i, in war and peace, are less concerned with accuracy than they are with portraying Hawai'i according to the needs of those on the US mainland. According to these representations, until Western settlers arrived Hawai'i used to be a desolate frontier inhabited by savages. It was their Manifest Destiny to 'develop' a 'virgin land' that was underutilized by its primitive, godless inhabitants. Westerners brought to Hawai'i civilization, laws, technology, 'progress,' and Christianity. These settlers have written the story of Hawai'i in a way that justifies their actions as beneficial and natural. In the twentieth century, the newly arrived medium of cinema reinforced these narratives. In the immediate aftermath of World War Two, the idea of 'American Hawai'i' helped Americans cope with their guilt at the atomic bombings of Japan, and deflected attention away from the racist nature of the Pacific war. In the late 1950s and 1960s, Hawai'i acted as a paradigm for the mainland on inter-racial harmony. It is little wonder the thought of Native Hawaiian Sovereignty is presently an anathema to the United States. For it, Hawai'i is the gift that keeps on giving.

# 5
# Hawai'i's Press and the Vietnam War

In a properly functioning democracy, the news media should play an adversarial role to those in positions of power. It should act as a watchdog, defending the people against governmental abuse of power. An inquisitive press could hold those in positions of power accountable for their actions. Participatory democracy requires that citizens make informed choices about issues that affect them, and the media could play a role in ensuring citizens remain engaged in the democratic process. Roger Hilsman, a State Department official in the Kennedy administration, states, 'If we are to maintain a democratic society, people must be able to have a say in policy decisions. Obviously, they will have a say only if they know what is going on. And it is equally obvious that the press is the only vehicle by which ordinary people can find out what is going on' (126). The reality is somewhat different, of course, reducing such noble ambitions to wishful thinking. In fact, the news media rarely questions systems of power and is often beholden to wealthy and influential interests. In wartime, these influences become more blatant while, at the same time, the processes behind such media manipulation are shrouded in secrecy and masked by discourses of national security and operational military requirements. In peacetime, many of these influences remain, but are often harder to detect.

This concluding chapter examines press coverage of the Vietnam War, and of Hawai'i's reaction to that war. The dominant mainstream newspapers in that period were the two dailies, the *Honolulu Advertiser* and the *Honolulu Star-Bulletin*. However, a burgeoning underground press movement developed in Hawai'i in the 1960s and early 1970s, which, at its peak, consisted of around 15 publications (Chapin 269) including *Carrion Crow* (1967–68), *The Roach* (1968–69), *Gathering Place* (1971–72), *Hawaii Free People's Press* (1969–70), and *Liberated Barracks*

(1971–74). The prevailing memory of the Vietnam era in Hawai'i remains one of docility and compliance. For example, according to journalist Francine du Plessix Gray, Hawai'i was almost untouched by the same anti-war protests that occurred in the United States. She cites, as evidence of this position, a rally held to protest the firing of University of Hawai'i faculty member and anti-war protester Rev. Larry Jones, when only about 50 students attended. According to Gray, most of them were 'half asleep on the grass' (11). Newspaper historian Helen Geracimos Chapin has, however, reached a different conclusion: 'There is the general notion that resistance to the Vietnam War was exercised locally by a vocal but small minority. To the contrary, Hawai'i, which was a staging area for the war, generated a higher ratio of underground papers than the national average' (269). These papers offer a window into a mostly forgotten period of countercultural activism and, contrary to Gray's assertion, even a cursory survey of their content reveals evidence of an active and vociferous anti-war movement.

Press coverage of the US military in Hawai'i adds credence to Michael Parenti's observation that, in the American news media, 'the United States' global, military and economic empire is nowhere to be seen' (*Make-Believe* 55). Parenti believes the role of newspapers in society is to maintain 'the hegemony of the corporate class and the capitalist system' (*Inventing* 3), a role Hawai'i's newspapers have dutifully played by supporting and disseminating the virtues of American capitalism and strategic ambition in the Pacific. In the 1840s, for example, New Englander James Jackson Jarves ran the *Polynesian*, the first and perhaps most famous newspaper produced in Hawai'i in the nineteenth century. As Chapin has recorded, Jackson despised Native Hawaiians, and celebrated the supposed superiority of American culture:

> Hawaiians, Jarves believed, were inferior and unable to compete with whites, who were their racial superiors. Polynesian culture had little value. Hawaiian speech was 'rude and uncultivated, destitute of literature' and not worth preserving. Hawaiians had 'only a few misty traditions, oral records of the sensualities and contests of the barbarous chiefs, the rites of inhuman religion.' In a classic example of blaming the victim, Jarves declared the Hawaiians at fault for beginning to die off after Captain Cook's arrival (27).

Henry M. Whitney, the first owner of the *Pacific Commercial Advertiser* (as *The Honolulu Advertiser* was originally known) was a descendant of American Protestant missionaries. According to Chapin, Whitney had 'a total belief in American culture and values. Or, as he boasted in his reminiscences, the *Advertiser* "was independent in politics always, but an ardent advocate of annexation to the United States"' (54). It was with attitudes such as these, Chapin finds, that 'print ... has enabled imperialism to spread its power across continents and oceans. The imposition of print upon the Hawaiian Islands coincided with the rise of America as an imperialist Pacific power. American-style newspapers were a major contributor to this expansion' (15).

Nowadays such outward manifestations of racism are gone, but the dominant patriotic discourse is as strong as ever. Today, as Haunani-Kay Trask affirms, 'there are no critical news stations or radical magazines in Hawai'i' (*Native* 162).[1] In addition, press coverage of the US military is usually supportive, and reporters tend to follow a narrow script, which helps produce and sustain patriotic military values, while marginalizing anti-military voices. This does not occur by chance: the military organizes community liaison groups, consisting of business leaders such as bank officials, tourism chiefs, and newspaper employees or owners. Politicians and influential civilians are invited to various military functions, parades, briefings, and ceremonies, and are rewarded for their support with 'red-carpet tours' and 'free rides on PACOM equipment' (Albertini 14).[2] Local politicians, business leaders, and news media moguls have little to gain by antagonizing the military: indeed, pro-military interests often insist that Hawai'i's economy depends, in large part, on a continuing military presence (Ferguson and Turnbull 34–7). Instead of an inquisitive press, an acquiescent and supportive culture has developed, and this limits public debate about the efficacy of the US military presence in Hawai'i, and beyond.

Might this situation be different if Hawaii had a thriving alternative media, as was evident in the 1960s and early 1970s? Would a more open debate about the US military be possible if the *Advertiser* and *Star-Bulletin* did not operate under self-imposed reporting constraints, making criticism of the military almost an anathema? A comparative analysis of mainstream and underground newspaper coverage of the Vietnam War reveals significant differences in attitude, not only about such issues as the underlying causes of American intervention, selective service, desertion, anti-war protests, and the conduct of the war, but also about the role of the press in a free society. This chapter engages with a wider debate about the media's role in the Vietnam War, and its attitude towards the US military. It also unearths some of the largely forgotten activities of Hawai'i's anti-war movement. In so doing, it illustrates how the absence of self-imposed restrictions by underground newspapers led to a broader discussion of the war, and to a wider understanding of the systems of power in which the US military operates.

## The traditional media: 'Watchdog of the State' or 'Fifth Column'?

Two divergent viewpoints have emerged about American media coverage of the war. On one side are 'mostly conservative policy analysts, intellectuals, politicians, government officials, and journalists' (McMahon 173), who believe the news media was politically and ideologically opposed to the war. They argue American forces were victorious on the battlefield, but because of press hostility, lost the war of American public opinion. Perhaps the most influential advocate of this interpretation is journalist Robert Elegant, who claims the press was 'instinctively "agin [sic] the Government" — and, at least reflexively, for Saigon's enemies' ('How to Lose' 138). A more nuanced view comes from journalist Peter Braestrup, whose analysis of the 1968 Tet Offensive is often cited as evidence that the press painted a 'portrait of defeat' in Vietnam, which 'veered so widely from reality' ('An Extreme Case' 153).

The opposing argument comprises a range of views, from those who believe the press functioned adequately, in difficult circumstances, to those who believe the press acted to disseminate official propaganda about the war. At the moderate end of that spectrum are war correspondents that were present in Vietnam from the earliest days of American involvement, 'courageous and imaginative' reporters such as Homer Bigart, David Halberstam, Neil Sheehan, Malcolm Browne and Peter Arnett (Wyatt 217). Most critical are those such as Michael Parenti or Noam Chomsky, who regard the press as 'gatekeepers' for the interests of the political elite. For example, Parenti has said that the news is 'little more than uncritical transmission of official opinions to an unsuspecting public' (*Inventing* 51), and Chomsky has argued that press coverage of the war showed 'no serious deviation from state doctrine' (*Rethinking* 112).

Historian C. Dale Walton claims that the 'hostility of the press to US policy towards Vietnam was a phenomenon that began well before the entry of US troops into the war and gained momentum over time' (35–6). However, the press's attitude to the war, and to the military, cannot be as easily categorized as this. In fact, from the early 1950s, American news coverage of Indochina was guided by a set of assumptions which arose from the bipartisan Cold War consensus that the United States was the leader of the free world, and that the need to 'contain' communism and protect free enterprise should define American foreign policy (Hodgson 67–8). In a speech to the American Newspaper Publisher Association in April 1961, just a few days after the failed Bay of Pigs invasion, President John F. Kennedy reminded the press of their patriotic responsibility: 'In time of war, the government and the press have customarily joined in an effort, based largely on self-discipline, to prevent unauthorized disclosures to the enemy. In times of clear and present danger, the courts have held that even the privileged rights of the First Amendment must yield to the public's need for national security' (Wyatt 36).

The overarching assumption about South East Asia in general, and Indochina in particular, was that post-World War Two nationalist movements were a façade for international communism. Just as China had been 'lost' to communism in 1949, it was assumed that other countries in Southeast Asia would fall like dominoes unless the West provided political direction and economic and military aid for what *New York Times* columnist Robert Trumbell called the 'free world's fight to contain aggressive communism' ('Week in Review'). In this climate, the press often acted as a conduit for the government's official version of events, particularly in the realm of foreign policy, and especially during any deployment of US armed forces.

Early press coverage of the American intervention in Indochina rarely questioned those underlying assumptions, as historian Marilyn Young explains:

> The American press ... in effect served as a branch of the U.S. enterprise in South Vietnam, cheering Diem's successes and praising his efforts to defeat communism in his country. The critical news reports of Scripps-Howard correspondent Albert Colegrove, which led to Congressional hearings on Vietnam in the summer of 1959, focused almost entirely on the inefficient and wasteful use of American aid. Colegrove, like many members of Congress, called for a closer supervision of funds rather than a reexamination of policy ... Wisconsin Democratic Representative Clement Zablocki ... wondered aloud if the public shouldn't be informed of the way in which Colegrove's criticism had given aid to the Communists (61).

Young's analysis is astute: there were, certainly, reporters such as the *New York Times*' David Halberstam, and Peter Arnett of the *Associated Press*, who were critical of the war effort, and of the corruption and incompetency of the Diem regime (Olson and Roberts 80–1). However, as journalist Phillip Knightley points out, such dissent was limited to the conduct of the war, not its underlying assumptions:

> the impression of those early years of Vietnam is of courageous and skilled correspondents fighting a long and determined action for the right to report the war as they saw fit. There is only one flaw in this: the correspondents were not questioning the American intervention itself, only its effectiveness. Most correspondents, despite what Washington thought about them, were just as interested in seeing the United States win the war as was the Pentagon ('Vietnam' 114).

For every dissenting journalist such as Arnett or Halberstam, there were others less critical of American efforts. Joseph Alsop, a leading syndicated columnist, and a key supporter of the Kennedy administration, spoke of 'intelligent, united, and energetic top-level leadership' and 'impressive combat-ready American officers,' which led to a 'marked improvement in the atmosphere and outlook of South Viet Nam,' and 'solid progress' in the military effort to 'repulse the communist attack' ('Firmness Called For'). Alsop called dissenting Saigon correspondents 'young crusaders,' and chided them for focusing only on negative aspects of the war.[3] Margaret Higgins of the *New York Herald Tribune*, accused her colleagues of misrepresenting the situation, and of being misled by media-savvy Buddhists opposed to Diem's government (Wyatt 120). She complained: 'Reporters here would like to see us lose the war to prove they're right' ('Foreign Correspondents').

To an extent, these opposing views can be explained by the reporters' geographic locality, which dictated what sources were available. By March 1968, 649 accredited journalists were in Vietnam. However, only 75–80 regularly accompanied US troops into combat (Sidle 110). Most of the rest lived in Saigon, at hotels such as the Caravelle and Continental, from where they filed their stories in relative safety and comfort. Washington-based journalists were even further from the action. Consequently, they tended to rely on official sources, which often contradicted the information coming from journalists based in Vietnam (Wyatt 122). George Reedy, President Lyndon Johnson's press secretary from 1964–65, argues that while some individual journalists learned quickly how the war was proceeding, 'the network of wire services, editors, and publicists who are responsible for the total product that reaches the readers — did not really catch up with the correspondents in the field' (121). Of course, those closest to combat are not necessarily best placed to report on wider aspects of the war. Pulitzer Prize-winning journalist William Tuohy argues, for example, that reporters 'in from the field' often took a more negative view of the US conduct of the war than was, perhaps, necessary (128). However, reporters closest to the troops were better placed to see the contradictions between the optimistic briefings of top-level government and military officials, and the often less promising facts on the ground. In the early stages of the war, these contradictions led to conflict between journalists and editors, and the press and the government. These inconsistencies also fuelled the myth that would later develop, that an unpatriotic press caused or contributed to the communist victory in Vietnam.

The popular perception of the journalist in Vietnam is probably that of a young, daring, and insubordinate reporter, willing to bend the rules and fight the establishment to get 'the truth.' The epitome of this image is, perhaps, photojournalist Sean Flynn, son of actor Errol Flynn, who was known for his risk-taking approach to life. Flynn, and fellow photojournalist Dana Stone, disappeared in Cambodia in 1971, and are both presumed dead. Such was Flynn's charisma that rock band The Clash named a song after him on their 1982 album, *Combat Rock*. He was also a character in Michael Herr's stylized, non-fiction account of his experiences in Vietnam, *Dispatches*. Alternatively, for those who blame the press for America's defeat in Vietnam, photographer Tim Page might personify their beliefs. Described by Michael Herr as the most 'bent, beaten [and] scarred' of the 'young, apolitically radical, wigged-out crazies running around Vietnam' (235–7), Page was the inspiration for the manic, drug-crazed photojournalist played by Dennis Hopper in Francis Ford Coppola's *Apocalypse Now* (1979). However, the most accurate image is probably George Beckworth (actor David Janssen), a character in John Wayne's anti-communist film, *The Green Berets* (1968). Beckworth is a jaded cynic, with vague pacifist leanings, and deeply distrustful of official accounts of the progress of the war. However, when the time comes for him to decide where his loyalties lie, Beckworth identifies more with the US military than with the enemy, and he files a patriotic story in support of the war effort.

A number of factors influenced the flow and content of news to the American public. Foremost were the reporters' own personal prejudices and opinions: reporters often claimed to present impartial news — just the 'facts,' devoid of any filtering or mediating process. This was particularly apparent in 'spot news' (breaking news, reported immediately), which focused on 'who, what, when, where, how many' (Wyatt 60). However, such impartiality is an illusion. In choosing what to include and omit, how they frame the information, and what images they use to illustrate the story, every journalist presents a point of view of some sort, so even the most seemingly impartial news report is not necessarily 'what was really happening' (Lederer 159), only a version of what happened.

More tangibly, correspondents operated under conditions of military censorship, which affected the scope and content of their reports. Restrictions were in place mainly for operational reasons. For example, the press was forbidden from discussing forthcoming US attacks, or providing details of troop movements. The military also placed restrictions on coverage of American casualties or damage inflicted by the enemy. In short, the press was constrained from providing information that could aid the enemy's conduct of the war. Such news could only be reported after the details had first been released by the Military Assistance Command, Vietnam (MACV) (Wyatt 159–60). It is significant that only one reporter, Jack Foisie of the *Los Angeles Times*, had his press credentials suspended for 30 days in 1966 for breaking a news embargo on a Marine landing in Quang Ngai province ('Ground Action'). This suggests the press was generally compliant with military censorship regulations, and challenges the argument that a hostile press actively undermined the military effort.

Contrary to the misleading image of the lone, rogue reporter, popularized in *Apocalypse Now*, most reporters in Vietnam were not independent agents. Instead, they worked for large news agencies such as Reuters, the Associated Press (AP) or United Press International (UPI), or major news outlets such as the *New York Times* or *Washington Post*. As such, they did not always have the freedom to follow their own leads, but instead had stories assigned to them by their employers. Many inexperienced journalist were instructed by editors to cover aspects of the war that were relatively uncontroversial, for example, stories about civilian healthcare or agricultural aid that showed the American effort in Indochina as beneficial and disinterested. Journalists who chose not to follow those instructions risked having their press credentials removed, which could lead to expulsion from Vietnam. Some were put in an untenable situation: seasoned *New York Times* correspondent Gloria Emerson was told by her managing editor, 'You've done some good writing on what is wrong with the war, now tell us what is working' (Emerson xx). Emerson, however, refused to change her ways, and, disillusioned, left the paper in 1972 (Applegate 83).

As most journalists relied on military transportation to and from locations distant from Saigon, the military could exert influence by denying access to combat zones, thus ensuring that journalists had to rely on official sources of information. For example, in February 1962, the Kennedy administration issued 'Cable 1006,' an instruction to the military to deny transport to unsympathetic reporters (Knightley, 'Vietnam' 110). The Army of the Republic of Vietnam (ARVN) was even more unsympathetic to the needs of the press: later that year, for example, Colonel Huynh Van Cao, commander of the Seventh Division operating in the Mekong Delta, issued a total ban on reporters in his area of operations (Wyatt 102). In an attempt to direct the flow of news, the US military and the ARVN held press conferences which soon became known as the 'five o'clock follies.' Journalists relying only on those sources received only the officially-sanctioned military perspective — stories David Halberstam claims, had 'the most constant use of misinformation and lack of verification' ('Role of Journalists' 113). Sometimes the military applied a more personal approach: for example, Admiral Harry D. Felt cornered AP reporter Malcolm Browne, and asked him 'Why don't you get on the team?' (Schlesinger 984). On occasion, US Military Intelligence was able to stop a sensitive story from being published: for instance, when UPI correspondent Kate Webb discovered a number of Chinese documents on the battlefield, which perhaps indicated collusion between Chinese and Vietnamese communist forces, Military Intelligence agents warned her that publicizing such information might widen the war. Webb chose not to send the story to UPI ('Highpockets' 85).

Successive South Vietnamese regimes also tried to control the flow of information to journalists. President Diem, in particular, had little sympathy for reporters critical of his policies. For example, after Francois Sully declared in her *Newsweek* article 'Vietnam: the Unpleasant Truth,' that the war was 'a losing proposition,' Diem issued an expulsion order against her, and she was forced to leave Vietnam a short time later (Knightley, 'Vietnam' 111). *The Village Voice*'s Judith Coburn suffered the same fate, refused an extension of her visa, in all likelihood because of her candid reporting of the war (Emerson xix). Sometimes interference with the press was more physical: during the Buddhist uprising in 1963, plainclothes police attacked and injured reporters Grant Wolfkill and John Sharkey of NBC, and David Halberstam ('Foreign Correspondents').

The US diplomatic mission in South Vietnam also sought to exert pressure on journalists. When Malcolm Browne's Pulitzer Prize-winning images of the self-immolation of a Buddhist monk were widely published, American diplomats cooperated with Diem's secret police to freeze official sources, tap the phones and closely monitor the activities of the press corps in Saigon (Knightley, 'Vietnam' 112–13). Gloria Emerson, who wrote many moving stories about the harsh effects of the war on the South

Vietnamese, claims that an American Embassy official warned her about the content of her reports (Applegate 82–3; Emerson xx). While American officials harassed or otherwise tried to cut off the flow of information to uncooperative journalists, other reporters who were more supportive of the Washington line — *Time-Life*'s Howard Sochurek, for instance, and Joseph Alsop — received every assistance, including jumping the queue for military helicopter rides. This caused considerable anger among Vietnam-based reporters: *New York Times* correspondent Homer Bigart threatened to quit unless his newspaper acted to secure a more even-handed approach (Wyatt 77, 97), while David Halberstam — having accompanied troops on more than 30 missions by that point — made caustic comments about Alsop's 'brief visit to Vietnam' ('Getting the Story' 33).

Back in the United States, newspaper editors often had the final say over what was printed and often, editorial restrictions set boundaries on what reporters could discuss. For example, Peter Arnett tells of an 'understanding' whereby he was unable to report the military skills of the NLF. Nor could he mention that the conflict in Vietnam had many attributes of a civil war, since that would undermine the underlying reason for American intervention (249). Arnett once received an instruction from AP foreign editor Ben Bassett, asking him to 'cover anything that might be considered positive or optimistic from the US point of view' (Arnett 137). Sometimes he experienced more direct editorial control: in 1970, in the wake of the deaths of four student protesters at Kent State University, Bassett refused to print an Arnett report about US forces looting the Cambodian town of Snoul. Bassett's reasoning was:

> We are in the midst of a highly charged situation in the United States regarding Southeast Asia and must guard our copy to see that it is down the middle and subdues emotion. Specifically today we took looting and similar references out of Arnett copy because we don't think it's especially news that such things take place in war and in present context this can be inflammatory (Arnett 267).

No US newspaper would publish Martha Gellhorn's harrowing accounts of Vietnamese civilian casualties and the dreadful conditions of orphanages and hospitals. Gellhorn was told, repeatedly, her stories were too disturbing for American readers. Although the *St. Louis Post Dispatch* eventually published two of her milder stories, the rest were published outside the US, in the UK's *Guardian* newspaper. Afterwards, the South Vietnamese refused Gellhorn's requests for a visa to return to Vietnam, and the stories seem to have ended her career as a war correspondent (Knightley, 'Vietnam' 125). In a similar vein, British journalist Nicholas Tomalin found it difficult to get his blunt account of 'gun-toting' General James F. Hollingsworth published in the US. In 'The General Goes Zapping Charlie Cong,' which was first published in the London *Times*, Tomalin's verbatim quotation of the general introduced readers to the harsh and unmediated language of war. For instance, when Tomalin asked Hollingsworth if he was worried about civilian casualties, the general replied: 'Aw, come, son, you think there's folks just sniffing flowers in tropical vegetation like that? Anyone left down there, he's Charlie Cong all right.' However, it was also, surely, Tomalin's descriptions of the haphazard nature of war — a US bulldozer accidentally falling off a bridge; Army trucks carelessly knocking the roof off a Buddhist pagoda — or the comparison Tomalin invites between the general's impatient demands for his troops to 'zap' or 'get to killin' VCs,' with their inability to find their elusive enemy, that deterred US newspaper editors from printing the story.

Various US administrations sought to exert control by contacting newspaper editors about unflattering stories that had run, or were due to run, or by complaining about uncooperative reporters. For example, after Sully's expulsion, the Kennedy administration pressured *Newsweek* into running a flattering story about Diem's sister-in-law Madame Nhu, and then *Time* into rewriting a story by reporters Charles Mohr and Merton Perry that was initially critical of the war effort. Kennedy persuaded *Time* to quash another story by Mohr and Perry about the conflict between the Saigon press corps and the US diplomatic mission. Instead of printing this story, *Time*'s managing editor, Otto Fuerbringer, wrote a new article highly critical of his own reporters, which caused Mohr and Perry to resign in disgust (Knightley, 'Vietnam' 113–14). Kennedy also applied personal pressure on *New York Times* publisher Arthur Sulzberger to reassign Pulitzer Prize winner, David Halberstam. Kennedy asked Sulzberger, 'You don't think he's too close to the story?' When Sulzberger said no, Kennedy asked for Halberstam's reassignment, which also met with a negative response. Unaccustomed to such defiance, Kennedy administration officials openly questioned Halberstam's patriotism, and sought ways to discredit the reporter and his colleagues (Giglio 246).[4]

Newspaper hierarchies closely resemble the military command structure, as sociologist Herbert Gans notes: 'News organizations are not democratic; in fact, they are described as militaristic by some journalists' (85). According to Gans, journalists are analogous to foot soldiers, editors are equivalent to the officer class, and the newspaper owners are the 'top brass.' Like the military, newspapers are primarily run by men. It is unsurprising, therefore, that two organizations that resemble each other would empathize in areas such as command structure, 'following orders,' and the need for secrecy. In addition, the mainstream press's supportive attitude to the war effort, at least in its early years, was due to a patriotic belief in the essential goodness of American values. It was beyond the comprehension of those journalists who had not experienced war first-hand that US soldiers could indulge in the kind of barbaric behavior Americans had always associated with the enemy (or indeed that their government would lie to them about the progress of the war). When the horrific reality of war was revealed, usually through television images or by photojournalists, it proved to be such a threat to the war effort that journalists were subject to coercion. For example, when CBS broadcast Morley Safer's report of a US Marine attack on the undefended Vietnamese village of Cam Ne in 1965, Americans were shocked by images of their troops participating in the type of immoral actions that had previously only been associated with the enemy. President Johnson personally phoned the President of CBS to complain, and then ordered FBI and CIA investigations against Safer (Engelhardt 187–93).

It is, therefore, not the case that individual reporters were entirely to blame for any bias in the press: in fact, there are many examples of individual reporters risking their lives (and sometimes losing them) to seek out stories that the Pentagon did not approve of. However, due to the various 'filters'[5] involved in getting a story published, the press as an institution proved to be conservative and generally provided a limited, very patriotic point of view. During the Vietnam War, these restrictions helped keep the full reality of the conflict hidden from the American public — at least until the Tet Offensive, when the realities of modern warfare could no longer be concealed from view.

## Hawai'i's underground press: Possibilities and limitations

As the credibility gap grew between what Americans read in press reports and what they learned from soldiers returning from the war, many turned to alternative media sources for information. Such was the popularity of underground newspapers like the *Los Angeles Free Press* and New York's *East Village Other* that by the end of the decade almost every sizable city and college town had an underground publication of some sort. For example, in 1970, Robert J. Glessing composed a list of 457 underground newspapers, with a readership of almost five million (178). These papers appealed mostly, but not exclusively, to a younger audience, and their subject matter reflected those issues of most concern to that audience, for instance, the civil rights of African-Americans, women's and gay rights, anger about the Vietnam War and the military draft, freedom of expression, growing awareness and concern about the power of American capitalism, and, of course, sex, drugs and rock-n-roll. Underground papers looked and felt different from their mainstream counterparts: a typical issue might feature a story about an atrocity in Vietnam, a poem about an ongoing social concern, topical song lyrics, a first-person description of a drugs 'trip,' frank advertisements by individuals or couples seeking sexual partners, a satirical cartoon depicting a politician or political issue of the day, and an editorial column which both championed and publicized forthcoming counter-cultural events in the local community. Many of these items featured slang and profanity, which set a tone distinguishing them from mainstream newspapers. They also experimented with new and innovative graphic and text layouts, such as eye-catching fonts, and dynamic art inspired by the alternative art and culture of the period.

In contrast to the establishment press, the alternative or underground media had an explicitly adversarial attitude towards those in positions of power, and it imposed few limits on what could or could not be reported. Its only constraints appeared to be lack of money and fear of libel suits. As large business interests did not fund them, underground papers had to use the cheapest materials and most basic methods. Glessing describes a typical routine: 'After all his copy is ready for the camera, the fledgling underground publisher simply rubber cements, or waxes, his copy blocks and art work to layout sheets and he is ready to go to the printer' (43). The technology behind *Carrion Crow* was, for example, 'a typewriter, a glue pot ... and an old press' (Chapin 272).

*Figure 5.1* *Carrion Crow* (1967–68). Hawai'i Pacific Collection, University of Hawai'i at Mānoa.

[Fig. 5.1] The resulting paper looked amateurish and informal, two factors that potential readers, disillusioned by mainstream American newspaper coverage, undoubtedly found attractive.

The editors of *Carrion Crow* (1967–68), Hawai'i's first underground newspaper of the 1960s, declared, 'The *Carrion Crow* will be totally irresponsible, dealing with whatever we feel like and published whenever we get around to it' ('Statement'). Thirteen issues of *The Roach* were produced from May to December 1968. Edited by John Olsen, a 25-year-old philosophy graduate from Maine, and with a staff of about a dozen

*Figure 5.2* *Hawaii Free Press* (1969–70). Hawai'i Pacific Collection, University of Hawai'i at Mānoa.

(Chapin 273–4), it described itself as 'one of the 100 or so underground presses which have grown up recently in the United States to print news which the Establishment Press sees fit to ignore or minimize' (Jun 4, 1968: 1). Olsen was also involved with *Hawaii Free Press* (1969–70), whose declared aim was to 'liberat[e] our media' and to create 'a new world, a new people' (Editorial, Jun 1969). [Fig. 5.2] *Gathering Place* (1971–72) described itself as 'an underground newspaper to the extent that we will use traditional underground sources — Liberation News Service, other underground papers — and in that we aren't controlled by any corporation.' Its favorite subjects were, 'ecology, dope, peace, liberation, food, music, and meaningful ways to live' ('What Gathering Place is'). *Liberated Barracks* (1971–74) was a 'GI Paper,' written and produced by disaffected American servicemen and local civilians. Its aim was to fill a void, 'the lack of a place where G.I.'s could get together and collectively work on solutions to problems that are a daily part of military life' ('Liberated Barracks Grew').

Collectively, these papers claimed to offer an alternative view to the mainstream media on a wide range of social, political and economic issues. They openly challenged the authority of traditional journalism, and its claims to accuracy and neutrality. For example, they embraced the 'New Journalism' of Tom Wolfe, or attempted to emulate the 'Gonzo' style of Hunter S. Thompson. Indeed, Todd Gitlin believes that New Journalism began in the underground, 'with first-person accounts of news events — demonstrations, press conferences, street scenes; writers began to treat their own notions and responses as part of the story, in revolt against the spurious objectivity of the mainstream' (22–3). In one sense, it could be argued that the alternative press was not journalism at all. Traditionally, journalists were expected simply to convey information, not to offer views or solutions: those would appear only in the opinion columns, or in the editorial section. However, New Journalism challenged the idea that mainstream journalists were impartial or neutral. Instead, the movement recognized that, consciously or unconsciously, journalists would always filter what they see, and their reporting would reflect that. New Journalism embraced this filtering process more honestly, by insisting that journalists' views were an essential part of the story.

New Journalism was based, in part, on author William Faulkner's idea that great fiction is truer than journalism could ever hope to be. Truth is, of course, subjective, and New Journalism is therefore no more truthful or untruthful than the medium it challenged. However, New Journalism was a more candid style of reporting in that it recognized and even flaunted its subjectivity, letting its readers decide on the wisdom or accuracy of its news and opinion. Finally, New Journalism was a form of rebellion against a media system that many thought had failed them, as Glessing notes:

> Since most underground editors assume the traditional media incapable of telling the truth about anything important, they reason, 'What's the point of objectivity?' It is perhaps its total distrust of American institutions that frees the underground press to attack anything and everything related to the American establishment (6).

Consequently, underground papers held great appeal for a new, younger audience, alienated by the newspapers their parents read, and attracted to the rebellious and exciting journalism of the alternative press. Such reporting was, according to author and *Rolling Stone* journalist Hunter Thompson, 'close to the bone ... and to hell with the consequences' (18). But what were those consequences? Did the underground papers really offer a broader perspective than professional journalists and newspapers? Is there merit to their claims of self-censorship by the mainstream press? The following section offers a comparison between underground and mainstream reporting of the war, of protest movements, draft resistance, and militarism in Hawai'i, and proffers some answers to these questions.

## Perceptions of war

An article in *Hawaii Free People's Press* illustrates the chasm in thinking between pro-war supporters and anti-war activists. 'Making the Military Mind' tells of a meeting at Tripler Army Hospital between army representatives and what the paper calls, in the colorful language of the movement, 'student worker slaves of the military machine.' By 1969, the US military realized not only was it fighting the Vietnamese, but also a war for the 'hearts and minds' of its own soldiers. The military therefore began a series of meetings that ostensibly were to address soldiers' concerns, but which were, according to the *Hawaii Free People's Press*, a calculated plan to have 'a series of chaplains, lawyers, and doctors speaking "man to man," hoping to steer the troops to programmed conclusions, parroting Establishment dogma.' The first speaker was a Company Commander who was unaware of his alienation from a section of his troops. When he enquired what his men wanted to talk about, the first response from a 'black militant' was to query why soldiers should have to salute officers and stand to attention. The soldier compared such military trappings to 'prostrating oneself before the emperor.'

When the Company Commander tried to reassure these men about racial issues, asking the black soldiers in attendance if they agreed that the condition of the 'Negro' in American had improved, he was, according to *Hawaii Free People's Press*, met first with silence before one apathetic soldier replied, 'Naw, nothing much has really been changed.' One soldier asked the Company Commander what his feelings were about war. His reply, which including such military-speak as 'specific objectives,' 'progressive execution,' and 'consummating in a tangible victory, fulfilling the specific objectives,' highlighted the gap not only between the soldiers and their officers, but also between the casual, 'hip' language of the alternative newspaper and the cold, machine-like language that was (and is) the military's preferred mode of communication. James Dawes, a literary theorist, claims that such terminology 'replaces the aversive incomprehensibility of war's inhuman scale with a finite collection of clean, containable units of information' that he calls 'disposable ... information' (32). Such disengaged language was a world away from the youth generation that had turned on, tuned in, and dropped out.[6]

In contrast, Hawai'i's mainstream newspapers shied away from criticizing the military or the underlying assumptions behind the war. For example, in June 1967, the *Honolulu Advertiser* provided space for Admiral US Grant Sharp, Commander in Chief of the US Pacific Command, to advocate large-scale bombing of Hanoi and other North Vietnamese targets (Marquis C15). Sharp warned *Advertiser* readers, 'If America stops bombing North Vietnam it will lead to more Americans being killed' ('Halt'). Sharp told his Chamber of Commerce audience, 'There is no cause for gloom or pessimism. We are winning a war essential to the security of the free world.' In response, the president of the Hawai'i Chamber of Commerce assured the Admiral that the war was doing great things for the local economy: 'military expenditures here had made marked advances, the garment industry should have its finest year, the pineapple industry [is] holding its own [and] [t]ourism has set a record pace.'

Soon after, Denis Warner, the *Advertiser*'s Southeast Asia Correspondent, acted as a conduit for the US military command, telling readers that US forces had 'broken the initial Viet Cong summer offensive in and around the demilitarized zone' ('Hanoi Troops'). Warner was no stooge: the Australian had been a war correspondent in World War Two, and he sometimes published news and opinions that annoyed those in authority. Yet just as often, Warner repeated the official military or political view of events.[7] This often occurred when journalists had no independent way of verifying what was happening on the ground. Editors required stories to fill pages, and the military provided many news stories suitable for this purpose, albeit heavily slanted towards a favorable American point of view. It was, therefore, perhaps as much for commercial reasons as ideological that 'standard practice' throughout the war was for journalists 'to report Washington pronouncements as fact, even in the extreme case when official statements were known to be false' (Herman and Chomsky 176–7).[8]

While reporters in underground papers spoke of an 'American invasion' of Vietnam (Hill, Hugo), perhaps to counteract the mainstream press's explanation that American troops were in Vietnam to stop a North Vietnamese 'invasion,' mainstream reporters failed to report that the National Liberation Front (NLF) was comprised almost entirely of South Vietnamese nationals. Instead, Warner reported that the NLF was foreign-controlled ('foreign' meaning North Vietnamese). Ignoring the historical and cultural reality, Warner accepted the illusion that Vietnam was comprised of two separate and sovereign countries. Only by framing the story in this way could the US intervention in Vietnam be viewed as anything other than a military invasion. Warner described North Vietnam as an aggressor, which 'intends to continue its conventional war on a much bigger scale.' As Herman and Chomsky have noted, 'from the point of view of the media ... there is no such event in history as the US attack against South Vietnam and the rest of Indochina. One would be hard put to find even a single reference within the mainstream to any such event, or any recognition that history could possibly be viewed from this perspective' (184).

*Crow* reporters were aware that use of language and labels acted as signposts for readers and framed the terms of the debate. For example, they used the term 'National Liberation Front,' instead of 'Viet Cong,' which was the name preferred by every US administration. The term 'Viet Cong' was first used by South Vietnamese President Diem in the 1950s and was 'the Vietnamese equivalent of "Commie"' (Young 63). Many American journalists followed Diem's lead in using loaded terminology to describe the enemy, which leads Herman and Chomsky to conclude: '[t]he enemy of the US government was the enemy of the press ... they were the "Viet Cong," a derogatory term of US-Saigon propaganda, not the National Liberation Front, a phrase "never used without quotation marks" by American reporters' (177). The effect of this was to shape the news into a Manichean battle of 'good versus evil,' for which the terms 'communism' and 'democracy' served a heuristic function. In choosing the language of the debate, newspapers directed public opinion along narrow, patriotic lines. For example, in dehumanizing the Vietnamese as communist drones or 'Reds,' newspapers excused some of the more inhumane aspects of American policy. It is after all, easier to kill a thing than a person, as James Dawes explains:

> if we call the [opposition] 'enemy,' 'criminal,' or 'animal,' we enable ourselves to feel about and act toward them in a certain way; if we instead call them 'combatant,' 'prisoner of war' or 'civilian' (agent-neutral terms that could easily be used to describe us or our own families), we are forced by the pressure of our own lexicon to think about and act toward them in a drastically different fashion (211).

## Draft resistance and desertion

Support for conscientious objectors, and others who refused to fight in Vietnam (branded, dismissively, as 'draft dodgers' in the mainstream press) was a recurring theme of the underground press in both the United States and Hawai'i. The tone of these reports was usually 'peaceful non-compliance,' evocative of the tenor of the civil rights movement. For example, in *Carrion Crow,* Bill Jaworski explained that although he had refused to enlist in the US Army, he would not flee to Canada to avoid prosecution. Instead, he would allow the legal process to unfold, so that he could highlight the injustices of the system. Jaworski wrote: 'I choose [to] stay here and fight in the courts where the people will be informed of the reasons for objection through the news media' ('Plato's Column').

Underground journalists helped create a support network for those involved in draft resistance, including for those who chose not to follow Jaworski's example. In a section entitled 'Travel Tips From Abroad,' for example, *Roach* journalist Bill Boyd advised potential deserters which foreign countries would be most welcoming and, at the opposite end of the scale, which would be most likely to extradite them back to the US. The paper mixed humor with practical advice, advising that this was 'a regular *Roach* column for military personnel who may wish to take extended vacations from their units, and for civilians who find this country politically uncomfortable.' [Fig. 5.3] In ways such as these, underground reporters were able to draw on a groundswell of resistance against the war, provide advice for those who were avoiding

*Figure 5.3* *The Roach* (1968–69). Hawai'i Pacific Collection, University of Hawai'i at Mānoa.

induction into the military, and help mobilize disjointed protesters into a coherent movement.

In contrast, the *Advertiser* and *Star-Bulletin* utilized a tone of disinterested neutrality when discussing draft 'evasion.' They presented only bare details of individual cases, and thus created a pretense of neutrality and objectivity. According to the Index to the *Honolulu Advertiser* and *Honolulu Star Bulletin 1929 to 1967*, the papers published only ten articles about draft evasion. In 1968, however, in the wake of the Tet Offensive and growing anti-war feeling, almost 100 stories on the draft or draft resistance appeared. Whilst most of these articles maintained the same factual tone as earlier stories, their disapproval was clearly evident. For example, the *Star-Bulletin* reported a speech by Senator Daniel Inouye with the headline, 'Inouye fires blast at draft dodging.' (A few days later, it printed the full text of the speech.) Inouye was a second-generation Japanese-American, who had proved his loyalty to the United States as a member of the 442nd Regimental Combat Team in World War Two. By providing an extended forum for the Senator to air his views, the *Star-Bulletin* created a hostile context for further draft evasion stories.

In its coverage of the trial of Heavyweight Boxing Champion Muhammad Ali for alleged draft evasion, the *Advertiser* maintained a neutral tone by providing basic details of events ('Cassius'). However, it gave prominence in its sports pages to remarks by boxer Jerry Quarry that 'Convicted draft evader Cassius Clay is acting like a man who has been "brainwashed" ... Clay seems to be reciting things that have been drummed into him by a brainwashing technique.' The article, entitled 'Quarry Says Clay Brainwashed,' dredges up long-held American fears about the irrationality of foreigners and people of color (Engelhardt 38). Like the Soviets who labeled dissidents 'insane,' the paper infers that Clay must surely be out of his mind to avoid the draft. Furthermore, both the *Star-Bulletin* and *Advertiser* refused to call Ali anything other than 'Cassius Clay,' a name Ali had rejected because of its slave connections and his newfound religious beliefs. Such reporting seems to confirm Chapin's conclusion that, in Hawai'i, the 'Establishment journalists' basic premise ... was that the draft was necessary' (273).

*Roach* actively encouraged soldiers, sailors and airmen to desert their posts. For example, it published a letter from a former University of Hawai'i student, involved with 'Info 67,' a Canadian organization that helped American deserters and draft resisters. The letter assuaged fears that Canada would deport deserters and assured potential deserters and draft resisters they would get jobs, accommodation, and even Canadian citizenship. The letter also advised how to avoid the FBI and how to determine if a phone was wiretapped ('Resisters, Deserters'). *Roach* also advertised a draft resistance meeting to discuss draft card burning ('What's Happening?').

A typical tactic used by the paper was to subvert traditional militaristic narratives of bravery and honor. For example, in its campaign against the draft, it quoted the most sobering sections of Inouye's pro-draft speech to the graduating class at St. Francis Convent at the Mid-Pacific

Institute, particularly where Inouye spoke of the desensitizing impact of war. Inouye said, '[it] converted me into a killing machine ... [I experienced] a sense of great joy and elation when I killed my first German soldier. After that I killed many, many more. Much as I try, I find that I cannot erase these dark pages from my life' ('What's Happening?'). No doubt, Inouye meant his talk to inspire. However, *Roach* gambled that its readers would find Inouye's 'Greatest Generation' rhetoric as uninspiring and dated as John Wayne's effort in *The Green Berets* (1968) to portray the Vietnam War as a World War Two lark. *Roach* also gave its support to Dana Park, who was on trial for draft evasion ('What's Happening?'). In contrast, the *Advertiser* and *Star-Bulletin* provided only the basic proceedings of Park's arrest, hearings, and trial, and made no effort to explain why Park resisted the draft (he took a moral stance against the war). Instead, they reported the case as they would any other criminal proceeding, thus equating Park's pacifism with the mundane immorality of the petty criminal.

Jacques Ellul argues that propaganda is effective when it 'short-circuit[s] all thought and decision. It must operate on the individual on the level of the unconscious. He must not know that he is being shaped by outside forces' (27). Consequently, when the *Star-Bulletin* or *Advertiser* presented its readers with only the bare details of a 'draft dodger' story, the papers had, in actuality, already conditioned them to consider Park, and other draft resisters, in negative terms, as cowards or shirkers who were unwilling to fight like their GI forerunners had in the 'good war' against German fascism and Japanese imperialism. *Roach* made no such pretence of objectivity. Instead, it simply gave its support to Park and other draft resisters, and urged its readers to do all they could to help. Like most underground newspapers, *Roach* viewed the mainstream press's supposed neutrality as a sham.

*Hawaii Free Press* opposed the military draft and actively encouraged draft resistance and desertion from the military. The paper began circulation in 1969, in the wake of the Tet Offensive in Vietnam, when even pro-war establishment newspapers were beginning to have doubts about the war's efficacy, if not its underlying ideology. By this stage, there was no real need to appeal to its readers to avoid the draft, as many young people were politically aware enough at that point to know the issues involved. *Hawaii Free Press*, therefore, simply provided information to help those who had already chosen to avoid military service. In an article entitled 'Canada Welcomes Deserters,' the paper assured military deserters and draft resisters that, 'Deserters from the U.S. Armed Forces will be welcome immigrants to Canada.' The paper advised those interested that they should 'enter Canada as a visitor or tourist and get in touch with one of the anti-military groups for counselling. Deserters should not apply at the border for immigration — even though such application is now permitted because it is essential that they be properly prepared to make application.' The paper then listed a contact address and provided a phone number that deserters or draft avoiders could use. Such detailed, practical information on how to escape military service and disrupt war planning shows just how far the anti-war movement had progressed by 1969. No longer were there calls to revolt as, to a large extent, the revolt had already happened. Instead, the paper provided matter-of-fact information on how to make the revolution go smoothly.

## Antiwar protests

Like many in the anti-war movement, *Roach* staff did not think of themselves as unpatriotic; instead, they believed they were reclaiming American values from militarists who had wrapped themselves in the US flag. On the front cover of the 18 June 1968 issue, for example, *Roach* quoted the full text of the Declaration of Independence, and a photograph of police arresting a protester at a 'Students for Academic Freedom' march ('This Means Revolution!'). *Roach* provided sympathetic coverage of anti-war demonstrations, such as the protest at Fort DeRussy on 13 May 1968, which disrupted a National Guard convoy. Police subsequently arrested nine students and a university professor for 'loiter[ing] ... loaf[ing] or idl[ing]' ('Ten Arrested'). In contrast, the *Advertiser* and *Star-Bulletin* endeavored to persuade readers that such protests were unpatriotic, dangerous to military morale, and disrespectful to soldiers fighting in Vietnam.

Michael Parenti has identified six methods used by the mainstream press to marginalize, trivialize, and otherwise damage the reputation of protesters (*Inventing* 99–102). These are, 'Scanting of Content': omitting the meaning of the protest and treating it as a 'spectacle.' 'Trivialization': reporting superficialities such as how protesters are dressed rather than discuss the central political or social issues. 'Marginalization': portraying protesters as abnormal and marginal characters with abstract, superficial ideas that are unrepresentative of the American people. 'False Balance': to appear evenhanded and present a false sense of objectivity, the mainstream press gives disproportionate consideration and coverage to counterdemonstrations, many of which are much smaller than the main demonstration. 'Undercounting': underestimating the numbers of protesters at a demonstration the newspaper is unsympathetic to, or alternatively, overestimating the numbers of counter demonstrators. 'Omission': failing to report what the demonstration is actually about.

The *Advertiser* and *Star-Bulletin* used all of these filters in their reports of a 1966 anti-war protest. For example, the *Star-Bulletin* ran a two-column-wide story entitled 'Rival Marches Are Scheduled' alongside a much more extensively reported story entitled 'Tension Mounts as Protesters March.' The larger story is replete with lurid warnings and innuendo about violent protest marches on the US mainland (although upon closer reading it becomes apparent that little or no violence occurred). The paper ensured that its readers understood which 'side' to be on by detailing the 'hecklers [who] spat at the marchers and shouted "chicken, scum, cowards, commies!"' The smaller story about the upcoming Honolulu demonstration suffers from 'guilt by association' with the mainland reports: in effect, the *Star-Bulletin* was preparing readers to expect violence from the Honolulu anti-war protesters. The paper also gave equal coverage to a counter demonstration, although the 'pro-war' march was much smaller in scale.

The *Advertiser's* coverage of this protest was headlined, 'Isle's Peacenik March is a Calm One.' Headlines help readers to interpret the story and reach a conclusion as to its significance. Here, the *Advertiser* assumed that violence was the norm for protest marches and the 'news' was that the march passed peacefully. The paper used a 'guilt by association' tactic, referring unnecessarily to the 'egg-throwing, police arrests and feverish speeches' of some mainland protests. Although no violence occurred, reporter David Butwin created a false sense of menace and inferred the march remained peaceful only because of the vigilance and professionalism of the authorities. He stated, 'If violence was brewing beneath the peaceful surface yesterday, the police kept it there. Some 50 Honolulu police officers, many in casual aloha dress, escorted the marchers ... with the care of mother hens.' Butwin gave no credit to the anti-war protesters for successfully marshalling their own peaceful demonstration: '[P]assion and violence took a holiday,' he claimed, reinforcing the headline's guidance to readers that violence was the norm, and this particular protest was, therefore, an atypical anti-war demonstration.

The *Advertiser* also gave prominent coverage to the smaller counter demonstration, although it was, by the paper's own admission, only a third the size of the anti-war protest. Butwin used a childish 'heads I win, tails you lose' verbal trick, stating, 'Some people heckled the anti-war group and some cheered the smaller body favoring U.S. policy in Viet Nam.' In contrast to his description of anti-war protesters, for whom he has little evident sympathy, Butwin described a pro-war demonstrator as 'one of the most attractive sights' there. He also claimed to hear a small child say, 'Here comes the good guys' when pro-war marchers approached. Butwin failed to provide any context for the protest, instead filling space with petty observations about a protester's 'straw sombrero' and a woman 'crocheting.' Such triviality seems to confirm Parenti's analysis that the mainstream press uses 'selective details to make light of [the protesters'] dress, age, language, styles, presumed lack of seriousness, and self-indulgent activities' (*Inventing* 99–100).

The papers' hostile attitude towards anti-war protesters continued into 1967. For example, in May of that year, the *Advertiser* again gave first page prominence to Admiral Sharp, who declared, 'peace demonstrations merely prolong the fighting ... The demonstrators get so much publicity that, to outsiders, the demonstrators are out of proportion to the depth of feeling in the majority of Americans' ('Adm. Sharp'). However, after the Tet Offensive created a major shift in public opinion against the war, both newspapers moderated their tone and softened their attitude (Schreiber 227). By that stage, resistance to the war was widespread and commonplace. Howard Zinn points out, for example, 'By mid-1965, 380 prosecutions were begun against men refusing to be inducted; by mid-1968 that figure was up to 3305. At the end of 1969, there were 33,960 delinquents nationwide' (485). Maintaining a hostile attitude towards protesters could, therefore, potentially alienate a significant section of the papers' readership. Nevertheless, *Advertiser* and *Star-Bulletin*' coverage of Vietnam War protests appears to substantiate Michael Parenti's observation that the media tends to associate 'protest with violence' (*Inventing* 98),[9] and supports his interpretation that the mainstream press 'spent more time attacking those who protested the enormities of the world than those who perpetrated those enormities' (*Inventing* 90).

## Expanding consciousness and coverage: Women, sex, drugs and rock-n-roll

Prior to 1967, the focus of the underground press in the US was on cultural issues such as drugs, gay rights, music, sex, and religion, with an occasional spotlight on political topics such as civil rights or the war in Vietnam. As the war progressed, and its violence was reflected in American streets, the underground press became more political. However, the swing from cultural to political emphasis was not permanent. Nixon continued his program of investigation and harassment of anti-war groups, including the most political and influential underground newspapers. Furthermore, when American troops began to withdraw from Vietnam under Nixon's strategy of 'Vietnamization,' some of the energy behind anti-war protests began to dissipate. As a result, many alternative papers shifted their focus from politics back to cultural issues. Robert Glessing notes, for example, 'By 1969 many underground editors were disillusioned and depressed by the failure of the Peace and Freedom Party, SDS, or the Black Panthers to get the youth movement together ... Many of the underground press's leaders had given up on cities, schools, and American institutions in general and

*Figure 5.4* *Gathering Place* (1971–72). Hawai'i Pacific Collection, University of Hawai'i at Mānoa.

were trying alternative ways of living' (66). *Gathering Place* is a prime example of this trend.

*Gathering Place*'s main focus was 'drugs and sex, gay news, and psychedelic art' (Chapin 277), and this was reflected in its cover imagery. For example, unlike the amateurish and sometimes poorly drawn covers of *Roach*, the covers of *Gathering Place* have artistic merit. [Fig. 5.4] *Roach*'s covers are mostly political cartoons, whereas the covers of *Gathering Place* tended to be psychedelic or idealized pastoral scenes of butterflies, frogs, flowers, naked women, temples and communes. In general, *Gathering Place*'s content reflected the cultural and artistic tenor of its front page. However, it sometimes printed stories critical of the American venture in Vietnam. For example, although the first issue of *Gathering Place* featured the above-mentioned cover of psychedelic flowers, frogs and butterflies, and a teaser which stated, 'inside: a study of 1000 Honolulu pot smokers,' it also featured an insightful biographical portrait of South Vietnamese general, Nguyen Cao Ky ('Who is Nguyen?'). The paper alleged that Ky was a drug smuggler, which, accurate or not, indicates the kind of subjects the underground press were interested in, which the mainstream newspapers largely ignored.

In the make-up of their staff, and in the content of their reports, papers like *Roach* tended to have a more inclusive attitude towards women than their mainstream rivals. In one sense, this reflected the attitudes of the combatants: while the NLF and NVA embraced the concept of female soldiers, American combat units were all-male in composition. Instead, American women could serve as nurses in the US Army Medical Corps or join a voluntary service such as the Red Cross. Nonetheless, as many as 55,000 of them were exposed to combat, or dealt with its consequences. This aspect of the war has largely been forgotten: as Marilyn Young notes, 'For women veterans the[ir] problem[s] [were] compounded by the initial inability of anyone ... to acknowledge that they too were combat veterans' (322). American newspapers generally failed to acknowledge the role of women on both sides of the war. The newspaper industry was a male-dominated profession, with only a small number of female reporters. Those few were often the subject of sexist practices and discrimination, as Helen Geracimos Chapin explains:

> When the men returned after World War II, and unlike many of their mainland counterparts, women kept their jobs, even when married to colleagues. They continued, however, to be underrepresented as reporters, and in news management, not to mention the back shop that is still largely male. When they were represented,

they were often trivialized, as in the *Star-Bulletin's* description of its excellent reporters, Helen Altonn and Harriet Gee, as 'little jewels in [the] newsrooms' (283–4).

Female American war correspondents were rare. When the *Advertiser* hired Denby Fawcett in May 1966 as its Vietnam correspondent 'specializing in feature stories in and around Saigon' (Chaplin 297), it already had two male reporters, Bob Krauss and Bob Jones reporting from the front lines. The *Advertiser* described Fawcett as an 'attractive 24-year-old' and admitted it hired her to cover positive stories — 'articles on men and women who are lending their teaching, building and medical skills to winning the peace' ('Newswoman'). The *Advertiser* patronized Fawcett,

*Figure 5.5* Vietnam War correspondent Denby Fawcett. Courtesy of Denby Fawcett.

*Figure 5.6* Vietnam War correspondent Denby Fawcett. Courtesy of Denby Fawcett.

and minimized her professional status by describing her as a 'shapely, green-eyed blonde about 5-feet, 4-inches tall' and 'a very pretty girl — many say the prettiest of the 10 or 12 women correspondents in Vietnam' ('For Denby'). [Fig. 5.5] [Fig. 5.6]

In contrast, Hawai'i's underground papers actively encouraged women to take part in anti-war activities, and the papers' coverage of Vietnamese women, particularly those fighting in the NLF, was positive to the point of being celebratory. For instance, *Roach* published a story entitled 'VN Women Liberation,' stating, 'in the course of the struggle against colonialist invaders, the Vietnamese women contributed greatly to the fighting ... and in the process are transforming their roles and consciousness.' Underground G.I. paper *Liberated Barracks* published a number of affirmative, non-sexist photographs of Vietnamese women, including one image of a female NLF soldier it called 'A Veteran of the Vietnam War' ('Who Is The Real Enemy?'). Occasionally, *Roach* used a lewd or obscene cartoon, but never gratuitously, or solely for titillation. For example, one drawing depicted a young woman, chained and vulnerable, apparently about to be raped. However, the woman was actually a representation of 'Lady Liberty' and the man bore a resemblance to President Richard Nixon (Jan 15–31, 1969: 5). Another *Roach* edition contained a picture of a near-naked woman, in a typical pornographic pose. However, the photo was headlined 'Break the Dull Steak Habit,' and the woman's body was marked into cuts like a butcher's carcass. The image did not promote a degrading view of women and instead sought to draw attention to such sexual objectification (Oct 23–Nov 4, 1968: 5).

Not every underground newspaper in the 1960s was as progressive as *Roach* or *Liberated Barracks*. As Todd Gitlin has noted, many papers were 'stupidly sexist' (23). In part, this was a reflection of the new culture of 'free love' in the 1960s, whereby men and women could more openly express their sexual needs and explore sexual freedom. However, even within the supposedly 'enlightened' political movements, some men were deeply sexist. For example, Marilyn Webb was shouted down when she spoke about sexism at a political rally. And when a young female activist at the University of Wisconsin met Tom Hayden for the first time, Hayden asked her to do his dirty laundry (DeGroot 290–1). Nevertheless, some of the outward manifestations of sexism in underground newspapers can be accounted for — to an extent at least — as reactions to intimidation and harassment from law enforcement agencies. Geoffrey Rips points out, for example, that the FBI pressured Columbia Records to withdraw its advertisements from the *Berkeley Barb*, which meant that the paper had to 'survive … on lewd sex ads' (Mackenzie 166).

## Conduct of the war

One of the major criticisms of press coverage of the war is that there was too much focus on drama and action, and not enough focus on mundane but important issues, such as America's pacification program. Peter Braestrup argues, for example, that too much emphasis on 'enemy threats and localized fighting … left many other crucial matters unexplored' (159). According to Braestrup, this imbalance left the American public with the impression that the war was being lost, when the opposite was the case. For the most part, Hawai'i's underground papers avoided combat reports, especially those with heavy American casualties. In part, this was because they had no reporters in Vietnam, and therefore did not have access to first-hand accounts of battle. Furthermore, underground papers rarely used stories from traditional news feeds such as AP, UPI, or Reuters. For example, *Gathering Place* used Liberation News Service, an agency based in New York, which focused on national and international news, rather than combat reporting. Hawai'i's underground papers focused mainly on political aspects of the war, or opposition to the draft and the military.

An occasional story did feature graphic descriptions of combat, but this was usually done to illustrate a wider point about the conduct of the war. For example, a *Gathering Place* story headlined 'Slain in Holdup — A Hero's Welcome ...' told how veteran Dwight Johnson had been shot and killed while robbing a grocery store. During the war, Johnson received the Medal of Honor for rescuing a wounded comrade from a burning tank. *Gathering Place* described how Johnson fought off NLF attackers, killing maybe 20 of them in hand-to-hand fighting. However, this was not 'combat reporting,' as such, as the battle occurred at least a year previously. Instead, these details were included to provide context for the story's larger point about the US Army's treatment of veterans (12). In contrast, the *Star-Bulletin* and *Advertiser* filled pages with dramatic stories of Americans in combat against an enemy the press often demonized. For instance, the *Star-Bulletin* described a successful NLF attack against American troops as a 'massacre' ('Tactical'). As historian Tom Engelhardt has revealed, framing stories in this way reverses the roles of invader and invaded. Engelhardt states, 'it was the Indians who, by the ambush, the atrocity ... became the aggressors, and so sealed their own fate' (5). Thus, the *Star-Bulletin* framed the story within acceptable boundaries, depicted the NLF as intruders or invaders, rather than indigenous South Vietnamese, and placed emphasis on American suffering rather than Vietnamese.

Hawai'i's underground papers were among the first to realize the extent of American atrocities in Vietnam. For instance, when news of the My Lai massacre finally broke in the mainstream newspapers, long after the alternative press had covered the story, *Gathering Place*'s Jon Olsen declared, 'My Lai, as most of us know, was not an isolated instance, but far too typical of US policy toward Asian people in practice, which is quite different from official pronouncements. Radical papers reported events like My Lai years ago, but because of rampant anti-communism, such reports were not given much credibility by non-radicals' (Olsen 11). Hawai'i's radical military newspaper, *Liberated Barracks*, made the same point, declaring, 'My Lai was not a single isolated incident but part of a general policy of genocide against the Vietnamese people which is promulgated very high up the chain of command' ('VVAW').

In 1969, as reports of this massacre began to appear, the *Star-Bulletin* gave considerable space to General Lewis Walt to deny the story. Under the headline 'U.S. General Discounts Massacre,' the paper summarized Walt's view that, 'reports of an alleged massacre in Vietnam exaggerated the civilian death toll for Communist propaganda purposes.' Walt stated, 'in any case, whatever may have happened at Song My [a nearby hamlet] would be contrary to any battle orders he, Gen. Westmoreland or Gen. Creighton Abrams ever put out.' No *Star-Bulletin* reporter challenged Walt's assertions. In due course, Americans discovered, to their horror, My Lai was a reality: the US military knew about it, and had instigated a cover up. My Lai was, in fact, 'part of an official policy of terrorizing and massacring all civilians deemed sympathetic to the insurgents' (Franklin 39). For example, in early 1971, Colonel Oran Henderson, the brigade commander whose unit carried out the My Lai massacre, told reporters: 'Every unit of brigade size has its My Lai hidden someplace' (Zinn 479).

Given conservative criticism of the press's supposed role in undermining the American war effort, ironically, it was not a crusading reporter who uncovered the My Lai atrocity; it was, in fact, a whistleblower named Ron Ridenhour. He was not present at the massacre, but subsequently gathered details about it from Army comrades. Ridenhour sent letters to Richard Nixon, members of Congress and top Pentagon officials, and this was the catalyst an official enquiry. Even then, however, the story received little attention from the press. It was only when Seymour Hersh, a young AP reporter, made his own investigations that the story gained momentum. Hersh offered it to *Life* magazine, but *Life* turned him down. Eventually the Dispatch News Service picked up the story, and it broke on 12 November 1969. A week later, *Life* ran its own story, as did *Time* and *Newsweek* (Wyatt 207–8; Oliver 248). Nevertheless, initial coverage of My Lai and other American atrocities suggests the underground press was more willing to investigate the darker side of war than their mainstream counterparts.

## Espionage and oppression

*Gathering Place* covered one of the largely forgotten stories of the Vietnam era, US military espionage against civilians. In its coverage of peace group Catholic Action's 'almost daily' anti-war leafleting campaign at the gates of Hickam Air Force Base, *Gathering Place*' journalists noticed US military personnel spying on the campaigners and taking photographs. This was, in all probability, the 710th Military Intelligence Unit (Chapin 275). The paper reminded its readers, 'Back in 1970 military intelligence agents admitted to Sen. Sam J. Ervin's subcommittee on constitutional rights that they had been spying on civilian protest groups for several years ... Soon the Army said they would stop this perfidious practice and told Ervin in March of 1970 that their data bank on civilians had been "discontinued and destroyed"' ('Propaganda Guerillas').

As journalist Aryeh Neier explains, these activities were revealed to a national audience by a 'whistleblower,' a former Army intelligence officer called Christopher Pyle:

> It was a revelation in January, 1970, that the United States Army was compiling dossiers on the political beliefs and associations of Americans that finally made political surveillance a matter of great public controversy. The revelation came in a magazine article by Christopher Pyle, a lawyer and a former Captain in the United States Army. Pyle ... eventually persuaded more than a hundred former military intelligence agents to join him in revealing publicly that they had spied on the peaceful political activities of their fellow Americans (15).

This exposure led to the Congressional investigation mentioned in *Gathering Place*, and to ACLU legal action. Although the lawsuit failed, the unwanted publicity generated by the Congressional investigation prompted the military to promise to desist from further spying on civilians. As Geoffrey Rips explains, however, the military did not keep that promise: 'When restrictions placed on military intelligence in 1971 called for destroying files on civilians, Army agents in Chicago, Cleveland, Pennsylvania, and Washington, D.C., gave the files instead to local and state police' (57). Furthermore, if *Gathering Place* was correct in its reporting of military intelligence spying on peace activists in Honolulu, it indicates that the military continued its espionage against civilians, in defiance of the US Congress.

The inaugural issue of *Hawaii Free Press* in July 1969 attacked the University of Hawai'i for accepting military research contracts for 'chemical-biological warfare research, ROTC, and the many other defense-stimulated projects being conducted at our universities' ('New Look'). The paper also alleged that 'personnel associated with the CIA' staffed many university departments. To many at the time, such statements must have seemed like a bizarre conspiracy theory. However, a small alternative magazine called *Ramparts* had already broken the story, as Michael Parenti recounts: 'many important and revealing stories are broken by small publications with only a fraction of the material resources and staff available to the mass media. The startling news that the CIA was funding cultural, academic, and student organizations was first publicized by the now defunct *Ramparts* magazine' (*Inventing* 53). At the request of the CIA, *Ramparts* was then audited by the IRS (Rips 75; Mackenzie 161).

In time, the *Hawaii Free Press* was proven correct on this issue, as peace activist Robert Witanek explains:

> Professors and CIA operatives with academic cover have worked extensively on campuses around the world ... they have written books, articles, and reports for U.S. consumption with secret CIA sponsorship and censorship; they have spied on foreign nationals at home and abroad; they have regularly recruited foreign and U.S. students and faculty for the CIA; they have hosted conferences with secret CIA backing under scholarly cover, promoting disinformation; and they have collected data, under the rubric of research, on Third World liberation and other movements opposed to U.S. intervention.

According to Noam Chomsky, the Political Science Department at Massachusetts Institute of Technology had links with the CIA. He states, 'Around 1960, the Political Science Department separated off from the Economics Department. And at that time it was openly funded by the CIA; it was not even a secret ... In the mid-1960s, it stopped being publicly funded by the Central Intelligence Agency, but it was still directly involved in activities that were scandalous' (*Cold War* 181).

## Rights of Native Hawaiians and Pacific Islanders

Unlike its mainstream counterparts, *Gathering Place* was prepared to criticize the US military presence in Hawai'i: 'The first windmill I'm going to attack is the US Army,' declared journalist Bob Shipley. Shipley was critical of the vast swathes of land reserved for military use, and out of bounds to Hawai'i residents. He criticized the Army's destruction of the environment and its unwillingness to compromise with local residents, stating, 'Various groups of responsible citizens have tried for years to play ball with the Army ... but the Army has consistently refused to even listen to what we have to say.'

*Hawaii Free People's Press* gave a voice to Native Hawaiian activists and exposed American abuses of Pacific Islanders. In a piece entitled 'An Open Letter to my Brothers and Sisters of Hawaii,' one activist explained how Hawaiians had 'take[n] out our anger and frustration on defenseless servicemen, hippies and tourists.' In a plea for Native Hawaiians to recognize the cause of their frustration as American imperialism and the theft of Hawaiian sovereignty, the writer reminded Hawaiians that, 'fear of the haole is ... shown by our irrational patriotism. We look upon draft avoiders, flag burners, and political activists as cowards and traitors.' This misplaced anger is the result of decades of exposure to militaristic narratives of US patriotism. As Ferguson and Turnbull have revealed, '[M]ilitary order is heavily written into Hawai'i' (xiv) in the Waikīkī War Memorial, the Army Museum of Hawaii, and in many other military sites which link the sacrifice of Hawaiians to the cause of American freedom. In consequence, some Native Hawaiians have come to see themselves in terms of the dominant American agenda. Sociologist Charles Cooley calls this effect 'the looking-glass self' (Montagu and Matson xxxi).

Whereas the mainstream press remained virtually silent about the effects of US nuclear testing in the Pacific, the underground press covered the story in depth. For example, a *Roach* article, entitled 'Micronesians Demand Decent Conditions,' highlighted the plight of the people of Eniwetok [sic] who suffered as a result of US nuclear testing ('Micronesians'). The 142 impoverished islanders of Enewetak, in the Marshall Islands, agreed to let the US use their land for atomic testing, in return for $175,000 compensation. The US evacuated the islanders in December 1947, relocating them to the island of Ujelang. Ujelang, however, provided less food and fresh water than Enewetak, and it was much smaller. This raw deal caused islanders to 'look ... back on their life in Enewetak as a golden age' (Firth 34). The military exploded three low-yield atomic bombs on Enewetak in 1948, and thereafter utilized the islands as a permanent nuclear testing facility. It was there that the US developed the world's first hydrogen bomb, and on 1 November 1952, it exploded an H-bomb the strength of 800 Hiroshimas on the island's northern side. Ten nuclear tests also took place on Enjebi Island to the north, which remains heavily contaminated and cannot support human habitation. Until 1968, the military used Enewetak as a target for long-range missiles launched from California. By that time, two of the atoll's islands had been completely vaporized.

*Roach* therefore demonstrated, not only the investigative vigor missing from mainstream papers, but also some much-needed compassion. It concluded, 'the past twenty years have been miserable for the people of Eniwetok,' and demanded that they be returned from exile. In part, the failure of the mainstream press to report on the plight of Pacific Islanders affected by nuclear testing can be explained by a 'stifling blanket of official secrecy' (Boyer, *Bomb's* 304) in the early years of atomic testing. Even so, official secrecy does not explain how or why the underground press was able to uncover the story, when Hawai'i's mainstream press could not. This lacuna suggests that a conservative ideology affected the *Advertiser* and *Star-Bulletin*'s reporting of such issues.

## G.I. blues

The US Army that began the Vietnam War was vastly different to the US Army that ended it. In 1965, the troops involved in the first large-scale military operations against the Vietnamese, were professional soldiers. They made up an all-volunteer army that had won an unprecedented series of battles from Revolutionary times until the Korean War. By the end of the Vietnam War, however, the US Army was almost unrecognizable. In a 1971 article published in *Armed Forces Journal* entitled, 'The Collapse of the Armed Forces,' Colonel Robert D. Heinl Jr. concluded,

> The morale, discipline and battleworthiness of the U.S. Armed Forces are, with a few salient exceptions, lower and worse than at anytime in this century and possibly in the history of the United States. By every conceivable indicator, our army that now remains in Vietnam is in a state approaching collapse, with individual units avoiding or having refused combat, murdering their officers and non commissioned officers, drug-ridden, and dispirited where not near mutinous.

As casualties mounted, so too did the number of disobedient soldiers. Many of these young men were anti-war to begin with, and most were conscripts. As such, they were unwilling to follow dangerous orders from over-eager officers. In the later years of the war, such 'combat refusals' became increasingly common. Racial animosity also undermined military discipline. For example, Black veteran Don F. Browne, who helped retake the American Embassy compound in Saigon after the Tet Offensive, recalls: 'When I heard that Martin Luther King was assassinated, my first inclination was to run out and punch the first white guy I saw' (Terry 167). Veteran Wallace Terry claimed the war had become a 'double battleground, pitting American soldier against American soldier. The spirit of foxhole brotherhood I found in 1967 had evaporated' (xv).

Underground newspapers were not the cause of G.I. unrest, but they did act as a catalyst and a conduit for it, as Howard Zinn explains:

> Near Fort Jackson, South Carolina, the first 'GI coffeehouse' was set up, a place where soldiers could get coffee and doughnuts, find anti-war literature, and talk freely with others. It was called the UFO, and lasted for several years before it was declared a 'public nuisance' and closed by court action. But other GI coffeehouses sprang up in half a

dozen other places across the country. An antiwar 'bookstore' was opened near Fort Devens, Massachusetts, and another one at Newport, Rhode Island, naval base. Underground newspapers sprang up at military bases across the country; by 1970 more than fifty were circulating. Among them: *About Face* in Los Angeles; *Fed Up!* In Tacoma, Washington; *Short Times* at Fort Jackson; *Vietnam GI* in Chicago; *Graffiti* in Heidelberg, Germany; *Bragg Briefs* in North Carolina; *Last Harass* at Fort Gordon, Georgia; *Helping Hand* at Mountain Home Air Base, Idaho. These newspapers printed antiwar articles, gave news

LIBERATED

Our symbol is a fist because if we are like an open hand our fingers may be broken one by one, but if we stick together like a fist we cannot be smashed.

BARRACKS

VOL. I NO. 3 PHONE 923-2503 NOVEMBER 1971

FREE TO GI's

FTA SHOW COMES TO HAWAII



NOVEMBER 25

DOD DIRECTIVE # 1325.6 SECTION IIIA: " The mere posession of unauthorized printed material may not be prohibited." THIS IS YOUR PERSONAL PROBERTY AND CANNOT BE CONFISCATED.

*Figure 5.7* *Liberated Barracks* (1971–74). Hawai'i Pacific Collection, University of Hawai'i at Mānoa.

> about the harassment of GIs and practical advice on the legal rights of servicemen, told how to resist military domination (494).

Hawai'i had its own G.I. paper in the *Liberated Barracks*, which began circulating in 1971. [Fig. 5.7] By this time, unrest among soldiers in Hawai'i had been ongoing for at least four years. Soldiers, sailors, and aviators took part in anti-war protests, wrote letters of support to underground papers like *Roach*, and participated in personal acts of dissent such as wearing peace signs or buttons on their uniforms or displayed on their cars. In 1968, 36 members of the military sought asylum in local churches (Chapin 277–8). In 1969, soldiers and civilians marched from Kapi'olani Park to Ala Moana Park to demand a 'bill of rights' for military personnel. In the aftermath of the march, up to 50 servicemen sought sanctuary at the Church of the Crossroads and the First Unitarian Church of Honolulu (Blanco).

*Liberated Barracks* began life as a G.I. coffeehouse for military men like these who were 'taking a stand against what they feel is a futile and senseless war' (Norwood 7). The coffeehouse opened in April 1971, and by September 1971, the first issue of this new G.I. paper was in print. It survived until 1974, covering numerous topics about military life in Hawai'i and the war in Vietnam. In the first issue, a column entitled 'Hawaii: Why So Much Military,' offered an interesting alternative to the mainstream media's adoration of the US military presence in the islands. For example, unlike the *Advertiser* or *Star-Bulletin*, which emphasized Hawai'i's supposed economic dependence upon the military, *Liberated Barracks* talked of the social and economic 'sacrifice' that military dependence brings, such as being asked to support the military's 'unjust' wars against 'people fighting for their self-determination and freedom.' *Liberated Barracks* spoke of the '38% of the land on Oahu ... controlled by the military, bottling land we need for food and housing. Our schools and other social institutions are pressured by the increased military migration of dependents, as is our housing crisis and work opportunities.' 'Hawaii: Why So Much Military' became an ongoing column, and in later editions would discuss other topics ignored by the mainstream press, such as nuclear weapon storage at Pearl Harbor (Feb 1972: 4), and how the military presence promotes prostitution (Mar 1972: 11).

*Liberated Barracks* also supported Native Hawaiian cultural and sovereignty issues. For instance, it advised its readers to buy the *Hawaii Pono Journal*, an alternative publication which focussed on Hawaiian social and cultural concerns, because 'Our G.I. struggle in Hawaii is very closely related to the over-all problems and struggles of Hawaii's people ... we must understand clearly our Hawaiian brothers and sisters problems and struggles' ('Hawaii Pono Journal'). The paper also supported student complaints about the absence of an ethnic studies program at the University of Hawai'i. It stated, 'From the time of the missionaries, Hawaiian history has been written by White people who thought that the Hawaiians were ignorant savages, and completely ignored the rich and beautiful culture that was already here.' An ethnic studies program was needed to counteract 'a school system based on Western values and thinking' ('Ethnic Studies').

*Liberated Barracks* disproves the myth that veterans despised, in toto, anti-war activists such as Jane Fonda (Burke). For instance, in its November 1971 edition, the paper promoted and sponsored a 'Free the Army' (FTA) show featuring Fonda, actor Donald Sutherland, and musician Country Joe McDonald, among others. The show took place at the Civic Auditorium on 25 November 1971, in front of an audience of approximately 4000 ('I Said "Keep On Truckin" ... '). According to the *Advertiser*, about 2500 of the audience were servicemen and their wives ('Rapping'). The *Star-Bulletin* claimed only 3500 people were in attendance ('F.T.A. Show is Biting'). This discrepancy may be due to the mainstream media's 'regular practice of undercounting the size of demonstrations' (Parenti, *Inventing* 97), in this case, undercounting the number of military personnel to minimize the scope of military dissent against militarism and the war in Vietnam. According to *Liberated Barracks'* publicity material, the show intended to 'reflect the attitudes, sentiments and feelings of the servicemen and women who struggle against the dehumanizing oppression of the American military machine' ('FTA Show Comes'). Although in the run up to the event, the *Advertiser* and *Star-Bulletin* recorded a few gripes about mainstream press exclusion from meetings between Fonda and *Liberated Barracks*, *Advertiser* and *Star-Bulletin* coverage of the show itself was neutral and even-handed, which can perhaps be explained by their new-found tolerance of the anti-war movement which, by 1971, had widespread support.

Military authorities despised underground G.I. newspapers and did their utmost to make life difficult for military personnel involved in producing, distributing, or simply receiving them, as Geoffrey Rips records:

> To control these underground publications, the command used disciplinary, judicial, and surreptitious tactics. Intimidation by rank and threats of prosecution by military courts often provoked self-censorship among writers in the military. Those who exercised their right to publish and write were harassed and verbally abused by

> their superiors. Sometimes they were transferred without advanced notice, demoted to menial assignments, and followed by military police and intelligence (139).

The military hierarchy faced two problems however. Firstly, the imposition of blatant censorship might prove counterproductive to troop morale, and risk 'increasing the interest in antiwar literature by banning such literature or by declaring it dangerous' (Glessing 141). Secondly, soldiers retain some Constitutional rights of free expression, as Chapin makes clear: 'In 1969, the U.S. Army issued a "Guidance on Dissent," which all of the services supposedly followed. This stated that the "publication of underground newspapers by soldiers off post, and with their own money and equipment, is generally protected under the First Amendment"' (279–80). Initially, the G.I. press welcomed this directive: one editor said, 'any lifer, officer, etc., who tries to bust you for having a copy of [an underground GI paper] can be charged with article 92a UCMJ — violation or failure to obey a Lawful general order' (Lewes 143). As both Chapin and Ripps point out, however, such was the power of the officer class in the military that local commanders often ignored these guidelines, without fear of retribution from their superiors. However, as G.I. newspapers reflected attitudes among soldiers, it proved impossible for the military to eradicate or silence them. As the military grew increasingly divided by the war, G.I. newspapers thrived. For example, writer Roger Lewis provided a 'far from complete' list of 45 papers available in 1972 (134). *Liberated Barracks* ceased publication in 1974, by which time most American soldiers had left Vietnam, the draft was winding down, and anti-war opposition was on the wane.

Author William Burroughs once remarked, 'What the American alternative press did in the 1960s is of inestimable value. Many of the gains in freedom that we take for granted ... were won due, in great part, to the efforts of the alternative press' (Ginsberg 34). Historian H. Bruce Franklin asserts, however, that:

> the role of the underground press during the Vietnam War soon disappeared into the black hole of national amnesia that has swallowed much of our consciousness ... everybody seems to have forgotten that the established press eventually lost its monopoly on reporting the war, as millions of Americans began to rely primarily on the unabashedly disloyal movement press for accurate and truthful reporting (90–1).

It is difficult to find fault with these assessments, although perhaps Franklin paints an overly rosy picture: underground press reporting was often biased and unreliable, and contributors could be insensitive and immature. However, as Abe Peck observes, they also offered 'an honest subjectivity in place of an "objectivity" that ignored its underlying political and cultural assumptions' (xv). Free of ties to the military, the government, and corporate financial interests, underground newspapers challenged the political, social and cultural orthodoxy. In so doing, they reflected the progressive radicalism of the time, and acted as a conduit for a generation's frustration with what had gone before.

Hawai'i's underground newspapers covered many issues unconnected to the Vietnam War and the US military presence in the state. Drugs, music, politics, style and sex, were favorite topics, with occasional stories about surfing or luaus. In the broadest sense, these were the same topics favored by the *Advertiser* and *Star-Bulletin*, although opposing ideologies and agendas ensured that each approached stories from different angles, revealing what former underground press editor Abe Peck has called a 'gulf in perspective' (xvi) between the often self-indulgent muckraking of the underground, and the supposed objectivity of the mainstream, whose values were 'white, middle-class [and] male' (xiv). However, it was the war and militarism that provided the fuel for the underground — the draft that discriminated against the poorest in American society, the senseless destruction of Vietnamese villages to 'save' the inhabitants from communism, the endless body counts, the lies, and the crimes.

The impact of the underground in Hawai'i is hard to assess. A loose coalition of students, activists, scholars, church groups and pacifists united, for a time, primarily to oppose the war in Vietnam, but also to champion the causes of racial, sexual and social equality. Campaigns by the *Free People's Press* against environmental damage and urban development, met with some success (Chapin 277), and the underground's support for Native Hawaiian rights helped sow the seeds for the sovereignty movement that developed in the following decades. In their defense of some of the most vulnerable in society, underground papers affected the lives of many individuals for the better. Moreover, they offered alternative viewpoints to the *Advertiser* and *Star-Bulletin* and, in so doing ensured Hawai'i's citizens received a wider perspective of the war, and were made aware of the militaristic agendas in Hawai'i. Chapin believes their most extensive influence was as a 'catalyst ... for change' (280), although it is difficult to gauge to what extent the papers affected change, or just reflected it. Indeed, historians have tended to concern themselves more with determining the impact of the mainstream press on American public opinion. A recurring allegation is that the media lost the war by swaying public opinion against it. The Tet Offensive is often cited as both a pivotal moment in the war, and a prime example of how supposedly biased press coverage influenced the war's outcome. Franklin calls this an 'absurd proposition' (90), but it remains a powerful hypothesis. How, then, did Hawai'i's establishment press report Tet? Were the *Advertiser* and *Star-Bulletin* 'disloyal,' or is Franklin's judgment valid?

## Reporting Tet: January–April, 1968

In January 1968, the NVA and NLF launched simultaneous attacks across all of South Vietnam, laid siege to the American base at Khe Sanh in the northern highlands, and for the first time brought major combat into urban areas such as Saigon and Hue. Tet represented a significant change in tactics on the part of anti-American forces, from hit-and-run guerrilla warfare, to full-scale frontal assaults on ARVN and American forces. The Tet Offensive was conceived by General Vo Nguyen Giap, commander of the North Vietnam Army. Giap hoped to achieve a significant military victory, but he also planned for maximum psychological and political effect in both Vietnam and the US. In using the Tet New Year ceasefire as cover for the attacks, Giap hoped to catch his enemy unawares. Additionally, however, he timed the offensive to coincide with the early stages of President Johnson's re-election campaign. The offensive was, initially, successful, inflicting heavy casualties on the ARVN and, to a lesser extent, on American forces. The American Embassy compound in Saigon was briefly over-run (although the main Embassy building remained secure); Saigon's Tan Son Nhut airport was attacked; Khe Sanh was under siege; the ancient citadel at Hue was occupied by NLF troops; five out of six major cities were assaulted, as well as 36 out of 44 provincial capitals (Herring 186). Within days, however, the tide of battle turned in favor of America and its allies. The siege at Khe Sanh failed and Saigon was quickly brought under control. The NLF bore the brunt of the fighting, and in exposing themselves to superior US firepower, suffered very heavy casualties. According to journalist Don Oberdorfer, Tet cost the NLF 'the best of a generation of resistance fighters' (329). Furthermore, the anticipated general uprising of the South Vietnamese people did not materialize, and, after US forces recaptured Hue on 24 February, it was obvious to most observers that the NVA and NLF had suffered a major military reverse.[10]

However, the political effect of Tet proved more effective than its military aspect. In 1967, President Johnson had waged a propaganda campaign in America to bolster support for his Vietnam policies. He recalled General Westmoreland from Vietnam so that Westmoreland could give optimistic briefings to the media about American progress in the war. Westmoreland dutifully declared, 'We are now in a position from which the picture of ultimate victory success may be viewed with increasing clarity' (Hallin 165). Tet proved that to be overly-optimistic at best. Westmoreland's outward optimism belied the private fears of many in the Johnson administration that the war was not progressing as was hoped. For instance, by 1967 Secretary of Defense Robert McNamara had decided that the war was unwinnable (Herman and Chomsky 217), and he asked Johnson to scale down his expectations, withhold sending more troops, and begin real negotiations with North Vietnam (Herring 176–7). So when CBS anchor Walter Cronkite said during Tet that the US was 'mired in stalemate' (Hallin 170), he was saying publicly what some in the Johnson Administration had already admitted in private.

Tet caused Lyndon Johnson to reconsider his Vietnam policy: in its wake, Johnson refused Westmoreland's request for a substantial troop increase, announced a bombing halt, and expressed a hope that peace negotiations in Paris could begin in earnest. Despite this, Johnson fared badly against anti-war candidate Eugene McCarthy in the New Hampshire primary election, and he faced anti-war demonstrations every time he appeared in public (Zinn 483). Disillusioned, and with the knowledge that he could lose the Democratic nomination to McCarthy or Robert Kennedy, Johnson announced in a national television broadcast that he would not seek or accept his party's nomination for another term as president. Tet had proved to be a military defeat, but a political victory for the communist effort in South Vietnam.

The main criticism of media coverage of the Tet Offensive is that it failed to report a resounding military victory for America and its allies (Braestrup 153). Critics contend that the offensive was a desperate gamble by an almost-defeated enemy, and, if reported accurately, would have been a defining moment in the war, in America's favor (Young 222). Instead of turning American public opinion against the war, this argument goes, accurate reporting would have demonstrated that the US and its South Vietnamese ally were on the road to victory. Among those who hold this view are Westmoreland, who claimed that 'a hostile and all-too-powerful media seized defeat from the jaws of victory by turning the public against the war and limiting the government's freedom of action just when the United States had a battered enemy on the ropes' (Herring

200). Journalist Phillip Knightley claims that media coverage emphasized the endurance of the enemy and suggested that America was losing the war. He concludes, 'most journalists got Tet wrong' ('Role' 107). It is beyond the scope of this work to assess the merits or otherwise of this interpretation of events. However, the following analysis of *Advertiser* and *Star-Bulletin* reporting of Tet situates this coverage within the wider debate about newspaper coverage of the offensive, and in addition, suggests that both papers stayed faithful to Washington's version of events.

Criticism of media coverage began a few weeks into the offensive, and it came directly from the top, from the Johnson administration. An *Advertiser* editorial dated 18 February 1968 quotes a cabinet member who accused the media of being 'ambitiously negative' and asked, 'Whose side are you on' ('Press & Vietnam'). However, the accusation that the media reported Tet as a military victory for the NLF is not borne out by analysis of *Advertiser* and *Star-Bulletin* coverage. For example, in the days before the offensive, the *Advertiser* printed an optimistic account of the progress of the war entitled 'Top Marine Says U.S. Winning War.' On the second day of the battle the *Star-Bulletin* quoted official military sources that listed enemy casualties as 1800 and American/ARVN casualties as 40 ('Viet Cong Troops'). On page two, the paper also quoted US Ambassador Ellsworth Bunker's erroneous observation that, 'Saigon is Secure Now' (fighting actually continued in and around Saigon for months afterward) (Franklin 95). This optimistic outlook dominated the *Star-Bulletin*'s reporting. It relied on, and reported only the official American military casualty figures, which showed that the NLF suffered a heavy defeat, whereas American and ARVN casualties were relatively light ('5-Day'). The *Advertiser* also reported Tet as a devastating defeat for communist forces. Typical were page one headlines such as 'Allied Tanks Smash Into Reds in Hue' (Feb. 2, 1968) and 'Red Force Fading in Saigon Battle' (Feb. 3, 1968). This optimistic tenor reached its zenith on 12 February, when a front-page *Star-Bulletin* story headlined 'Reds won the headlines at record cost' assured readers, 'Things are not so bad as they might seem ... the Communists won the world's headlines [but] have suffered a major military defeat.'

Report after report suggests the *Star-Bulletin* followed Washington's lead. For example, a 1 February 1968 editorial entitled 'Attacks of Desperation,' assured readers the Tet Offensive should not 'undermine the assumption that our basic war plan is sound and succeeding.' According to the paper, Tet was a 'suicidal' effort, prompted by 'desperation,' a 'climactic final effort,' which when defeated will lead to the tide of war 'flowing in our favor even more strongly than before.' An official military censor could not have written a more favorable editorial. In fact, the following day the *Star-Bulletin* repeated Marine Lieutenant General Victor Krulak's remarks that the attacks were 'acts of desperation' and the enemy 'captured no territory … have not slowed the powerful Allied machine [and] have not altered either our plans or our purposes' ('Krulak'). On 4 February, the *Advertiser* quoted Major-General Fillmore K. Mearns, commander of the 25th Division, based in Hawai'i, that the Tet Offensive was an 'ill-advised' and 'foolhardy' effort by the NVA and NLF, and that 'it is not a military victory' ('25th's General'). A *Star-Bulletin* editorial on 9 February informed readers they must 'keep … cool,' that the war was 'just,' and that victory was still attainable ('Keep'). The paper assured readers the US was 'still very much in control of South Vietnam' and demanded that Americans 'rally round and do our utmost to defeat the enemy.' These are hardly the words of a press attempting to convince Americans that the war was lost or that Tet was a resounding communist success.

The images the papers used to illustrate their stories were also sympathetic to the American position. Ferguson and Turnbull's observation that in war memorials, US soldiers are nearly always shown 'slumped in exhaustion, acting bravely in battle, and being kind to children' (127) could as easily apply to images used by the *Advertiser* and *Star-Bulletin*. For example, a photograph given prominence on page two of one edition shows an ARVN officer carrying a dead child in his arms. The photograph is entitled 'Viet Cong Executed Her,' and the accompanying text states, 'A South Vietnamese officer carries his dead child from his home. The officer's family was executed by the Viet Cong when they overran his home in a military compound in a suburb of Saigon. He was out leading his troops in Saigon street fighting.' A prominent page-two photograph a few days later entitled 'Marine Rescues Girl,' showed a US soldier carrying a Vietnamese child with the accompanying text, 'A U.S. Marine carries a seriously wounded Vietnamese girl through a shattered wall of her home in Hue during heavy street fighting.'

The *Advertiser* used front-page images of injured or distressed Vietnamese civilians on consecutive days from 2 February to 4 February. While their propaganda value is obvious, the paper's use of the imagery of the home is, perhaps, less so. The photographs suggest that the NLF were outsiders, wild men from the jungle, who attacked the domiciles of America's 'civilized' Vietnamese allies. Moreover, they depicted US and ARVN troops as protectors of innocent children, threatened and brutalized by the enemy. For Americans, depictions of the home under attack by savages may invoke cultural memories of the frontier experience, as historian Jill Lepore reveals: 'When John Foster engraved a map of New England to accompany William Hubbard's Narrative, he marked English territory with tiny houses and church steeples, and Indian territory with trees' (83). The home represents civilization, a safe haven from the savage beasts of the forest, who were, in this instance, the NLF. In contrast to the prominence given to photographs sympathetic to the American cause, on 14 February 1968 the *Star-Bulletin* relegated one of the most famous photographs of the war, Eddie Adams's horrific image of the execution of a bound NLF prisoner by South Vietnam police chief, General Nguyen Ngoc Loan, to page E8. In any event, the *Star-Bulletin* assured readers the man deserved his fate, having been captured 'Carrying a pistol and wearing civilian clothes.'[11]

To be sure, both the *Advertiser* and *Star-Bulletin* displayed some doubts about the US response to Tet, and the overall progress of the war. For instance, the *Advertiser*'s Joseph Kraft queried the impact of American bombing of Saigon and Hue, which resulted in heavy civilian casualties, and the *Star-Bulletin* published a similar report by Tom Wicker on February 21. However, the reporters did not take an oppositional stance; instead, they only echoed concerns shown by the military about the negative propaganda impact of such heavy destruction and loss of life. Wicker stated, 'American military men are not happy about this; they know the result is bound to be thousands upon thousands of homeless refugees [and] human misery.' Furthermore, both papers compared the siege at Khe Sanh to the 1954 French defeat at Dien Bien Phu, and thereby raised the possibility of a humiliating American defeat ('New Dien?'; 'Through Rosy-Hued'). However, they were hardly alone in worrying about the situation at Khe Sanh: for example, President Johnson and General Westmoreland stated publicly that a major assault at Khe Sanh was imminent ('Fighting Intense'), so if a siege atmosphere had developed, the newspapers again took their lead from Washington.

Perhaps the best evidence of this is *Star-Bulletin* coverage of the NLF assault on the US Embassy in Saigon, an event Peter Braestrup cites as a prime example of misleading reporting. Braestrup notes that some reporters initially recorded the fall of the Embassy to communist forces. These reports created a sense of disbelief and pessimism: if US forces could not even protect their own Embassy in Saigon, what hope was there for the rest of the country? (Wyatt 183–4). Yet the *Star-Bulletin* reported on 31 January that the attack on the Embassy had been successfully repelled ('Attack on Embassy'). *Advertiser*' coverage was equally conformist: like the *Star-Bulletin*, it quoted military intelligence sources which confirmed that enemy insurgents had breached the Embassy grounds, but had not been able to enter the Embassy building. American troops soon recaptured the grounds and killed the insurgents. So while there may be some validity to Braestrup's general contention, the evidence suggests, however, that both the *Advertiser* and *Star-Bulletin* rarely strayed from the official line.

## Conclusion

Tom Engelhardt argues that in the decades after World War Two, the US 'was a triumphalist society that lacked a defeat to make tangible its deepest despairs and anxieties' (*History Wars* 239). This triumphalism arose, in part, because US forces had never been defeated in a major war. Americans held a collective belief in their country's exceptional place in history, as a champion of democracy and bastion of freedom. When Communism threatened American values, American newspapers leapt to their country's defense. Americans, journalist Robert Scheer states, believe they are the 'repositories of all virtue' and the enemy 'the repositories of all evil,' a belief system that 'was at the root of the problems of reporting the Vietnam War' ('Difficulties' 119). In his exhaustive study of the media in Vietnam, writer Daniel Hallin observes that American reporters were 'deeply committed to the "national security" consensus that had dominated American politics since the onset of the Cold War, and acted as "responsible" advocates of that consensus' (9). In addition, Herman and Chomsky accuse the media of having a 'pervasive, docile, and unthinking acceptance of a set of patriotic assumptions,' which ensured critical reporting of America's intervention remained within acceptable boundaries (186).

There is considerable merit in these interpretations: as noted previously, supposedly radical journalists like Halberstam and Sheehan expressed concern at the conduct of the war, rather than its underlying causes or its moral validity. Like most American journalists, both wanted their country to be on the winning side — a point missed by many hawkish critics. Jurate Kazickas, a freelance reporter in Vietnam from 1967–68, claimed to be 'passionate about seeing an end to the war,' but was 'deeply offended' by the chants of anti-war protesters. She blamed this on her 'feeling of patriotism' which was 'too strong to march against my own country' (150–1). So while individual journalists recorded events and conditions in Vietnam which often contradicted the official position, it was only after Tet that they began to question the causal reasons for American policy. Mostly, this was a result of the obvious challenge Tet made to the unduly optimistic statements of the Johnson administration and US military commanders, rather than any liberal bias, but it was also a reflection of the public mood, which had begun to turn against the war in 1967 (Zinn 476).

General Westmoreland wrote to the *Advertiser* to express his appreciation for Bob Krauss and Bob Jones' reporting, which he called 'thorough and accurate' (Chaplin 260), and the army awarded Fawcett a citation for 'outstanding coverage of the American soldier as an individual in combat' (Chapin 290–1). However, reporters are only on the first rung of the ladder in the process of getting a story to the American public. Other factors beyond their control often meant the American public was misled about the war, or was sheltered from its harshest aspects. By minimizing enemy gains, quoting official casualty figures, projecting a positive outlook, and looking forward to an American victory, the Honolulu-based establishment press never strayed far from the optimistic military and political point-of-view emanating from Washington.

# Afterword
# Alternative Futures — A Demilitarized Hawai'i

The Hawaiian Islands are often portrayed in tourist brochures and movies as paradise isles, where life is slower and less complicated than in the contiguous United States. To maintain this illusion, however, the American military presence has to be concealed. This is achieved by physical means, such as restricting civilian access to military installations. However, such heavy-handed and obvious actions are, by themselves, inadequate, and must be accompanied by propaganda that makes the military seem natural, welcome, and friendly, and portrays counter-narratives as unpatriotic, unreasonable, impractical, and dangerous to 'national security.' The prevailing political situation is an obstacle to productive discussion about the militarization of Hawai'i. Such issues are not often raised in mainstream Republican/Democratic Hawai'i politics (and are almost completely ignored by politicians in the United States). Furthermore, Hawai'i has become so imbued with militarism that few notice or give much thought to its role, or the problems it causes. Ferguson and Turnbull state,

> For something to be in plain sight it must mark a variety of spaces, projecting itself into a number of landscapes. For something to be hidden it must be indiscernible, camouflaged, inconspicuously folded into the fabric of daily life. The key to this incompatibility is a series of narratives of naturalization imbricate military institutions and discourses into daily life so that they become 'just the way things are.' The narratives of reassurance kick in with a more prescriptive tone, marking the military presence in Hawai'i as necessary, productive, heroic, desirable, good (xiii).

While US military activities are often 'hidden in plain sight,' the problems they cause are obvious and ongoing. Anti-military activists point, for example, to land use issues, economic dependency, the sex trade industry, environmental concerns, destruction of native archeological sites, militarization of Hawai'i's youth, misuse of financial resources, and danger from unexploded ammunition as significant problems caused by the ongoing military presence (Kajihiro, 'Brief'). It is difficult to counteract the effects of decades of pro-military propaganda: Haunani-Kay Trask worries, for example, about the psychological damage of colonialism on her people (*Native* 3), and is concerned that many Hawaiians today conform and behave according to the demands of dominant colonialist ideology. For example, ROTC programs in Hawai'i's schools ensure that, from a young age, students are exposed to the mind-set that militarism is a natural and normal state of affairs. A result of this is, as one female student recalls, 'boys are apathetic, they've had this military crap beat into them by the *haoles* since they're babies to make them docile' (Gray 15). At the very least, such conditioning trains young Hawaiians for careers in the service industries, as bellhops or doormen, waiters and waitresses, or perhaps as policemen and National Guard soldiers. As Albert Memmi has revealed, the colonialist's image of the colonized appears so often, it conditions colonized people to view that image as their own. Memmi states, '[the image of] the colonized as seen by the colonialist [is] widely circulated in the colony and often throughout the world (which, thanks to his newspapers and literature, ends up by being echoed to a certain extent in the conduct and, thus, in the true appearance of the colonized)' (55).

However, militarism is not natural or normal, and its production has always to be underpinned and reinforced by patriotic propaganda. Michael Parenti has identified some of the basic components of propaganda as, 'omission, distortion, and repetition' (*History* 209), and, as I have shown, these mechanisms are a recurring feature of pro-militaristic narratives justifying the US military's role in Hawai'i. There are, however, counter-narratives: Trask's view of military as an occupation force (*Native* 176) gathers weight, as more is revealed about the true nature, cost, and effects of militarism. In 2008, the American Friends Service Committee celebrated 40 years of peace activism, and it continues to work towards the demilitarization of Hawai'i. [Fig. A.1] The Hawaiian Sovereignty Movement has won some notable victories, including ending military live-fire exercises on Kaho'olawe island (Trask, *Native* 68) and interrupting or halting military live-fire exercises at Makua Valley ('U.S. Military Out').

Other anti-military activists offer economic alternatives to the islands dependence on US military spending. Supporters of the military presence

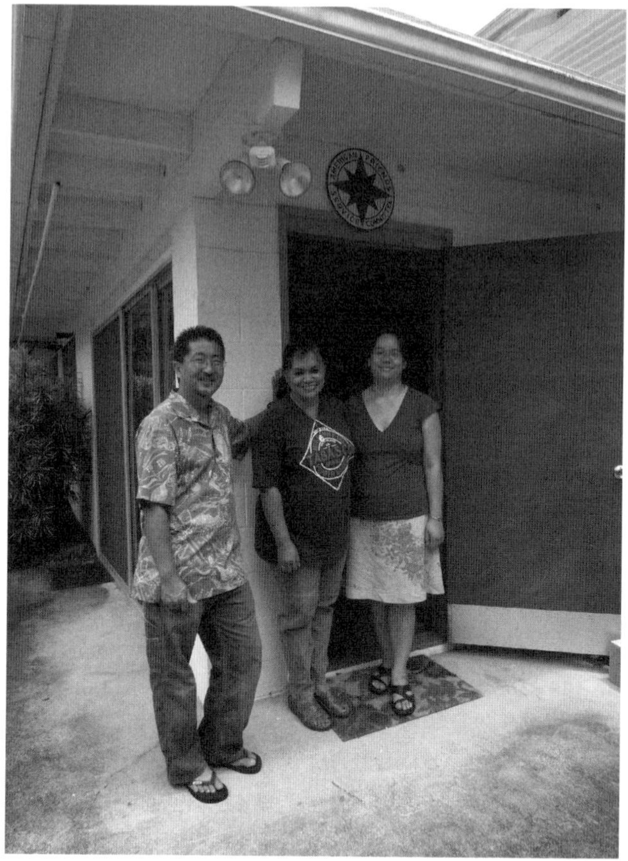

*Figure A.1* American Friends Service Committee, Hawai'i. Photo by Brian Ireland.

argue demilitarization would have a significant detrimental impact on Hawai'i's economy. The military does, after all, provide jobs for 15,000 civilians, spending $3731 million in the year 2000 alone (Schmitt, *Hawai'i Data* 158). Leroy Laney, vice president and chief economist of First Hawaiian Bank states, 'when one balances the known economic contributions from military use against the possible benefits of any proposed civilian use, it is far from clear that the latter is more desirable ... As tourism slows, agriculture fades, and diversification into new export industries eludes the state, keeping the military is all the more important' (278). However, the military is, essentially, a massive Federal program, and if the money invested in what is euphemistically called 'defense' is, instead, spent on job creation, many more civilian jobs could be created than those presently supported by military spending (Albertini *et al* 63). Albertini *et al* state:

> It has long been taken for granted that massive Pentagon expenditures are a great asset to Hawai'i's development. A closer examination of the economic facts, however, indicates that Hawai'i's military is not necessarily a healthy force in the economy of the Aloha state (62).

Only 5 percent of the companies in the state get 62 percent of all military contracts; these companies are multi-national and not solely dependent on military orders. Furthermore, most of the land on O'ahu currently controlled by the US military was donated by the State of Hawai'i, either free-of-charge, or for a nominal amount. The state does not, therefore, profit from renting land to the military. Nor do military personnel contribute as much to the economy of Hawai'i as their supporters, or their own boosterism, claims. Much of their spending takes place at on-base 'PX' stores, which, like the soldiers themselves, do not pay state income taxes. The military, therefore, *competes* with local business rather than supports them. In addition, because 20 percent of military personnel live off base, they add to the general housing shortage in the state and to overcrowding, particularly on O'ahu (Albertini *et al* 63–4).

In 1960, *National Geographic* declared that the US military presence aided the tourist industry, which still competes with military spending as the State's main source of income. If it was ever true, as the magazine states, that, '[t]heir presence ... does much to generate tourist travel to the islands' (Simpich Jr. 9), the extant relationship between the military and the tourist industry is generally one of competitors fighting over dwindling resources such as land and water. For example, the tourist industry relies on the continuing physical beauty of the islands, whereas the military has little interest in such things. As Trask notes, when the military appropriates land, it files the environmental impact statements required by law, and 'takes the heat' at public hearings. However, its interests, and those of the environment, are often in opposition. As such, it is difficult to find fault with Trask's observation that, 'the military ... has never cared much for the environment' ('Stealing' 266).[1]

Native Hawaiians traditionally have close spiritual ties to their land or *'āina*. There is an obvious conflict of interest, therefore, when the military controls 25 percent of the land on O'ahu, and in Hawai'i, 7.5 percent in total (Trask, 'Stealing' 266). Much of this land was originally set aside to build homes for Hawaiians. However, the State of Hawai'i later reserved it for military use only (Kajihiro, 'Brief' 3). Furthermore, the military often competes with the local community for resources. For example, fresh water supplies on crowded O'ahu are constantly under threat from pesticides and general overuse. However, priority seems to be given the US military needs: in 1980, for example, 'the Honolulu Board of Water supply was limited to 77 million gallons a day, while the Army and Navy alone took 27 million gallons daily' (Albertini *et al* 64). Despite the prevailing view that the economy of Hawai'i would suffer without the military, in fact, the military adds significantly to the shortage of land, amenities, and resources in the islands, and on O'ahu in particular.

There are alternatives to militarism, but piercing the military's public relations and propaganda 'ring of steel' is difficult. Through a process of propaganda, disinformation, and limiting the political debate, the militarization of Hawai'i is portrayed most often as beneficial, protective, and natural. Such is the dominance of pro-military narratives that discussions about demilitarization are silenced, ignored, or made to appear as radical ideas at the margins of sensible political discussion. For example, few people today know of the vibrant underground press that, in the 1960s and early 1970s, opposed militarism in Hawai'i, and the war in Vietnam. Instead, the prevailing memory of that time is of a largely supportive public, and of Hawai'i as a welcoming rest and recreation area for returning troops. Hawai'i's war memorials and monuments tell a patriotic story of duty and honor, and its military graveyards a similarly monoglossic tale of noble sacrifice for American values. Honolulu's Army Museum creates a history of the islands which justifies American military intervention, and supports the continued military presence. When the military writes its own history of the islands, it utilizes a unitary, centripetal language, reaching self-serving conclusions based on martial themes of regulation, discipline, and order. And cinematic depictions of Hawai'i situate the islands in a cautionary tale of sneak attack by envious foreigners, and ongoing warnings about military unpreparedness.

Cracks are, nevertheless, starting to appear in the 'sugar-coated fortress,' as it has proved increasingly difficult to silence the eloquent, compelling and strident claims of modern-day sovereignty and peace activists. For many Americans, Hawai'i is simply an exotic holiday location, a warm and welcoming place, different enough to offer a taste of the unusual, but also familiar enough to be a non-threatening home away from home. If they ever ponder questions of sovereignty and ownership, the patriotic memory of their countrymen's blood sacrifice at Pearl Harbor no doubt reassures them of the secure status of their 50th state. In contrast, a growing minority in Hawai'i have come to recognize their homeland as little more than a militarized outpost of empire, a one-time American colony, now annexed and integrated into the state, whose native inhabitants, nevertheless, remain an oppressed and exploited minority in their own land.

# Notes

## Introduction

1 According to Schmitt, the highest number of military personnel in Hawai'i was 400,000 during World War Two. More recently, the highest number of military personnel and dependents peaked at 134,000 in 1988 (*Hawai'i Data* 158).
2 In a 1926 study of the US invasion of the Philippines, authors Moorfield Story and Marcial Lichauco tell how 'the President of the United States [in 1925] still asserts that the islands came to us "unsought"' (Loewen, *Lies Across* 141).
3 Unless stated, all other data is from this source.
4 For example, in his book *John Tyler: the Accidental President*, historian Edward P. Crapol describes a 'classic display of French gunboat diplomacy' in the islands (137), and a second incident of 'unauthorized gunboat diplomacy' by the British (158). However, he chooses not to describe similar actions by Americans as 'gunboat diplomacy.'
5 A notable exception is Professor William R. Chapman, Director of the Graduate Program in Historic Preservation at the University of Hawai'i. As a preservationist, Chapman believes the memorial is an important part of Hawai'i history and should be conserved. He states, 'There are so few major important buildings from the territorial period that to lose any one at this point would be a tragedy' (Leidemann).

## Chapter 1 War Stories: A Militarized History of Hawai'i

1 The 'ap' in Captain Thomas ap Catesby Jones, is a Welsh term meaning 'son of'.
2 According to Ralph S. Kuykendall, conspirator Lorrin Thurston would later admit that the new constitution 'was not in accordance with law' (371). The source for this quote, Kuykendall's *Hawaiian Kingdom*, is listed in *Pearl's* bibliography (405).
3 Most historians who have written about Hawai'i could not speak Hawaiian and therefore only had access to English-language sources. More recently, however, a new generation of Hawaiian historians has unearthed a wealth of sources written in their native language, including newspaper archives and, in the case of Noenoe Silva, an anti-annexation petition signed by over 21,000 people. The petition is the basis for Silva's remarkable book, *Aloha Betrayed*, in which she details the extent of resistance to the overthrow of Lili'uokalani's government.
4 'Revisionist' in a positive sense: as Paul Boyer notes, 'all good scholars are "revisionists," continually questioning an revising standard interpretations on the basis of new evidence, deeper analysis, or the fresh perspectives offered by the passage of time' ('Whose History?' 131).

5 The Museum of the Pacific War in Fredericksburg, Texas, for example, is notable according to Loewen more for 'things not mentioned' than its actual contents. These omissions include visual images — a lack of photographs or representations of dead bodies — and also historical events or narratives that contradict the commonly held view of World War Two as the 'good war.' Loewen concludes that 'The Nimitz Museum not only prettifies the Pacific War, it also prettifies America's role in it' (188–95).

6 A rare example of a dispute that did raise public consciousness occurred in 1995. To commemorate the 50th anniversary of the end of World War Two, the Smithsonian Institution's National Air and Space Museum planned to exhibit the *Enola Gay*, the airplane which was the delivery vehicle in the atomic bombing of Hiroshima in 1945. The theme of the exhibit was that the bombing not only ended World War Two but also, in effect, started the Cold War. Conservative politicians and commentators such as Senator Bob Dole, Rush Limbaugh, Newt Gingrich and Pat Buchanan claimed the exhibit was divisive and unnecessarily 'political.' World War Two was the 'good war,' after all, and the divisive arguments of Vietnam-era politics should not be brought to bear on the 'greatest generation.' Conservatives argued that the proposed exhibit made America the villain and the Japanese the victims of World War Two. Furthermore, the inclusion of a narrative about the beginning of the Cold War brought into question the decision to drop the bomb. If allowed to proceed, conservatives argued, the exhibit would dishonor America's war veterans. Under pressure from politicians, the American Legion, and a section of the general public that had been motivated to act by the controversy, the museum eventually backed down and its director resigned. As Edward Linenthal and Tom Engelhardt note in *History Wars*, 'The fiftieth anniversary of any major event that put large numbers of people in peril naturally tends to establish a protective membrane around the commemorative moment. This accounts for the outrage.' (4) However, it also seems clear that at least some of the uproar occurred because of the public's fear that 'revisionist' history (in the negative sense of the word) had penetrated the hallowed halls of the Smithsonian Museum, which, until that moment, had been seen as a metonymy for historical integrity and truthfulness.

7 I use the word 'partially' because land was still passed down to descendants of the *ali'i* by *kauoha* (verbal will) as if they were all their own *Mō'ī*.

## Chapter 2 Remembering and Forgetting at Waikīkī's Great War Memorial

1 From this point on the *Pacific Commercial Advertiser* will be referred to as the *Advertiser*.

2 These organizations included the Outdoor Circle, Chamber of Commerce, Rotary Club, Ad Club, Free Kindergarten, Hawaiian Historical Society, Child Welfare Commission, Humane Society, Outrigger Club, Pan-Pacific Club and the Daughters of Hawai'i. Reclaiming land was, in many cases, doublespeak for appropriating it from small landowners, who were mostly Asian and Native Hawaiian. This lack of concern for small-ownership land rights was not unusual for either the rich elites in Hawai'i or for the *Advertiser*.

Some 20 years before, when 38 acres of Chinatown was destroyed by fire, the *Advertiser* had stated that 'the fire would give the white man's business district room to expand' (Daws 303).

3 Although not considered one of the Big Five, the Dillingham family had dredging, construction and real estate interests that coincided with the interests of the ruling economic oligarchy (Kent 72; Cooper and Daws 3).

4 These included the Daughters of Hawai'i, Rotary Club, Outdoor Circle, Pan-Pacific Union, Central YMCA, Hawaiian Societies, Junior Auxiliary, Hawaiian congregation, St Andrew's Cathedral, War Camp Community Service, Hawaiian Women's Guild, Kamehameha Alumni Association, Hawaiian Civic Club, Order of Kamehameha, Longshoremen's Mutual Aid Association, Knights of Pythias, House of the Chiefs of Hawai'i, and the Ad Club.

5 See also 'Memorial Project Takes Real Shape'; 'Pan-Pacific Art Committee to Plan Memorial'; 'Statue or Memorial Hall Issue Must Be Determined'; 'Proposes Aid For Memorial Funds' and 'Rotary Club to Honor Officials of Old Republic.'

6 One wonders if the title of this article was intended to remind readers of D.W. Griffith's *Birth of a Nation* (1915), a movie which championed white supremacy.

7 Revealingly, Hathaway applies the term 'unprincipled' only to those who organized labor unions, but not those involved in the overthrow of the sovereign state of Hawai'i or the theft of native lands.

8 Burnham was a well-known architect responsible also for the design of the United Spanish War Veterans Memorial (aka The Spirit of '98) situated at the Wadsworth Hospital Center, West Los Angeles, erected in 1950. Text from the plaque on the memorial reads: '1898 — To Those Who Volunteered and Extended the Hand of Liberty to Alien Peoples — 1902.'

9 All further references to Fairbanks or his proposed monument are from this source unless otherwise stated.

10 In John Ford's 1943 documentary *December 7*, 'Uncle Sam' describes the process of 'civilization' undertaken by *haole* missionaries and business men as 'a pioneering story that compares favorably with the opening of the West.'

11 The use of Native Hawaiian imagery in the designs is especially problematic since it appears that they were excluded from the whole process. With the exception of Prince Jonah Kuhio, whose name appears in only one early account of the War Memorial Committee, there does not appear to be any input from the Native community at all ('Statue Or Memorial'). It cannot be taken for granted that Kuhio represented Native Hawaiian interests on the War Memorial Committee. Although he had been imprisoned for his role in defending Queen Lili'uokalini during the 1895 uprising, Kuhio later accepted a role in the Republican Party running in opposition to Home Rule candidate Robert Wilcox in the 1902 election for delegate to Congress. Perhaps Kuhio thought that in this role he could best defend the interests of the Hawaiian people. Certainly his efforts as delegate after he was triumphant in the election seem to suggest this. For example, in the 1904 Territorial elections he pushed for devolution of local government powers away from Honolulu and towards the larger individual Hawaiian islands. He was also instrumental in the establishment of the Hawaiian Homes Commission Act of 1920. However, as a figurehead for Hawai'i's *haole* business elites, Kuhio attracted many Native

Hawaiian votes away from the decidedly pro-Native Hawaiian Home Rule Party. Within ten years of Robert Wilcox's defeat at the hands of Kuhio, the Home Rule Party was finished (Daws 293–302).

12 For a fuller discussion of these masquerades, see Deloria.

13 These photographs, of clothed white explorers dwarfed by nature, demonstrate a familiar theme of American photography and painting. For instance, Thomas Cole (1801–1847) was a member of the Hudson River School of American artists. This was the first batch of American artists who focused on painting American landscapes instead of European. Cole's painting *Pastoral* (1836), from his quartet of paintings *The Course of Empire*, shows, for example, a toga-clad and bearded man who embodies white civilization foregrounded against uncivilized nature — massive trees and threatening mountains and skies. Similarly, Asher Brown Durand's *Kindred Spirits* shows two white males peering over a cliff against a mountainous backdrop. And Thomas Moran's *The Grand Canyon of the Yellowstone* shows two miniscule white travelers in contrast with the vastness of the Grand Canyon.

14 The Natatorium was a form of control over the uncontrollable — a lesson to the locals perhaps that nature can be defeated by Western knowhow. It served yet another more practical purpose too: in the 1920s the majority of Americans could not swim. Although ancient cultures like the Egyptians have practiced swimming as long ago as 2400 years, in the West, swimming did not become a popular pastime until the mid-1800s. Indeed, in the Middle Ages, communal swimming was seen as a way to spread disease and was thus discouraged by organized religion. Swimming did not even become an Olympic sport until the 1890s. In the early twentieth century, the profession of life guarding on open beaches was in its embryonic stages, and some early tactics, such as that of a lifeguard carrying a rope out to a troubled swimmer who would then be reeled in by two other lifeguards, was not successful or practical because it required three lifeguards to save one person (*History of the Beach*). While Native Hawaiians had been surfing for at least a thousand years, and were rightly reputed to be strong swimmers, many tourists stayed away from the water because they could not swim. As authors Lena Lencek and Gideon Bosker note, 'In those days, most bathers were seriously unprepared for the sea' (147). The spate of natatorium building in the US in the late nineteenth century occurred, therefore, as a direct result of the American population's poor swimming skills. In comparison to the open sea, in a natatorium poor swimmers could easily be saved, or save themselves. In that Hawai'i was being molded into a popular tourist destination in the 1920s, the erection of a natatorium can therefore be considered as O'ahu's first modern man-made tourist attraction.

15 Mullgardt was well-known both locally and nationally: he designed the Theo H. Davis Building in Bishop Street (1919–1921) and, along with Bernard Maybeck, Mullgardt was on the Architectural Commission the Panama-Pacific International Exposition in San Francisco (February 20–December 4, 1915).

16 The Chicago Columbian Exposition of 1893 directly inspired many of America's *beaux-arts*-designed buildings that date from the early part of the twentieth century. *Beaux-arts*-style buildings include the Nebraska State Capitol in Lincoln (1916–1928), Charles McKim's Boston Public Library (1888–1895), Carnegie Hall, Grand Central Station, the Rush Rhees Library at the University of

Rochester, and the New York Public Library. The Exposition's master plan was a classic example of *beaux-arts* arrangement, emphasizing symmetry and uniformity of color with a white marble effect. The idea of designers Burnham and Root was to show that America's past was a European one. In an era of rising immigration by the supposedly inferior Southern Europeans, and of American imperialism in the Pacific, the Exposition's White City exhibited foreigners in racially derogatory ways. The midway featured ethnological exhibitions, including examples of Native Hawaiians, for the amusement of white Americans. It invited Americans to contrast the 'barbarous' and 'uncivilized' antics of these supposedly inferior races with the grandeur of the European style architecture in other parts of the Exposition. William H. Jordy notes, 'White City conjured a vision of a marble America from the urban styles of Europe ... In its Roman and baroque trappings, moreover, the imperial flavor of the White City accorded with the imperial flavor of American culture at the end of the century.' Not only did the Exposition emphasize America's 'civilized' European origins, through the uniformity of its layout it also asked visitors to contrast the refinement and sophistication of the city as opposed to the disorder of nature, rural, and the frontier. Jordy states 'It was not merely, or even principally, the imperialism of foreign affairs which the symbolism of the Exposition made concrete, but the hegemony of the metropolis' (79).

17 These atavistic, social-Darwinist ideas were fueled by pseudo-scientific research at America's universities. For example, Stanley Porteus, head of the Psychology department at the University of Hawai'i from 1922 to 1948 states in *Temperament and Race*, 'During the last 400 years [western races] have been carrying the burden of an almost endless struggle for liberty' (330). Porteus believed it was the 'white man's burden' in Hawai'i to educate and 'free' lesser races. He repeated Nietzsche's repugnant arguments about eugenics: 'Side by side with the growth of medical science has been the development of this impulse towards preserving and perpetuating the unfit' (331) and advocated selective sterilization as a 'sensible measure' in place of natural selection which modern medicine has interfered with (333). Porteus, an Australian by birth, believed that countries such as Canada, United States and Australia 'belong to the white race by right of peaceful conquest,' that they are now 'Nordic strongholds' and that any lessoning of suspicion towards [for example] the Japanese would amount to 'race suicide' (336).

18 A few years later, in 1925, the Legion's national Headquarters in Indianapolis would be built in that fashion. That building, half of which's fourth floor is designed to replicate a senate chamber, has been described as 'combining all the advantages of Greek beauty and modern efficiency' (Duffield 14).

19 Even the addition of the 'Three Soldiers' statue and flag, considered by many conservatives as a more patriotic design than the wall itself, caused controversy — Maya Lin referred to it contemptuously as 'drawing a moustache' on her design (Young 328). Indeed, it is hard to imagine any design for a Vietnam Veterans Memorial that was imbued with such ceremonial importance as to be situated in Washington DC, the nation's capital 'which was consciously designed as the ceremonial center of the nation' (Linenthal, *Sacred* 2).

20 These figures may be underestimates: there was also a Naval Militia of the Territory of Hawai'i, which was established in 1915. At the outbreak of the war

with Germany, the Naval Militia was federalized and 50 enlisted men and officers were accepted into federal military service (Warfield 69–70).

21 Whereas in the United States, the Bureau of Naturalization normally denied citizenship to most aliens of Asian ancestry, deeming them to be 'non-white' and therefore ineligible under current citizenship laws, in Hawai'i, federal district court judge, Horace W. Vaughan, took the view that all who had been drafted were entitled to US citizenship (Salyer 853–7). Given Vaughan's aforementioned opposition to Japanese language schools, his uncharacteristically liberal views on soldier naturalization remain hard to fathom. Salyer determines, somewhat unconvincingly, that it was a 'change of heart, moved by the rhetoric of militaristic patriotism.'

## Chapter 3 'Unknown Soldiers': Remembering Hawai'i's Great War Dead

1 The League played its part in Bureau of Investigation raids against Industrial Workers of the World (IWW) halls in September 1917. The raids were politically motivated, but many of the charges against IWW members that ensued were related to draft dodging. The League later took part in the March 1918 'slacker raids' to round up draft resisters.

2 The seven soldiers killed in action in France are Private Louis J. Gaspar, Sergeant Apau Kau, Private Antone R. Mattos, Private John R. Rowe, Private Henry K. Unuivi, Manuel G.L. Valent Jr. (rank unknown), and Captain Edward Fuller.

3 Not only is there US government involvement in the sites of memory discussed here, through authorization, funding, construction, and maintenance, the history the sites present carries the imprimatur of official history by claiming to speak for the nation. For example, the inscriptions at the National Cemetery of the Pacific use the first person plural pronoun 'we,' to ensure visitors are aware the sacrifices made were for their benefit, and also so that they can bask in the military victory that was achieved.

4 For example, Benigno Rivera, whose grave marker (A1066) reads, 'Private, U.S. Army, World War I, DEC 16 1893–DEC 5 1980.'

5 Unless otherwise noted, most of the raw statistical data has been extracted from document reference M-477, 'United Veterans' Service Council Records' (UVSCR), from the Hawai'i State Archives.

6 Paul Auerbach, Richard Catton, Henry Chapman, Alexander Cornelison, Carel De Roo (born in Holland), Frank Dolin, George Dwight, Henry Evans, Edward Fuller, Ivan Graham, Francis Green, Edmund Hedemann (father was Danish Consul in Hawai'i), John Kana (born in Cardiff, Wales), Kenneth Marr, Philip Mills, George O'Connor, John O'Dowda, Frank Raymond (born in France), William Riley (a Canadian citizen), William Scholtz, Moses Thomas, George Turner, Charles Warren, Clarence Watson and David Withington.

7 Adam Aki, Frank Aki, Archibald Bal, Ephraim Ezera, Abraham Hauli, Daniel Io(e)pa, Edward Iskow, Herman Kaaukea, Kuulei Kaea, Edward Kahokuoluna, Sam Kainoa, Charles Kalailoa, Rolph Kauhane, Charles Kino, Edward Kuaimoku, John Makua, Sam Moke, Peter Naia, Joe Puali, John Rowe, Henry Unuivi, James Waialeale and Levi Waihoikala.

8 Bragee Arcilo, Louis Gaspar, Manuel Gouveia, Antone Mattos, Manuel Rames, Richard Rodriques, Pablo Santos, John Silva, Manuel Valent and Frank Viera.
9 Frederick Char, Apau Kau, Han Lee, and George Tom.
10 Chin Sung Chuy.
11 See *History of the USS Schurz* at: http://www.ecu.edu/maritime/projects/2000/schurz/history_of_the_uss_schurz.html and *U.S. Navy Ships Sunk or Damaged from Various Causes during World War I* at: http://www.usmm.org/ww1navy.html both (accessed 9 August 2003).
12 The Waikīkī War Memorial refers to Manuel Ramos, not Rames. All other sources suggest his correct surname is Rames. See, for example, the United States Transport Service's passenger list, printed in the *The New York Times* on 9 February 1918, which refers to Private M. Rames of Maui, attached to the 20th Engineers, Company E, 6th Battalion. A list of the deceased published in the same paper a few weeks later mentions Manuel Rames, son of Marira Rames of Paia, Maui ('New Tuscania List'). In addition, the United States Department of Veterans Affairs, Nationwide Gravesite Locator website, lists a Manuel Rames, a private in Company E of the 20th Engineers, who died on February 5th, 1918, and is buried at section WH EU SITE 1321 in Arlington National Cemetery.
13 The other two are Henry Kolomoku Umuivi, whose name appears on the West Virginia Veterans Memorial, located in the State Capitol grounds in Charleston; and Philip Overton Mills, who is commemorated on four separate memorials.
14 Notable volunteers included writer John Dos Passos and poet E.E. Cummings (Carr, Virginia 127–8).
15 As journalist Michael Sledge points out, 'A soldier's widow had the highest priority in determining disposition of remains. After her, the choice fell to the children, oldest son first. If there were no widow or children, the soldier's father had the right to decide. If he were deceased, then the mother could decide. Following her were all brothers, oldest first, then all sisters, oldest first. If the deceased had no surviving father, mother, or siblings, uncles and then aunts decided' (141).
16 Another two were disinterred and reburied in the United States. These were Captain Edward Fuller, who is (buried at the United States Naval Academy Cemetery at Annapolis, Maryland, and Manuel Rames, who is buried at Arlington National Cemetery.
17 The full text of the inscriptions at the cemetery is available in the American Battle Monuments Commission's publication, *Honolulu Memorial, National Memorial Cemetery of the Pacific, Honolulu, Hawaii.*
18 They are Videl Agar (states 'Agan' on headstone), Bragee Arcilo, Ariston Arozal, Cipriano Bega, Anastacio Bueno, Esteban Castillo, Chin Sung Chuy (states 'Sung Choy Chin' on headstone), Bidal Ciempoon (states 'Clempoon' on headstone), Julian Daguman, Juan De La Cruz (states 'Juan Cruz' on headstone), Rufino Esbra, Anatelio Eugenio (states 'Anatalio' on headstone), Mariano Monsieur (states surname as 'Mariano' and forename as 'Monseuir' on headstone), Aurelio Orbe (states 'Arilo' on headstone), Juan Quibal, Pablo R. Santos (states 'Santes' on headstone), Jose Sarsosa (states 'Kase Sarosa' on headstone), Rufo Tenebre, and Paustino Tingking (states 'Paustino King' on headstone). The discrepancies suggest that either the US Army records are incorrect or,

perhaps more likely, some of the names listed on the plaque at the war memorial in Honolulu have been listed incorrectly.

19 The others are Paul Harold Auerbach, Esteban Castillo, Frederick Char, Carel J. De Roo, George K. Dwight, Henry J. Evans, Edmund Hedemann, Herman Kaaukea, John Stephen O'Dowda, William Kalauaikaumakoawakea Scholtz, George B. Tom, and Clarence J. Watson.

20 Paul Harold Auerbach, Richard Belmont Catton, George K. Dwight, Henry J. Evans, and William K. Scholtz.

21 Ephraim Ezera who died of tuberculosis at Schofield Barracks on 7 July 1918, Edward Kahokuoluna who died of pneumonia at Dept. Hospital on 10 July 1918, Abraham Hauli who died of pneumonia at Honolulu on 7 February 1919, and Charles Kino who died of pneumonia at Dept. Hospital Honolulu on 18 September 1918.

## Chapter 4 Hooray for Haolewood? Hawai'i on Film

1 In attempting to make sweeping statements about a large number of movies across a number of decades, it is perhaps useful to recall Michael Parenti's disclaimer: 'Do I select only the [movies and television shows] that paint the entertainment media in the worst possible light? If anything, I give disproportionately greater attention to the relatively few quality films and programs of progressive hue' (intro.). In this study, I focus on those movies about Hawai'i and the Pacific that are generally considered as the best examples of the genre, such as *White Shadows in the South Seas* and *From Here to Eternity*. Parenti also reminds his critics that, 'For almost every criticism I make of the "make-believe media", one could find some exceptions' (intro.).

2 Kahanamoku did appear in two post-war movies, *Wake of the Red Witch* (1948), and *Mister Roberts* (1955), neither of which are about Hawai'i.

3 Of the 1946 strike, one labor union leader stated, 'This victory makes Hawaii part of the United States for all Hawaiians, especially the workers. It is no longer a feudal colony' (Kent 135).

4 For example, Americans elected President Jimmy Carter, a relatively unknown Washington outsider, untainted by the Vietnam War or political scandals, partly on his promise to heal America's wounds. Movies also reflected this sense of healing: the main characters in *The Deer Hunter* (1978) sing, for example, a unifying, patriotic anthem, 'God Bless America,' in the film's climactic scene. Film critic Gilbert Adair states, '[Director Michael] Cimino's intentions were ... to restore his audience's confidence in their country's regenerative powers' (90).

5 Ellul's definition of propaganda is, 'a set of methods employed by an organized group that wants to bring about the active or passive participation in its actions of a mass of individuals, psychologically unified through psychological manipulations and incorporated in an organization' (61).

## Chapter 5 Hawai'i's Press and the Vietnam War

1 Trask did not mention *Honolulu Weekly*, which was first published in 1991, two years before the first edition of her book. The *Weekly* prints many news items and editorials critical of the US military.

2 In February 2001, one of these 'freebies' led to tragedy: the US nuclear submarine *Greeneville,* carrying a number of civilians on a 'fact-finding' trip, accidentally sunk a Japanese training ship *Ehime Maru* killing nine Japanese civilians, including a number of high school students. Despite an official military enquiry, the exact circumstances of the accident remain unclear.

3 Reporter Carl Bernstein claimed in a 1977 *Rolling Stone Magazine* article, that Alsop was one of over 400 American journalists who, during the Cold War, secretly carried out assignments for the Central Intelligence Agency in what became known as Operation Mockingbird ('CIA and the Media').

4 Such was the confidence of government and Pentagon officials in their ability to manage the news by pressurizing editors and owners that by 1965, Arthur Sylvester, who was President Johnson's Assistant Secretary of Defense for Public Affairs, was confident or arrogant enough to tell a group of reporters, 'I don't even have to talk to you people. I know how to deal with you through our editors and publishers in the States' (Carpenter 138).

5 In the documentary *Manufacturing Consent*, Noam Chomsky identifies six of these filters: (i) selection of topics, (ii) distribution of concerns, (iii) emphasis, (iv) framing of issues, (v) selection of information, and (vi) setting the boundaries of debate.

6 *Carrion Crow* used similar tactics: although its inaugural issue was only four pages long, *Crow* devoted a full page to anti-war issues, including a letter/poem by a soldier on leave from Vietnam. In it he stated, 'I'm really a kid ... I don't want to kill. Military discipline is coercion of the moral sense' ('Letter From Vietnam'). Below the letter is a cartoon drawing of the White House with the caption 'black is white, night is day, war is peace,' which infers that the official version of history is a façade, and that underground press readers were privy to information that mainstream newspaper readers lacked.

7 Warner's analysis portrayed the South Vietnamese insurgency as a foreign-led communist uprising, although evidence was available at that time of the corruption of South Vietnamese officials, the weakness of President Diem, America's policy of undermining the Geneva Accords, and its scorning of North Vietnamese goodwill. Although he was a communist, Ho Chi Minh had, for example, declared Vietnamese independence after World War Two using the terminology of the American Declaration of Independence (Young 10–11). Historian John Stoessinger believes that Ho was 'as much a Vietnamese nationalists as a Communist' (100), not just a pawn of Soviet or Chinese communists. This Vietnamese regime demonstrated this in 1978, when it invaded Cambodia to defeat the Khmer Rouge, and in its conflict with Chinese communist forces in 1979. Ho was not prepared to allow outside communist powers to threaten Vietnam's independence. It seems clear now, as it did to many dissident voices in the US at the time, that if Vietnam had been allowed its independence according to the terms of the Geneva Accords, it would have developed into an independent state analogous to Tito's Yugoslavia, not just a puppet state under the control of either China or Russia.

8 Under the Johnson administration, a policy of 'maximum candor' had replaced the previous administration's strategy of providing as little information as possible. Ostensibly, the purpose of this new policy was to aid the press's coverage of the war. However, its true goal was to direct press coverage, and ensure that the American public received only the most optimistic version

of events. Reporters had previously spoken of a 'credibility gap' between what they were told, and what they saw. Cooperation from official sources was unforthcoming, so reporters like Halberstam and Sheehan sought their own stories and provided their own analysis and context. In practice, maximum candor bombarded journalists with information, and therefore ensured that the official version of events received maximum coverage. The purpose of this policy was, therefore, to set the agenda and manage the flow of news. According to Clarence R. Wyatt, maximum candor achieved its goals: 'It made the press dependent upon the government for information and, consequently, usually made what the government wanted told the first and most prominent aspect of any particular story' (163).

9 See also the *Advertiser's* coverage of mainland peace protests such as 'N.Y. War Protesters Battle Police in Village' and 'Chicago Police Battle Rioters.'

10 Certainly, the Tet Offensive failed if judged only in terms of land won and lost, or casualties inflicted balanced against casualties incurred. For instance, while 9000 American or South Vietnamese lives were lost during Tet, over 58,000 North Vietnamese and NLF combatants died — equal to the number of American deaths in the whole of the war. However, the offensive freed as many as 200,000 prisoners, which more than made up for NVA and NLF combat losses (Franklin 95).

11 A few weeks previous to this, the *Advertiser* featured an API picture of a communist suspect being tortured by American forces. The suspect had a towel placed over his face, and was held down by two soldiers while another poured water into his mouth. While one might expect a degree of outrage from the paper, instead the *Advertiser* describes this coyly as soldiers 'Prying answers out of an uncooperative Viet Cong' (Jan 23, 1968: A2).

## Afterword

1 The Defense Department has, for example, decided to station the Stryker Brigade Combat Team in Hawai'i, despite the concerns of 2000 citizens who contributed to a Final Environmental Impact Statement, and the opposition of three Native Hawaiian organizations. A Stryker is a 19-ton, eight-wheeled Armored Personnel Carrier. This new unit will add 300 of these vehicles to Hawai'i's fragile landscape and will require 28 construction projects, including extensive building work at Schofield Barracks and Pohakuloa Training Area on the Big Island, and the construction of new road links to and from Schofield Barracks, Helemano Military Reservation and Dillingham Military Reservation (Rhen; Cole, William).

# Works Cited


'Actual Work on Waikiki Project Almost in Sight.' *Pacific Commercial Advertiser* June 27, 1920: 1, 3.

'Ad Club Warned Americans Must Fight Radicals.' *Pacific Commercial Advertiser* Sep 25, 1919: 1.

Adair, Gilbert. *Hollywood's Vietnam*. London: Heinemann, 1989.

'Adm. Sharp Believes Peace Protests Harmful.' *Honolulu Advertiser* May 10, 1967: 1.

Akaka, Daniel Kahkina. 'In Tribute to Private John Rowe,' Memorial Day, Oahu Cemetery, May 27, 2002. Accessed July 3, 2009. http://akaka.senate.gov/public/index.cfm?FuseAction=Speeches.Home&month=5&year=2002&release_id=987

Albertini, Jim, Nelson Foster, Wally Inglis and Gil Roeder. *The Dark Side of Paradise: Hawaii in a Nuclear World*. Honolulu: Catholic Action of Hawaii/Peace Education Project, 1980.

Alderson, William T. and Shirley P. Low. *Interpretation of Historic Sites*. Nashville: American Assoc. for State and Local History, 1976.

'Allied Tanks Smash Into Reds in Hue.' *Honolulu Advertiser* Feb 2, 1968: A1.

Alsop, Joseph. 'Firmness Called for in Southeast Asia.' Editorial. *The Free-Lance Star* (Fredericksburg, VA.) May 5, 1962: 4.

Ambrose, Stephen E. *Rise to Globalism: American Foreign Policy Since 1938*. Harmondsworth, Middlesex, England & New York: Penguin, 1983.

'American Legion Plans Memorials at Waikiki Park.' *Pacific Commercial Advertiser* Aug 10, 1920: 1.

'American Legion to Meet Tonight.' *Pacific Commercial Advertiser* Sep 18, 1919: 4.

'American Legion Urges Anti-Alien Land Law Passage.' *Pacific Commercial Advertiser* Mar 2, 1920: 2.

'American Legion Wants Schools to Teach U.S. Ideals.' *Pacific Commercial Advertiser* Apr 1, 1920: 3.

'Americanism is Part of Library Work.' *Pacific Commercial Advertiser* May 8, 1920: 3.

'Americanization of Islands One of Chief Duties of Legion, Says Commander As Convention Opens.' *Pacific Commercial Advertiser* Feb 24, 1920: 5.

'An Open Letter to my Brothers and Sisters of Hawaii.' *Hawaii Free Press* July 1969: 2.

Anthony, Joseph Garner. *Hawaii Under Army Rule*. Honolulu: UP of Hawaii, 1975.

Anzaldúa, Gloria. *Borderlands: The New Mestiza*. San Francisco: Aunt Lute, 1987.

Apollo [Movie] Guide. http://www.angelfire.com/film/pearlharbormovies/eternity.html Accessed July 24, 2003.

Applegate, Edd. *Literary Journalism: a Biographical Dictionary of Writers and Editors*. Westport, Conn.: Greenwood, 1996.

'Are We in Danger of Losing a Good Neighbor? The Army in Hawaii.' *Midweek* May 10, 2000.

Arnett, Peter. *Live From the Battlefield: From Vietnam to Baghdad: 35 Years in the World's War Zones*. New York: Simon & Schuster, 1994

Ashford, Clarence W. 'Republic Only in Name: A Hawaiian Exile's Experiences Graphically Told.' *New York Times* Mar 29, 1895: 2.

'Assignments of Artillery.' *New York Times* Mar 21, 1899: 5.

'Attack on Embassy is Repulsed.' *Honolulu Star-Bulletin* Jan 31, 1968: A1.

'Attacks of Desperation.' Editorial. *Honolulu Star-Bulletin* Feb 1, 1968: A16.

'Back Home.' *Honolulu Advertiser* Mar 15, 1922: 3.

Bakhtin, Mikhail. *The Dialogic Imagination: Four Essays*, Ed. Michael Holquist, trans. Caryl Emerson & Michael Holquist. Austin: U of Texas P, 1981.

Bailey, Beth and David Farber. *The First Strange Place: Race and Sex in World War II Hawaii*. Baltimore & London: Johns Hopkins UP, 1992.

Barber, Bernard. 'Place, Symbol, and Utilitarian Function in War Memorials.' *Social Forces* 28.1 (1949): 64–8.

Barry, John. 'China: A New Pacific Strategy.' *Newsweek* May 7, 2001: 49.

'Beautiful Park is Dedicated to Memory of Men in Great War.' *Pacific Commercial Advertiser* Nov 12, 1919: 1.

Bederman, Gail. *Manliness & Civilization: A Cultural History of Gender and Race in the United States. 1880–1917*. Chicago: U of Chicago P, 1995.

Bernstein, Carl. 'The CIA and the Media.' *Rolling Stone* Oct 20, 1977. http://www.carlbernstein.com/magazine_cia_and_media.php Accessed Aug 20, 2009.

*Big Jim McLain*. Dir. Edward Ludwig. With John Wayne and James Arness. Warner Brothers, 1952.

'Bill for Buying Site for Memorial Park is Prepared.' *Pacific Commercial Advertiser* Mar 29, 1919: 1.

*Bird of Paradise*. Dir. King Vidor. With Joel McCrea, Dolores Del Rio, and Lon Chaney Jr. RKO Radio Pictures, 1932.

*Bird of Paradise*. Dir. Delmer Daves. With Debra Paget and Louis Jourdan. Twentieth Century Fox, 1951.

*Birth of a Nation*. Dir. D.W. Griffith. With Lilian Gish and Mae Marsh. Mutual, 1915.

'Birth of Nation Observed by City in Fitting Rites.' *Pacific Commercial Advertiser* July 5, 1919: 3.

Blaisdell, Kekuni. 'Sovereignty' in Robert H. Mast and Anne B. Mast, *Autobiography of Protest in Hawai'i*. Honolulu: U of Hawai'i P, 1996: 363–73.

Blanco, Sebastian. 'GI Sanctuary.' *Honolulu Weekly* Mar 12, 2003. http://www.honoluluweekly.com/archives/coverstory%202003/03-12-03%20Sanctuary/03-12-03%20Sanctuary.html Accessed Oct 23, 2009.

*Blount Report*. United States Congress. Executive Document No. 47. 53rd Congress, 2nd Session, 1893.

*Blue Hawaii*. Dir. Norman Taurog. With Elvis Presley and Joan Blackman. 1961.

Blum, John M. *Years of Discord: American Politics and Society, 1961–1974*. New York: Norton, 1991.

Bodnar, John. 'Public Place in an American City: Commemoration in Cleveland' in *Commemorations: the Politics of National Identity*. Ed. John R. Gillis. Princeton UP, 1994: 74–89.

——. *Remaking America: Public Memory, Commemoration, and Patriotism in the Twentieth Century*. New Jersey: Princeton UP, 1992.

'Boost The Game.' *Pacific Commercial Advertiser* Nov 1, 1919: 4.

Borreca, Richard. *Sugar yields sweet deal for 'Big Five' firms*. http://starbulletin.com/1999/07/12/millennium/ story1.html Accessed Oct 23, 2009.

Boyd, Bill. 'Travel Tips From Abroad.' *Roach* June 18, 1968: 10.

Boyer, Paul. *By the Bomb's Early Light: American Thought and Culture at the Dawn of the Atomic Age*. New York: Pantheon, 1985.
——. 'Whose History is it Anyway? Memory, Politics, and Historical Scholarship' in *History Wars: The Enola Gay and Other Battles for the American Past*. Ed. Linenthal, Edward T. and Tom Engelhardt. New York: Metropolitan, 1996: 115–39.
Boylan, Dan. 'Keeping Peace in the Pacific.' *Midweek* May 30, 2001: 1, 32, 50.
Braestrup, Peter. 'An Extreme Case' in *The American Experience in Vietnam: A Reader*. Ed. Grace Sevy. U of Oklahoma P, 1991: 153–62.
Brennan, Joseph L. *Duke: The Life Story of Hawai'i's Duke Kahanamoku*. Honolulu: Ku Pa'a, 1994.
Breslau, Karen and Evan Thomas. 'A Captain's Story.' *Newsweek* Apr 2, 2001: 28–30.
Brown, Dee. *Bury My Heart at Wounded Knee: An Indian History of the American West*. New York: Henry Holt, 1970.
Brown, DeSoto. 'Ebb Tide.' *Honolulu Weekly* Oct 10–16, 2001: 6–8.
*Burials and Memorials*. United States Department of Veterans Affairs. http://www.cem.va.gov/hist/history.asp Accessed June 22, 2009.
Burke, Carol. 'Why They Love to Hate Her: The Civilian Female in Soldier Lore.' *Nation* 278.11 (March 22, 2004): 14.
Burleigh, Anne. 'Save the Natatorium.' *Hawaii Architect* July 1973: 12–13.
Burlingame, Burl. 'Carving a Link to the Past.' *Honolulu Star-Bulletin* Mar 1, 1999.
'Burnham Design for War Memorial Expresses Spirit of Brave Hawai'i.' *Pacific Commercial Advertiser* May 14, 1919: 1, 3.
Bushnell, Andrew F. 'The "Horror" Reconsidered: An Evaluation of the Historical Evidence for Population Decline in Hawai'i, 1778–1803.' *Pacific Studies* 16.3 (1995): 115–61.
Butler, John K. Letter to Governor McCarthy. Mar 23, 1921. Hawai'i State Archives.
Butwin, David. 'Isle's Peacenik March is a Calm One.' *Honolulu Advertiser* Mar 28, 1966: 1.
Cameron, Duncan F. 'The Museum, a Temple or the Forum.' *Journal of World History* 14.1 (1972): 189–202.
'Canada Welcomes Deserters.' *Hawaii Free Press* July 1969.
Carlson, Doug. *Hill of Sacrifice: The National Memorial Cemetery of the Pacific at Punchbowl*. Honolulu: Island Heritage, 1982.
Carpenter, Ted Galen. *The Captive Press: Foreign Policy Crises and the First Amendment*. Washington, D.C.: Cato Inst., 1995.
Carr, E.H. *What is History*. Knopf: New York, 1962.
Carr, Virginia Spencer. *Dos Passos, a Life*. New York: Doubleday, 1984.
'Cassius Clay Goes to Trial Tomorrow.' *Honolulu Advertiser* June 18, 1967: E4.
Chapin, Helen Geracimos. *Shaping History: The Role of Newspapers in Hawai'i*. Honolulu: U of Hawai'i P, 1996.
Chaplin, George. *Presstime in Paradise: The Life and Times of The Honolulu Advertiser, 1856–1995*. Honolulu: U of Hawai'i P, 1998.
Chapman, William, 'Saving the Natatorium.' *Honolulu Advertiser* Apr 12, 1998: B4.
Char, Tin-Yuke. *The Sandalwood Mountains: Readings and Stories of the Early Chinese in Hawaii*. Honolulu: UP of Hawaii, 1975.

—., and Wai Jane Char. *Chinese Historic Sites and Pioneer Families of the Island of Hawaii*. Honolulu: U of Hawai'i P, 1983.

Chan, Gaye and Andrea Feeser. *Historic Waikīkī*. Honolulu: U of Hawai'i P, 2006.

'Chicago Police Battle Rioters.' *Sunday Star Bulletin and Advertiser* Apr 28, 1968: A4.

Chomsky, Noam. *9–11*. New York: Seven Stories, 2001.

——. *Rethinking Camelot: JFK, the Cold War, and US Political Culture*. Boston: South End, 1993.

——. 'The Cold War and the University' in *The Cold War and the University*. Ed. David Montgomery. New York: New Press, 1997: 171–94.

Churchill, Ward. *Fantasies of the Master Race: Literature, Cinema and the Colonization of American Indians*. Ed. M. Annette Jaimes. Monroe, Maine: Common Courage, 1992.

'Civilians on Sub Were Taken to Control Room After Lunch.' *Irish Examiner* Feb 22, 2001.

CJS Group Architects. *Final Historical Background Report Waikiki War Memorial Park and Natatorium*. City and County of Honolulu Dept. of Parks and Recreation. 1985.

Clifford, James. 'On Ethnographic Allegory' in *Writing Culture: the Poetics and Politics of Ethnography*. Ed. James Clifford & George E. Marcus. Berkeley: U of California P, 1986: 98–121.

Cole, Thomas. *The Course of Empire: The Pastoral or Arcadian State*. New-York Historical Soc.

Cole, William. 'Lawsuit Opposes Stryker Brigade.' *Honolulu Advertiser* Aug 18, 2004: http://the.honoluluadvertiser.com/article/2004/Aug/18/ln/ln25a.html Accessed Oct 23, 2009.

'The Complete Passenger List of the Lost American Transport Tuscania.' *New York Times* Feb 9, 1918: 6.

Cooper, George and Gavan Daws. *Land and Power in Hawaii*. Honolulu: U of Hawai'i Press, 1990.

Cragg, Dan. *Guide to Military Installations*. Harrisburg PA: Stackpole, 1988.

Crapol, Edward P. *John Tyler: The Accidental President*. Chapel Hill: U of North Carolina P, 2006.

*Creating Hawai'i Debuts at the National Museum of American History*. Smithsonian Asian Pacific American Program: news and Events blog. http://apanews.si.edu/2009/08/20/creating-hawaii-debuts-at-the-national-museum-of-american-history/ Accessed Oct 23, 2009.

Cripps, Thomas and David Culbert. 'The Negro Soldier (1944): Film Propaganda in Black and White' in *Hollywood as Historian: American Film in a Cultural Context*. Ed. Peter C. Rollins. UP of Kentucky, 1983: 109–33.

Damon, Ethel M. *The Stone Church at Kawaiahao 1820–1944*. Honolulu: Trustees of Kawaiahao Church, 1945.

'Dana R. Park Imprisoned.' *Roach* July 16, 1968: 1–2.

'David Withington Dies in the East: Honolulu Boy Falls Victim to Spanish Influenza.' *Pacific Commercial Advertiser* Oct 8, 1918: 1.

Daws, Gavan. *Shoal of Time: A History of the Hawaiian Islands*. Honolulu: U of Hawai'i P, 1974.

Dawes, James. *The Language of War: Literature and Culture in the U.S. From the Civil War through World War II*. Cambridge Ma.: Harvard UP, 2002.

'A Day Aboard the USS Greenville.' *Midweek* Feb 21, 2001: 22.

*December 7*. Dir. John Ford. With Walter Huston and Harry Davenport. U.S. Navy, 1943.

*The Deer Hunter*. Dir. Michael Cimino. With Robert DeNiro and Christopher Walken. Universal Pictures, 1978.

DeGroot, Gerald J. *The Sixties Unplugged: A Kaleidoscopic History of a Disorderly Decade*. Cambridge MA & London: Harvard UP, 2008.

Deloria, Philip J. *Playing Indian*. New Haven & London: Yale UP, 1998.

Deloria Jr., Vine. *Red Earth, White Lies: Native Americans and the Myth of Scientific Fact*. New York: Scribner, 1995.

Dening, Greg. *The Death of William Gooch: A History's Anthropology*. Honolulu: U of Hawai'i P, 1995.

Department of the Army. *American Military History 1607–1953*. ROTCM 145–20, 1956.

Desmond, Jane. *Staging Tourism: Bodies on Display From Waikiki to Sea World*. Chicago: U of Chicago P, 1999.

Desser, David. 'Charlie Don't Surf: Race and Culture in the Vietnam War Films' in *Inventing Vietnam: The War in Film and Television*. Ed. Michael Anderegg. Philadelphia: Temple UP, 1991: 81–102.

*Diamond Head*. Dir. Guy Green. With Charlton Heston and Yvette Mimieux. Columbia Pictures, 1963.

Dingeman, Robbie. 'Natatorium Faces Another Study.' *Honolulu Advertiser*, June 21, 2006. http://www.savekaimanabeach.org/archives/the.honoluluadvertiser.com/article/2006/Jun/21/ln/0~FP606210341.html Accessed Sep 20, 2007.

Dower, John. *War Without Mercy: Race and Power in the Pacific War*. New York: Pantheon, 1993.

Drinnon, Richard. *Facing West: The Metaphysics of Indian-Hating and Empire-Building*. New York: New American Library, 1980.

Dubin, Steven C. *Displays of Power: Memory and Amnesia in the American Museum*. New York & London: New York UP, 1999.

Duffield, Marcus. *King Legion*. New York: Cape, 1931.

Dunne, John Gregory. 'The American Raj: Pearl Harbor as Metaphor.' *New Yorker* May 7, 2001: 46–54.

Durand, Asher Brown. *Kindred Spirits*. New York Public Library.

Dye, Tom. 'Population Trends in Hawai'i Before 1778.' *Hawaiian Journal of History* (1994): 1–20.

*Economic History Services*: http://eh.net/hmit/ppowerusd/ Accessed Oct 23, 2009.

Editorial. *Hawaii Free Press* June 1969.

Editors of the Army Times. *Pearl Harbor and Hawaii: A Military History*. New York: Bonanza, 1971.

'Edmund Hedemann Dies in Service.' *Pacific Commercial Advertiser* Mar 21, 1919: 1.

Eisenhower, Dwight D. Farewell Address to the American People. Washington, Jan 17, 1961. The Dwight D. Eisenhower Presidential Library, Abilene, Kansas. http://eisenhower.archives.gov Accessed Oct 23, 2009.

Elegant, Robert. 'How to Lose a War: Reflections of a Foreign Correspondent' in *The American Experience in Vietnam: A reader*. Ed. Grace Sevy. U of Oklahoma P, 1991: 138–42.

Ellul, Jacques. *Propaganda: The Formation of Men's Attitudes*. New York: Knopf, 1965.

Emerson, Gloria. 'Remembering Women War Correspondents in Vietnam' in Tad Bartimus *et al. War Torn: Stories of War From the Women Reporters Who Covered Vietnam*. New York: Random House, 2002: xv–xxi.

*Enchanted Island*. Dir. Alan Dwan. With Dana Andrews and Don Dubbins. Warner Brothers, 1958.

Engelhardt, Tom. *The End of Victory Culture: Cold War America and the Disillusioning of a Generation*. U of Massachusetts P, 1998.

Engle Merry, Sally. *Colonizing Hawai'i: The Cultural Power of Law*. Princeton UP, 2000.

Enloe, Cynthia. *Bananas, Beaches and Bases: Making Feminist Sense of International Politics*. Berkeley: U of California P, 1990.

'Ethnic Studies.' *Liberated Barracks*. Mar 1972: 11.

Fairbanks, Eugene. 'The Lincoln Landscape Sculptural Commemorations of Abraham Lincoln by Avard T. Fairbanks.' *Journal of the Abraham Lincoln Association* 26.2 (2005): 49–73.

Ferguson, Kathy E. and Phyllis Turnbull. *Oh, Say, Can You See? The Semiotics of the Military in Hawai'i*. Boderlines 10. Minneapolis: U of Minnesota P, 1999.

'Fighting Intense on Vietnam Fronts.' *Honolulu Star-Bulletin* Feb 2, 1968: A1.

'Final Decision on Memorial is Expected Today.' *Pacific Commercial Advertiser* Mar 24, 1919: 6.

Firth, Stewart. *Nuclear Playground*. Honolulu: U of Hawai'i P, 1987.

'5-Day Viet Toll: 15,000 Reds.' *Sunday Star-Bulletin and Advertiser* Feb 4, 1968: A1.

Fletcher, Danvers. Letter. *Midweek* May 9, 2001: 4.

*Flirtation Walk*. Dir. Frank Borzage. With Dick Powell and Ruby Keeler. Warner Brothers, 1934.

'For Denby, Rigors of War are Tempered by Kindness.' *Honolulu Advertiser* Nov 6, 1966: A17.

'Foreign Correspondents: The Saigon Story.' *Time* Oct 11, 1963: 55–6.

Franklin, H. Bruce. *Vietnam and Other American Fantasies*. Amherst: U of Massachusetts P, 2000.

French, Brandon. *On the Verge of Revolt: Women in American Films of the Fifties*. New York: Ungar, 1978.

*From Here to Eternity*. Dir. Fred Zinnemann. With Burt Lancaster, Montgomery Clift and Frank Sinatra. Columbia Pictures, 1953.

'FTA Show Comes to Hawaii.' *Liberated Barracks* Nov 1971: 4–5.

'F.T.A. Show is Biting, Disrespectful, Well Done.' *Honolulu Star-Bulletin* Nov 26, 1971: B8.

Fuchs, Lawrence. *Hawaii Pono, a Social History*. New York: Harcourt Brace, 1961.

'Funeral Services for Lieutenant O'Dowda Held at 3 P.M. Today.' *Honolulu Advertiser* Aug 7, 1921: 3.

Fussell, Paul. *The Great War and Modern Memory*. Oxford UP, 2000.

——. *Wartime: Understanding and Behavior in the Second World War*. New York: Oxford UP, 1990.

Gaff, Alan D. *Blood in the Argonne: The 'Lost Battalion' of World War I*. U of Oklahoma P, 2005.

Gaffney, Angela. *Aftermath: Remembering the Great War in Wales*. Cardiff: U of Wales P, 1998.

Gans, Herbert J. *Deciding What's News: A Study of CBS Evening News, NBC Nightly News, Newsweek, and Time*. New York: Vintage, 1979.

Gapp, Frank W. *The Commodore and the Whale*. New York: Vantage, 1996.
——. 'The Kind-Eyed Chief: Forgotten Champion of Hawai'i's Freedom.' *Hawaiian Journal of History* (1985): 101–21.
Gatchell, Charles. Interview with D.W. Griffith: 'The Filming of 'Way Down East.' http://www.televisiontoys.com/waydowneast3.htm Accessed Aug 22, 2004.
Gellermann, William. *The American Legion as Educator*. New York: Teachers College Colombia UP, 1938.
*Gidget Goes Hawaiian*. Dir. Paul Wendkos. With Deborah Walley and James Darren. Columbia, 1961.
Giglio, James N. *The Presidency of John F. Kennedy*. American Presidency Series. UP of Kansas, 1991.
Ginsberg, Allen. 'Smoking Typewriters' in *Unamerican Activities: The Campaign Against the Underground Press*. Eds. Anne Janowitz and Nancy Peters. San Francisco: City Lights, 1981: 31–5.
Gitlin, Todd. 'The Underground Press and Its Cave-In' in *Unamerican Activities: The Campaign Against the Underground Press*. Eds. Anne Janowitz and Nancy Peters. San Francisco: City Lights, 1981: 19–30.
Glessing, Robert J. *The Underground Press in America*. Bloomington and London: Indiana UP, 1970.
Good, Peter. *Language For Those Who Have Nothing: Mikhail Bakhtin and the Landscape of Psychiatry*. Cognition and Language: A Series in Psycholinguistics. London: Springer, 2001.
'Governor's Plan to Reclaim Duck Ponds Approved.' *Pacific Commercial Advertiser* Oct 19, 1919: 1.
Grant, Glenn, Kenneth Kipnis, Jon M. Van Dyke and Mitch Yamasaki. *Hawai'i Under Army Rule: 1941–1944*. Honolulu, ?: 1991.
——. Introduction. *Fort DeRussy Days: Letters of a Malihini Army Wife, 1908–1911*. By Winslow. Ed. M. Winslow Chapman. Honolulu: Folk Press Kapiolani CC, 1998: ix–xiv.
Gray, Francine du Plessix. *Hawaii: The Sugar-Coated Fortress*. New York: Vintage, 1973.
*Great American Monuments: The War Memorials*. Drimmer, Host: Roger Mudd, Narrator: Paul Kirby. A&E Television Networks, 1994.
*Griffith's 20 Year Record*. http://www.cinemaweb.com/silentfilm/bookshelf/7_dwg_2.htm Accessed Oct 23, 2009.
Griswold, Charles L. 'The Vietnam Veterans Memorial and the Washington Mall: Philosophical Thoughts on Political Iconography.' *Critical Enquiry* 12.4 (Summer 1986): 688–719.
'Ground Action Takes Heavy Viet Cong Toll.' *St. Petersburg Times* Feb 1, 1966: 12A.
Hack, Brian Edward. 'Spartan Desires: Eugenics and the Sculptural Program of the 1915 Panama-Pacific International Exposition.' *PART: Journal of the CUNY PhD Program in Art History*, Part 6 http://web.gc.cuny.edu/dept/ArtHi/part/part6/articles/bhack.html Accessed Oct 23, 2009.
Hagan, Kenneth J. *American Gunboat Diplomacy and the Old Navy 1877–1889*. Contributions in Military History 4. Westport, Connecticut: Greenwood, 1973.
Halberstam, David. 'Getting the Story in Vietnam.' *Commentary* Jan 1965: 30–4.
——. 'The Role of Journalists in Vietnam: A Reporter's Perspective' in *Vietnam Reconsidered: Lessons From a War*. Ed. Harrison E. Salisbury. New York: Harper and Row, 1984: 113–16.

Hallin, Daniel C. *The 'Uncensored War': The Media and Vietnam*. New York: Oxford UP, 1986.

'Halt to Bombing is Error: Sharp.' *Honolulu Advertiser* June 2, 1967: 8.

'Harvard Athlete Killed in France.' *New York Times* Aug 22, 1918: 4.

'Hawaii Boy Dies Fighting: Details of Death of Lieut. James Bryant Are Learned.' *Pacific Commercial Advertiser* Jan 4, 1920: 8.

*Hawaii Calls*. Dir. Edward F. Cline. With Bobby Breen and Ned Sparks. RKO, 1938.

'Hawaii Did Her Part on France's Blood-Red Fields: Manhood of Isles Sacrifice Life on Land and Sea in Cause of Liberty.' *Honolulu Star Bulletin* May 10, 1919: 3.

'Hawaii Men Who Wear Wound Stripes: War Leaves Its Mark on 14 Island Heroes.' *Honolulu Star-Bulletin* May 10, 1919: 3.

'Hawaii Pono Journal.' *Liberated Barracks* Oct 1971: 2.

*Hawaii State Cemeteries*. Honolulu: Department of Accounting and General Services State of Hawaii/Hawaiian Memorial Park Cemetery Assoc., 1987.

'Hawai'i, the Islands of Aloha.' Hawaii's Official Tourism Site. http://www.gohawaii.com/ Accessed Oct 23, 2009.

'Hawaii to Have Organization of American Legion.' *Pacific Commercial Advertiser* Sep 4, 1919: 1.

'Hawaii: Why So Much Military.' *Liberated Barracks* Sep 1971: 3.

'Hawaii's First Victim of War Here for Burial.' *Honolulu Advertiser* Sep 9, 1921: 1–2.

*Hearts and Minds*. Dir. Peter Davis. Rainbow Pictures/Janus Films, 1974.

*Hearts of Darkness: A Filmmaker's Apocalypse*. Dir. Eleanor Coppola, Fax Bahr, and George Hickenlooper. American Zoetrope, 1991.

Heckathorn, John. 'Western Diseases in Hawaii: An Interview with David Stannard' *Honolulu Magazine* 1989. Accessed Oct 23, 2009. http://www2.hawaii.edu/~johnb/micro/m130/readings/stannard.html

'Heiau Found at La Pietra.' *Honolulu Star-Bulletin* Feb 6, 1968: A-8.

Heinl Jr. Robert D. (Colonel). 'The Collapse of the Armed Forces.' *Armed Forces Journal* (June 7, 1971): 30–7.

Herman, Edward S. and Noam Chomsky. *Manufacturing Consent: The Political Economy of the Mass Media*. New York: Pantheon, 1988.

Herman, RDK. 'The Aloha State: Place Names and the Anti-Conquest of Hawai'i.' *Annals of the Association of American Geographers* 89.1 (1999): 76–102.

Herr, Michael. *Dispatches*. London: Picador, 1978.

Herring, George C. *America's Longest War: The United States and Vietnam, 1950–1975*. America in Crisis. New York: Wiley, 1979.

Hill, Harold Charles. *A History of the American Legion Department of Hawaii*. Honolulu: American Legion, 1947.

Hill, Hugo. 'The Middle-Class Liberation Front.' *Roach* Mar 23–Apr 6, 1969: 4.

Hilsman, Roger. 'Difficulties of Covering a War Like Vietnam' in *Vietnam Reconsidered: Lessons From a War*. Ed. Harrison E. Salisbury. New York: Harper and Row, 1984: 124–7.

*Historic Guide: Schofield Barracks, Hawaii*. Tropic Lightning Museum, Schofield Barracks.

*History of Government Furnished Headstones and Markers*. http://www.cem.va.gov/hmhist.htm Accessed Aug 9, 2003.

'History of Hawai'i: The Pokiki: Portuguese Traditions.' *Islander Magazine*. http://www.islander-magazine.com/port.html Accessed Aug 9, 2003.

*The History of the Beach: The Turning Tides of History*. Dir. Laura Verklan. A & E Television Networks, 2003.

*History of the USS Schurz*. http://www.ecu.edu/maritime/projects/2000/schurz/history_of_the_uss_schurz.html Accessed Aug 9, 2003.

Hitchins, Christopher. *The Trial of Henry Kissinger*. London: Verso, 2001.

Hodgson, Godfrey. *America in Our Time: From World War II to Nixon — What Happened and Why*. Princeton UP, 2005.

Hoe, S. H. 'America Invaded by Oriental Foes' *The Baseball Magazine* XII.5 (Mar 1914): 69.

*Honolulu*. Dir. Edward Buzzell. With Eleanor Powell and Robert Young. Metro-Goldwyn-Mayer, 1939.

*Honolulu Memorial, National Memorial Cemetery of the Pacific*. American Battle Monuments Commission. http://www.abmc.gov/memorials/memorials/hn_base.pdf Accessed Oct 23, 2009.

'Honolulu Will Pay Tribute to Soldier Dead.' *Honolulu Advertiser* Sep 14, 1921: 1, 6.

'Honor Roll of Those Who Subscribed to Victory.' *Honolulu Star-Bulletin* May 10, 1919: 4.

'100 Percent of Americanism is Demand Made by U.S. Legion.' *Pacific Commercial Advertiser* Oct 24, 1919: 1–2.

'I Said "Keep On Truckin".' *Liberated Barracks* Apr 1972: 1.

*The Idol Dancer*. Dir. D.W. Grifith. With Richard Barthelmess and Clarine Seymour. First National, 1920.

Imada, Adria L. 'The Army Learns to Luau: Imperial Hospitality and Military Photography in Hawaii.' *The Contemporary Pacific* 20.2 (2008): 328–36.

*In Harm's Way*. Dir. Otto Preminger. With John Wayne and Kirk Douglas. Paramount, 1965.

*Index to the* Honolulu Advertiser *and* Honolulu Star Bulletin *1929 to 1967*. 5 vols. Department of Education: State of Hawaii, 1968.

*Index to the* Honolulu Advertiser *and* Honolulu Star Bulletin *1968*. Department of Education: State of Hawaii, 1968.

'Information on Hawaii Boys in War is Sought.' *Pacific Commercial Advertiser* Oct 19, 1919: 3.

'Inouye Fires Blast at Draft Dodging.' *Honolulu Star-Bulletin* May 27, 1968: A1.

'Irwin Property Makes Ideal Site for Park as Memorial to Men of Hawai'i Who Served.' *Pacific Commercial Advertiser* Mar 30, 1919: 1.

'Irwin Property on Beach Sought for Memorial.' *Pacific Commercial Advertiser* Mar 25, 1919: 1.

Jacobson, Matthew Frye. *Barbarian Virtues: The United States Encounters Foreign Peoples at Home and Abroad 1876–1917*. New York: Hill & Wang, 2000.

*The Japanese in Hawaii: A Century of Struggle*. The Official Booklet of the Oahu Kanyako Imin Centennial Committee. Honolulu: The Hawaii Hochi, 1985.

Jaworski, Bill. 'Plato's Column.' *Carrion Crow* May 9, 1967.

*Joe Versus the Volcano*. Dir. John Patrick Shanley. With Tom Hanks and Meg Ryan. Amblin Entertainment, 1990.

Jones, Edgar L. 'One War is Enough.' *Atlantic Monthly* Feb 1946. http://www.theatlantic.com/unbound/bookauth/battle/jones.htm Accessed Oct 23, 2009.

Jones, James. *From Here to Eternity*. New York: Dell, 1991.

Jordan, Winthrop D. *The White Man's Burden: Historical Origins of Racism in the United States*. Oxford UP, 1974.

Jordy, William H. *American Buildings and Their Architects: Progressive and Academic Ideals at the Turn of the Twentieth Century*. Garden City: Anchor, 1976.

Kajihiro, Kyle. 'No Peace in Paradise: The Military Presence in the Hawaiian Islands.' Koohan Paik, Jerry Mander *et al. The Superferry Chronicles: Hawaii's Uprising Against Militarism, Commercialism and the Desecration of the Earth*. Kihei, HI: Koa Books, 2009: 272–83.

——. 'A Brief Overview of Militarization and Resistance in Hawai'i.' Hawaii: DMZ-Hawai'i/Aloha 'Aina, March 1, 2007.

Kakesako, Gregg K. 'Soldier Receives Belated Tribute.' *Honolulu Star-Bulletin* May 27, 2002. http://starbulletin.com/2002/05/27/news/story1.html Accessed Oct 23, 2009.

Kame'eleihiwa, Lilikalā. *Native Land and Foreign Desires*. Honolulu: Bishop Museum, 1992.

Kazickas, Jurate. 'Those Hills Called Khe Sanh' in Tad Bartimus *et al. War Torn: Stories of War From the Women Reporters Who Covered Vietnam*. New York: Random House, 2002: 150–1.

'Keep the Goal in Sight.' Editorial. *Honolulu Star-Bulletin* Feb 9, 1968: A10.

Kelly, Anne Keala. 'Haolewood: The Last Epidemic.' *Honolulu Weekly* July 10–16, 2002: 6–8.

Kelly, Marion. 'Foreign Investment in Hawai'i.' *Social Process in Hawaii* 35 (1994): 15–39.

Kennedy, David M. *Over Here: The First World War and American Society*. Oxford: Oxford UP, 1980.

Kent, Noel J. *Hawaii: Islands Under the Influence*. New York: Monthly Review Press, 1983.

King, Alex. *Memorials of the Great War in Britain: The Symbolism and Politics of Remembrance*. Oxford & New York: Berg, 1998.

Kirch, Patrick V. Rev. of *Before the Horror: The Population of Hawai'i on the Eve of Western Contact. The Contemporary Pacific* 2.2 (1990.): 394–6.

Knightley, Phillip. 'The Role of Journalists in Vietnam: A Feature Writer's Perspective' in *Vietnam Reconsidered: Lessons From a War*. Ed. Harrison E. Salisbury. New York: Harper and Row, 1984: 106–9.

——. 'Vietnam 1954–1975 (The First Casualty)' in *The American Experience in Vietnam: a reader*. Ed. Grace Sevy. U of Oklahoma P, 1991 107–37.

Kraft, Joseph. 'Lesson From the Nightmare.' *Honolulu Advertiser* Feb 8, 1968: C2.

'Krulak Calls Raids Acts of Desperation.' *Honolulu Star-Bulletin* Feb 2, 1968: A2.

Kuykendall, Ralph S. *Hawaii in the World War*. Honolulu: The Historical Commission, 1928.

——. *The Hawaiian Kingdom 1874–1893, the Kalakaua Dynastism*. Honolulu: U of Hawaii P, 1967.

Landauer, Lyndall B. & Donald A. Landauer. *Pearl: The History of the United States Navy at Pearl Harbor*. S Lake Tahoe, CA: Flying Cloud, 1999.

Laney, Leroy. 'Just How Important is the Military to Hawai'i's Economy?' *The Price of Paradise*. Vol. II. Ed. Randall W. Roth. Honolulu: Mutual, 1993: 273–8.

*Larry King Weekend*. CNN. May 5, 2001.

Laughy, Lisa. Email to the Author. Aug, 7, 2009.

Least Heat Moon, William. *Blue Highways: A Journey into America*. New York: Ballantine, 1984.

Lederer, Edith. 'My First War' in Tad Bartimus *et al. War Torn: Stories of War From the Women Reporters Who Covered Vietnam*. New York: Random House, 2002: 154–85.

'Legion Action on Alien Employes [sic] Arouses British.' *Pacific Commercial Advertiser* Mar 3, 1920: 1.

'Legion Convention to Take Action on Language Press.' *Pacific Commercial Advertiser* Feb 7, 1920: 1.

'Legion Decides Against Action on Land Measure.' *Pacific Commercial Advertiser* May 21, 1920: 5.

'Legion Objects and Ideals Told to Ad Clubbers.' *Pacific Commercial Advertiser* Mar 11, 1919: 5.

'Legion Plans to Erect Monument in Memorial Park.' *Pacific Commercial Advertiser* May 9, 1920: 4.

'Legion to Demand Translation of Japanese Papers.' *Pacific Commercial Advertiser* Feb 19, 1920: 3.

Leidemann, Mike. 'Natatorium Debate at Crucial Junction.' *Honolulu Advertiser* Sep 20, 2009. http://the.honoluluadvertiser.com/article/2004/Jun/20/ln/ln01a.html Accessed Oct 23, 2009.

Lencek, Lena and Gideon Bosker. *The Beach: The History of Paradise on Earth*. New York: Viking, 1998.

Lepore, Jill. *The Name of War*. New York: Knopf, 1998.

'Letter From Vietnam.' *Carrion Crow* May 2, 1967.

Lewes, James. 'Envisioning Resistance: The GI Underground Press During the Vietnam War.' *Media History* 7.2 (2001): 137–50.

Lewis, Roger. *Outlaws of America: The Underground Press and its Context*. Harmondsworth: Penguin, 1972.

'The Liberated Barracks Grew Out.' *Liberated Barracks* Sep 1971: 1

'Lieut. O'Dowda Killed in France.' *Pacific Commercial Advertiser* Dec 6, 1918: 1.

'Lightfoot Calls Legion Members into Conference.' *Pacific Commercial Advertiser* Mar 4, 1920: 1.

'Lightfoot is Told Legion Backs its Alien Labor Stand.' *Pacific Commercial Advertiser* Mar 5, 1920: 1.

Limerick, Patricia. *The Legacy of Conquest: The Unbroken Past of the American West*. New York: Norton, 1988.

Lind, Ian Y. 'Ring of Steel: Notes on the Militarization of Hawaii.' *The Political-Economy of Hawaii, Social Process in Hawaii* (1984/85): 25–48.

Linenthal, Edward Tabor. *Sacred Ground: Americans and Their Battlegrounds*. Urbana: U of Illinois P, 1991.

——. and Tom Engelhardt. *History Wars: The Enola Gay and Other Battles for the American Past*. New York: Metropolitan, 1996.

Linn, Brian. M. *Guardians of Empire: The U.S. Army and the Pacific, 1902–1940*. Chapel Hill: U of North Carolina P, 1997.

Lipsitz, George. *Dangerous Crossroads: Popular Music, Postmodernism, and the Poetics of Place*. London & New York: Verso, 1994.

Loewen, James. *Lies Across America: What Our Historic Sites Get Wrong*. New York: New Press, 1999.

——. *Lies My Teacher Told Me: Everything Your American History Textbook Got Wrong*. New York: Simon & Schuster, 1996.

Lott, Eric. 'Love and Theft: The Racial Unconscious of Blackface Minstrelsy.' *Representations* 39 (1992): 23–50.

——. *Love and Theft: Blackface Minstrelsy and the American Working Class*. New York: Oxford UP, 1993.

Lyons, Paul '"They Will Eat Us Up": Remembering Hawai'i.' *American Literary History* 16.3 (2004): 543–57.

*Ma and Pa Kettle in Waikiki*. Dir. Lee Sholem. With Marjorie Main and Hilo Hattie. Universal-International, 1955.

MacCaughey, Vaughan. 'Race Mixture in Hawaii.' *The Journal of Heredity* 10.1 (Jan 1919): 41–7.

Mackenzie, Angus. 'Sabotaging the Dissident Press' in *Unamerican Activities: The Campaign Against the Underground Press*. Eds. Anne Janowitz & Nancy Peters. San Francisco: City Lights, 1981: 159–70.

Macomber, Ben. *The Jewel City: Panama-Pacific International Exposition 1915*. San Francisco: Williams, 1915.

Mahan, Alfred Thayer. 'Hawaii and Our Future Sea Power.' *The Interests of America in Sea Power*. Boston: Little, Brown, 1918.

——. *The Influence of Sea Power Upon History 1660–1783*. Boston: Little, Brown, 1890.

'Major Heiau Found on Diamond Head.' *Honolulu Advertiser* Feb 4, 1968: 1, 4.

'Making the Military Mind.' *Hawaii Free Press* June 1969.

*Manufacturing Consent: Noam Chomsky and the Media*. Dir. Mark Achbar and Peter Wintonick. Zeitgeist Video, 2002.

'Many Honor Lieutenant O'Dowda.' *Honolulu Advertiser* Aug 8, 1921: 4.

'Marine Rescues Girl.' *Honolulu Star-Bulletin* Feb 8, 1968: A2.

Marquis, Christopher. 'Ulysses S. Grant Sharp Jr., Vietnam War Admiral, 95.' *New York Times* Dec 18, 2001: C15.

Marshall, John D. Letter. *Midweek* Mar 7, 2001: 4.

Marshall, S.L.A. (Brig. Gen). 'Our Viet Forces See the Improvements.' *Sunday Star-Bulletin and Advertiser* Nov 6, 1966: B3.

Martin, Calvin. *The Keepers of the Game: Indian-Animal Relationships and the Fur Trade*. Berkeley: U of California P, 1978.

'Mass Meeting to Pass on Memorial.' *Pacific Commercial Advertiser* Feb 12, 1919: 1–2.

Matson, Floyd. 'Hollywood Goes Hawaiian' in *Viewers' Guide: East-West International Film Festival* Honolulu: East-West Film Festival 1984: 40–1.

Mayo, James M. *War Memorials as Political Landscape: The American Experience and Beyond*. New York: Praeger, 1988.

——. 'War Memorials as Political Memory.' *Geographical Review* 78.1 (1988): 62–75.

McMahon, Robert J. 'Contested Memory: The Vietnam War and American Society, 1975–2001.' (SHAFR Presidential Address) *Diplomatic History* 26.2 (Spring 2002): 159–84.

McNally, Dennis. *Desolate Angel: Jack Kerouac, the Beat Generation, and America*. New York: Random House, 1980.

Melville, Herman. *Typee: A Peep at Polynesian Life*. New York: New American Library, 1964.

Memmi, Albert. *The Colonizer and the Colonized*. Boston: Beacon, 1967.

'Memorial Architects to Look Over Plans.' *Honolulu Advertiser* June 14, 1922: 3.

*The Memorial Church of Harvard University. World War I Memorial.* http://www.memorialchurch.harvard.edu/history/ww1.shtml Accessed June 13, 2009.

'Memorial Park Proposal Wins Warm Approval.' *Pacific Commercial Advertiser* Mar 28, 1919: 1.

'Memorial Project Takes Real Shape.' *Pacific Commercial Advertiser* Feb 25, 1919: 5.

'Men of Action Needed to Save Nation.' *Pacific Commercial Advertiser* Oct 29, 1919: 8.

'Micronesians Demand Decent Conditions.' *Roach* Jan 15–31, 1969: 6–7.

*Midway*. Dir. Jack Smight. With Charlton Heston and Henry Fonda. Universal Studios, 1976.

Miles, L. Wardlaw. *A History of the 308th Infantry, 1917–1919*. New York: Putnam, 1927.

*Military Times Hall of Valor*. http://militarytimes.com/citations-medals-awards/recipient.php?recipientid=8704 Accessed July 11, 2009.

Miller, Char. Rev. of *Before the Horror: The Population of Hawai'i on the Eve of Western Contact. American Ethnologist* 17.3 (1990): 563–4.

Miller, Henry. *The Air-Conditioned Nightmare*. New York: New Directions, 1945.

Millett, Allan Reed and Jack Shulimson. *Commandants of the Marine Corps*. Naval Inst., 2004.

Mills, Barbara. *A Trip Through Hawaii's Military History: Exploring the U.S. Army Museum of Hawaii*. The Hawaii Army Museum Soc., 2000.

*Mister Roberts*. Dir. John Ford and Mervyn LeRoy. With James Cagney, Jack Lemmon, and Henry Fonda. Warner Brothers, 1955.

Montagu, Ashley and Floyd Matson. *The Dehumanization of Man*. New York: McGraw-Hill, 1983.

Moran, Thomas. *The Grand Canyon of the Yellowstone*. Department of the Interior.

Moriarty, Catherine. 'The Material Culture of Great War Remembrance.' *Journal of Contemporary History* 34.4 (1999): 653–62.

——. 'The Absent Dead and Figurative First World War Memorials.' *Transactions of the Ancient Monuments Society* 39 (1995): 7–40.

Mosse, George L. *Fallen Soldiers: Reshaping the Memory of the World Wars*. New York & Oxford: Oxford UP, 1990.

'Mother Hawai'i Sending Forth Her Sons to Battle on Sea and Land.' *Pacific Commercial Advertiser* June 28, 1919: 2.

*Mutiny on the Bounty*. Dir. Lewis Milestone. With Marlon Brando and Trevor Howard. Metro-Goldwyn-Mayer, 1962.

'A Natatorium.' *Paradise of the Pacific* Oct 1, 1905: 8.

*National Memorial Cemetery of the Pacific*. Information sheet prepared by the 100th Infantry Battalion Veterans Club.

Nationwide Gravesite Locator. United States Department of Veterans Affairs. http://gravelocator.cem.va.gov/j2ee/servlet/NGL_v1 Accessed June 14, 2009.

Neier, Aryeh. 'Surveillance as Censorship' in *Unamerican Activities: The Campaign Against the Underground Press*. Eds. Anne Janowitz and Nancy Peters. San Francisco: City Lights, 1981: 9–17.

'A New Dien Bien Phu?' Editorial. *Honolulu Advertiser* Feb 6, 1968: B2.

'The New Look at the U of H.' *Hawaii Free Press* June 1969.

'New Tuscania List: War Department Obtains Names of 16 Identified Dead.' *New York Times* Feb 24, 1918: 3.

*New York Times Film Reviews*. Rev. of *Flirtation Walk* Nov 29, 1934. New York: New York Times & Arno, 1970.

——. Rev. of *From Here to Eternity* Aug 6, 1953. New York: New York Times & Arno, 1970.

——. Rev. of *Honolulu* Feb 23, 1939. New York: New York Times & Arno, 1970.

——. Rev. of *Mutiny on the Bounty* Nov 9, 1962. New York: New York Times & Arno, 1970.

——. Rev. of *Submarine Raider* June 22, 1942. New York: New York Times & Arno, 1970.

——. Rev. of *Waikiki Wedding* Mar 25, 1937. New York: New York Times & Arno, 1970.

'Newswoman, 24, Joins Advertiser's Viet Staff.' *Honolulu Advertiser* May 31, 1966: B1.

Ng, Wendy. *Japanese American Internment During World War II: A History and Reference Guide*. Westport Ct. and London: Greenwood, 2002.

Norwood, Frank. 'G.I. Organizing ... The Liberated Barracks.' *Gathering Place* June 1971: 7, 13.

'N.Y. War Protesters Battle Police in Village.' *Sunday Star Bulletin and Advertiser* Apr 28, 1968: A4.

Oberdorfer, Don. *Tet!: The Turning Point in the Vietnam War*. Baltimore: Johns Hopkins UP, 2001.

Obeyesekere, Gananath. *The Apotheosis of Captain Cook: European Mythmaking in the Pacific*. Princeton, N.J. Honolulu, Hawai'i: Princeton UP; Bishop Museum, 1992.

'Obituary for Don Landauer.' *Tahoe Daily Tribune* June 6, 2006. http://www.tahoedailytribune.com/article/20060606/Obituaries/106060014/-1/OBITUARIES Accessed July 14, 2009.

'Objection to Bringing Home Soldier Dead.' *New York Times* Jan 18, 1920: 9, 11.

Odo, Franklin and Kazuko Sinoto. *A Pictorial History of the Japanese in Hawai'i 1885–1924*. Honolulu: Hawai'i Immigrant Heritage Preservation, Department of Anthropology, Bernice Pauahi Bishop Museum, 1985.

Okihiro, Gary Y. *Cane Fires: The Anti-Japanese Movement in Hawaii, 1865–1945*. Philadelphia: Temple UP, 1991.

Oliver, Kendrick. 'Atrocity, Authenticity and American Exceptionalism: (Ir)rationalising the Massacre at My Lai.' *Journal of American Studies* 37.2 (2003): 247–68.

Olsen, Jon. 'Judgement Daze.' *Gathering Place* 1.4 (1971): 11.

Olson, James S. and Randy Roberts *Where The Domino Fell: America and Vietnam 1945–1995*. Revised 5th edition. Malden, MA: Blackwell, 2008.

Onishi, Albert. Letter. *Midweek* Apr 4, 2001: 30.

*Operation and Financial Support for Military Museums*. Fiscal Year 2007 Annual Report to Congress. Office of the Deputy Under Secretary of Defense Installations and Environment.

Osman, Wali M. *An Update on French Polynesia*. Bank of Hawaii (August 2000). https://www.boh.com/econ/reports/pacFP0008.pdf Accessed Sep 30, 2009.

Osorio, Jonathan Kay Kamakawiwo'ole. *Dismembering Lāhui: A History of the Hawaiian Nation to 1887*. Honolulu: U of Hawai'i P, 2002.

*Our Letter Box* (Amateur Athletic Foundation of Los Angeles http://www.aafla.org [sports library].) Accessed Oct 23, 2009. http://www.la84foundation.org/SportsLibrary/BBM/1915/bbm3v.pdf

Packer, Peter and Bob Thomas. *The Massie Case*. New York: Bantam, 1966.

'Pan-Pacific Art Committee to Plan Memorial.' *Pacific Commercial Advertiser* Feb 19, 1919: 4.

Parenti, Michael. *Inventing Reality: The Politics of the Mass Media*. New York: St. Martin's, 1986.

——. *Make-Believe Media*. New York: St. Martin's, 1992.

——. *History as Mystery*. San Francisco: City Lights, 1999.

'Park as a Memorial.' *Pacific Commercial Advertiser* Mar 28, 1919: 4.

Paske-Smith, M. 'Early British Consuls in Hawaii.' *The Mid-Pacific Magazine of the Pan-Pacific Union*. Honolulu: Oct–Dec, 1936: 227–62.

Patterson, Emma C. 'The Radnor War Memorial, part 2' *Your Town and My Town* July 20, 1951. Radnor Historical Society. Accessed June 13, 2009. http://radnorhistory.org/collection/articles/ytmt/?tag=radnor-war-memorial

Peck, Abe. *Uncovering the Sixties: The Life and Times of the Underground Press*. New York: Pantheon, 1985.

Peek, Jeannette Murray. *Stepping Into Time: A Guide to Honolulu's Historic Landmarks*. Honolulu: Mutual, 1994.

Photographic Album of the Americans Soldiers' Graves in Islay. The Glasgow Islay Association. http://www.willdo4u.com/argon/burial.pdf Accessed June 14, 2009.

Piehler, Kurt G. *Remembering War the American Way*. Washington: Smithsonian Inst., 1995.

Porteus, Stanley D. *Temperament and Race*. Boston: Gorham, 1926.

Pratt, Mary Louise. 'Fieldwork in Common Places' in *Writing Culture: the Poetics and Politics of Ethnography*. Eds. James Clifford and George E. Marcus. Berkeley: U of California P, 1986: 27–50.

'The Press & Vietnam.' Editorial. *The Sunday Star-Bulletin and Advertiser* Feb 18, 1968: B2.

Preston, Anthony and John Major. *Send a Gunboat! A Study of the Gunboat and its Role in British Policy, 1854–1904*. London: Longmans, 1967.

'Propaganda Guerillas Invade Hickam.' *Gathering Place* II.3 (1972): 9.

'Proposed Memorials for War Heroes are Widely Discussed.' *Pacific Commercial Advertiser* Feb 15, 1919: 4.

'Proposes Aid for Memorial Funds.' *Pacific Commercial Advertiser* Jan 9, 1919: 1.

'Promotion Body Talks Memorial.' *Pacific Commercial Advertiser* Jan 15, 1919: 2.

Purnell, Nanette Napoleon. *O'ahu Cemetery Burial Ground and Historical Site*. Honolulu: O'ahu Cemetery Assoc., 1998.

'Quarry Says Clay Brainwashed.' *Honolulu Advertiser* June 23, 1967: B9.

Rampell, Ed and Luis Reyes. *Pearl Harbor in the Movies*. Honolulu: Mutual, 2001.

'A Rapping Good Time With Jane.' *Honolulu Advertiser* Nov 25, 1971: A6.

'Red Force Fading in Saigon Battle.' *Honolulu Advertiser* Feb 3, 1968: A1.

'Reds Won the Headlines at Record Cost.' *Honolulu Star-Bulletin* Feb 12, 1968: 1.

Reedy, George. 'Difficulties of Covering a War Like Vietnam' in *Vietnam Reconsidered: Lessons From a War*. Ed. Harrison E. Salisbury. New York: Harper and Row, 1984: 120–3.

Reid, Brian Holden. 'America and War' in *A New Introduction to American Studies*. Eds. Christopher Bigsby and Howard Temperley. London: Pearson, 2005: 302–24.

'Resisters, Deserters Welcome in Canada, However Living Costs Higher Than US.' *Roach* May 13, 1968: 9.

'Returning American Dead.' *New York Times* Aug 1, 1920: 25.

Rev. of *The Idol Dancer*. *New York Times* Mar 22, 1919. http://www.silentsaregolden.com/idoldancerreview.html Accessed Oct 23, 2009.

Rev. of *The Idol Dancer*. *New York Times* June ?, 1920 http://www.silentsaregolden.com/idoldancerreview.html Accessed Oct 23, 2009.

*The Revolt of Mamie Stover*. Dir. Raoul Walsh. With Jane Russell and Richard Egan. 20th Century Fox ,1956.

Reyes, Luis and Ed Rampell. *Made in Paradise: Hollywood's Films of Hawai'i and the South Seas*. Honolulu: Mutual, 1995.

Rhen, Bradley Staff Sgt., 'Hawaii Gets Approval for Stryker Brigade.' ARNews: *Army News Service*. http://www4.army.mil/ocpa/read.php?story_id_key=6148 Accessed Oct 23, 2009.

Richardson, James D. *A Compilation of the Messages and Papers of the Presidents* Vol. 4. BiblioBazaar, LLC, 2008.

Rifkin, Mark. 'Debt and the Transnationalization of Hawai'i.' *American Quarterly* 60.1 (2008): 43–66.

Rips, Geoffrey, 'The Campaign Against the Underground Press' in *Unamerican Activities: The Campaign Against the Underground Press*. Eds. Anne Janowitz and Nancy Peters. San Francisco: City Lights, 1981.

'Rival Marches Are Scheduled.' *Honolulu Star-Bulletin* Mar 26, 1966: 1.

Rosen, Jim. Letter. *Midweek* May 2, 2001: 4.

'Rotarians Interested in Plans for Memorial for War Dead.' *Pacific Commercial Advertiser* Feb 22, 1919: 5.

'Rotary Club to Honor Officials of Old Republic.' *Pacific Commercial Advertiser* Aug 12, 1919: 6.

Rumer, Thomas A. *The American Legion: An Official History 1919–1989*. New York: M. Evans & Co, 1990.

Said, Edward W. *Culture and Imperialism*. New York: Knopf, 1993.

'Sailors, Soldiers and Hawaiians Stage Riot at Midnight; Blood Flows in Incipient Revolution.' *Pacific Commercial Advertiser* July 6, 1919: 1.

Salyer, Lucy E. 'Baptism by Fire: Race, Military Service, and the U.S. Citizenship Policy, 1918–1935.' *The Journal of American History* 91 (2004): 847–76.

Samson, Jane. *Imperial Benevolence: Making British Authority in the Pacific Islands*. Honolulu: U of Hawai'i P, 1998.

Savage, Kirk. *Standing Soldiers, Kneeling Slaves: Race, War, and Monument in Nineteenth-Century America*. Princeton UP, 1999.

Scarry, Elaine. *The Body in Pain: The Making and Unmaking of the World*. New York: Oxford UP, 1985.

Schaefer, Christina K. *The Great War: A Guide to the Service Records of all the World's Fighting Men and Volunteers*. Baltimore: Genealogical, 1998.

Scheer, Robert. 'Difficulties of Reporting a War Like Vietnam' in *Vietnam Reconsidered: Lessons From a War*. Ed. Harrison E. Salisbury. New York: Harper and Row, 1984: 117–19.

Schell, Jonathan. *The Fate of the Earth*. New York: Avon, 1982.

Schlesinger, Arthur Meier. *A Thousand Days: John F. Kennedy in the White House*. New York: Houghton Mifflin Harcourt, 2002.

Schmitt, Robert C. *Hawai'i Data Book: A Statistical Reference to Hawai'i's Social, Economic and Political Trends*. Honolulu: Mutual, 2002.

——. *Hawai'i in the Movies 1898–1959.* Honolulu: Hawaiian Historical Soc., 1988.

——. 'Hawai'i's War Veterans and Battle Deaths.' *Hawaiian Journal of History* (1998): 171–4.

Schreiber, E.M. 'Antiwar Demonstrations and American Public Opinion on the War in Vietnam.' *British Journal of Sociology* 27.2 (1976): 225–36.

*The Searchers.* Dir. John Ford. With John Wayne and Natalie Wood. Warner Brothers, 1956.

'Service Flag Bears White Star for George K. Dwight.' *Pacific Commercial Advertiser* Jan 30, 1918: 8.

Shipley, Bob. 'Crash, Burn and Wipeout Dept.' *Gathering Place* 1.2 (1971): 9.

Sidle, Winant. 'The Role of Journalists in Vietnam: An Army General's Perspective' in *Vietnam Reconsidered: Lessons From a War.* Ed. Harrison E. Salisbury. New York: Harper and Row, 1984: 111–12.

Silva, Noenoe K. *Aloha Betrayed: Native Hawaiian Resistance to American Colonialism.* Durham and London: Duke UP, 2004.

Simpich Jr., Frederick. 'Hawaii, U.S.A.' *National Geographic* July, 1960: 1–47.

Singletary, Milly. *Punchbowl: National Memorial Cemetery of the Pacific.* Honolulu: Sunset, 1981.

Sklar, Robert. *Movie-Made America: A Cultural History of American Movies.* New York: Vintage, 1994.

'Slain in Holdup — A Hero's Welcome ...' *Gathering Place* 1:5 (1971): 12, 21.

Sledge, Michael. *Soldier Dead: How We Recover, Identify, Bury, and Honor Our Military Fallen.* New York: Columbia UP, 2005.

Smith, Bradford. *Yankees in Paradise: The New England Impact on Hawaii.* Philadelphia: Lippincott, 1956.

Smyser, A.A. 'Vietnam and Hawaii.' *Honolulu Star-Bulletin* July 31, 1965: 7.

Sobchack, Thomas and Vivian Sobchack. *An Introduction to Film.* Boston: Little, Brown, 1980.

Speakes, Larry and Robert Pack. *Speaking Out: The Reagan Presidency From Inside the White House.* New York: Scribner, 1988.

Stannard, David E. *American Holocaust: Columbus and the Conquest of the New World.* New York: Oxford UP, 1992.

——. *Before the Horror: The Population of Hawai'i on the Eve of Western Contact.* Honolulu: U of Hawai'i P, 1989.

——. 'The Hawaiians: Health, Justice, and Sovereignty.' *Cultural Survival Quarterly* (Spring 2000): 15–20.

——. *Honor Killing: How the Infamous 'Massie Affair' Transformed Hawai'i.* New York: Viking, 2005.

'Statement of Policy.' Editorial. *Carrion Crow* May 2, 1967: 1

'Statue or Memorial Hall Issue Must Be Determined.' *Pacific Commercial Advertiser* Jan 11, 1919: 5.

Stauffer, Robert H. 'The Hawai'i-United States Treaty of 1826.' *Hawaiian Journal of History* (1983): 40–63.

Steere, Edward and Thayer M. Boardman. *Final Disposition of World War II Dead 1945–51.* US Army, Quartermaster Corps, QMC Historical Studies, Series II, No. 4. Washington, D.C.: Historical Branch Office of the Quartermaster General, 1957.

Stewart, A.M. *A Visit to the South Seas in the U.S. Ship Vincennes, During the Years 1829 and 1830*. Vol. 2. New York, 1831.
Stirling, Yates (Rear Admiral USN Ret.). *Sea Duty*. New York: Putnam's, 1939.
Stoessinger, John George. *Why Nations Go to War*. New York: St. Martin's, 1993.
Sturken, Marita. *Tangled Memories: The Vietnam War, the Aids Epidemic, and the Politics of Remembering*. Berkeley: U of California P, 1997.
——. 'Absent Images of Memory: Remembering and Reenacting the Japanese Internment' in *Perilous Memories: The Asia-Pacific War(s)*. Eds. Fujitani, T., Geoffrey M. White and Lisa Yoneyama. Durham, NC: Duke UP, 2001: 33–49.
'Successful Architects Conception of Hawaii's $250,000 Memorial.' *Honolulu Advertiser* June 21, 1921: 1.
'A Suggestion.' Editorial. *Paradise of the Pacific* Feb 1, 1921: 3.
Tabrah, Ruth M. *Hawaii: A History*. New York: Norton, 1980.
'Tactical Errors Blamed for Ambush and Massacre.' *Honolulu Star-Bulletin* Aug 31, 1966: 9.
Takaki, Ronald. *Double Victory: A Multicultural History of America in World War II*. Boston: Little, Brown, 2001.
——. *Strangers From a Different Shore: A History of Asian Americans*. Boston: Little, Brown, 1989.
Tamura, Eileen H. 'The English-Only Effort, the Anti-Japanese Campaign, and Language Acquisition in the Education of Japanese Americans in Hawaii, 1915–1940.' *History of Education Quarterly* 33.1 (1993): 37–58.
'Ten Arrested for Fort DeRussy Sit-In.' *Roach* June 4, 1968: 8.
TenBroek, Jacobus, Edward N. Barnhart and Floyd W. Matson. *Prejudice, War and the Constitution*. Berkeley: U of California P, 1954.
'Tentative Sketch of Memorial Natatorium Proposed by American Legion.' McCarthy — Territorial Departments War Memorial Commission. Hawai'i State Archives.
'Tension Mounts as Protesters March.' *Honolulu Star-Bulletin* Mar 26, 1966: 1
Terry, Wallace. *Bloods: An Oral History of the Vietnam War*. New York: Ballantine, 1991.
'Text of Inouye's Speech.' *Honolulu Star-Bulletin* May 29, 1968: C2.
*The Official History of the 315th Infantry U.S.A.: Being a true Record of its Organization and Training, of its Operations in the World War, and of its Activities Following the Signing of the Armistice. 1917–1919*. Philadelphia: Historical Board of the 315th Infantry, 1920.
Theimer, J.E. (Maj. Gen.) 'Sentry at the Crossroads of the Pacific: The U.S. Army in Hawaii.' *Army Information Digest* 15 (July 1960): 2–13.
'This Means Revolution!' *Roach* June 18, 1968: 1.
Thompson, Hunter. S. *Fear and Loathing: On the Campaign Trail '72*. New York: Fawcett, 1974.
Thompson, Mark. 'Driving Blind: How the U.S. Navy is Trying to Undo Damage From a Fatal Hawaiian Practice Dive.' *Time* Feb 26, 2001.
'Threefold Plan for Memorial is Heard by Legion.' *Pacific Commercial Advertiser* Aug 24, 1920: 6.
'Through Rosy-Hued Glasses.' *Honolulu Star-Bulletin* Feb 21, 1968: A23.

*Tin Pan Alley*. Dir. Walter Lang. With Betty Grable and Alice Faye. 20th Century Fox, 1940.
Ting, Yu Shing. 'Saluting Army Heroes.' *Midweek* Nov 14, 2001: 50.
Toland, John *Infamy: Pearl Harbor and Its Aftermath*. Garden City, NY: Doubleday, 1982.
'Top Marine Says U.S. Winning War.' *Honolulu Advertiser* Jan 17, 1968: A5.
Toplin, Robert B. *History by Hollywood: The Use and Abuse of the American Past*. U of Illinois P, 1996.
'Tragic Death Comes to Captain Green and Forestalls His Arrest Yesterday.' *Pacific Commercial Advertiser* Jan 13, 1918: 1, 4.
Trask, Haunani-Kay. *From a Native Daughter: Colonialism and Sovereignty in Hawai'i*. Honolulu: U of Hawai'i P, 1999.
——. 'Settlers of Color and "Immigrant" Hegemony: "Locals" in Hawai'i.' *Amerasia Journal* 2 (2000): 1–24.
——. 'Stealing Hawaiian Lands for the War Machine' in Koohan Paik, Jerry Mander *et al*. *The Super Ferry Chronicles: Hawaii's Uprising Against Militarism, Commercialism and the Desecration of the Earth*. Kihei, HI: Koa, 2009: 264–9.
Trumbell, Robert. 'Week in Review.' *New York Times* Feb 18, 1962.
Tsai, Michael. 'Military-Hawai'i Ties.' *Honolulu Advertiser*, Aug 16, 2009. http://www.honoluluadvertiser.com/article/20090816/STATEHOOD01/908160339&template=statehood/Military-Hawai+i+ties Accessed Sep 17, 2009.
Tuohy, William. 'Difficulties of Covering a War Like Vietnam' in *Vietnam Reconsidered: Lessons From a War*. Ed. Harrison E. Salisbury. New York: Harper and Row, 1984: 128.
'Tuscania Survivor Lauds British Sailors.' *New York Times* Mar 2, 1918: 8.
'25th's General Sees No Victories for Viet Reds.' *Honolulu Advertiser* Feb 4, 1968: A3.
*United Veterans' Service Council Records*. Hawai'i State Archives.
*University of Oregon Department of Architecture. 2002–2003 Advising Handbook*. http://architecture.uoregon.edu/index.cfm?mode=programs&page=arch Accessed June 10, 2009.
'U.S. Allies Call Off Cease-fire in North.' *Honolulu Star-Bulletin* Jan 29, 1968: A3.
*The U.S. Army Museum of Hawaii: A Most Unusual Glimpse into the Past*. U.S. Army Museum of Hawaii.
'U.S. General Discounts Massacre.' *Honolulu Star-Bulletin* Nov 26, 1969: 2.
*U.S. Military Out of Mākua Valley*. Refuse & Resist! Hawai'i Chapter.
*Variety Film Reviews*. Rev. of *Flirtation Walk* Dec 4, 1934. New York & London: Garland, 1983.
——. Rev. of *From Here to Eternity* July 29, 1953. New York & London: Garland, 1983.
——. Rev. of *Honolulu* Feb 1, 1939. New York & London: Garland, 1983.
——. Rev. of *The Idol Dancer* Mar 26, 1920. New York & London: Garland, 1983.
——. Rev. of *Midway* June 16, 1976. New York & London: Garland, 1983.
——. Rev. of *Waikiki Wedding* Mar 31, 1937. New York & London: Garland, 1983.
——. Rev. of *White Shadows in the South Seas* Aug 1, 1928. New York & London: Garland, 1983.
'Vaughan to Tell Why He Opposes Nippon Schools.' *Pacific Commercial Advertiser* Nov 9, 1919: 6.

'Veterans Plan to Launch a Post of Legion Here.' *Pacific Commercial Advertiser* Aug 29, 1919: 1.

Vidal, Gore. *Perpetual War for Perpetual Peace*. New York: Nation, 2002.

'Viet Cong Executed Her.' *Honolulu Star-Bulletin* Feb 5, 1968: A2.

'Viet Cong Troops Seize Part of Hue.' *Honolulu Star-Bulletin* Jan 31, 1968: 1

'VN Women Liberation.' *Roach* Dec 17–31, 1968: 8.

'VVAW Winter Soldier Investigation.' *Liberated Barracks* Oct 1971: 2.

*Waco Morning Star* XV.3 (July, 1915): 91.

Waddle, Scott (Cmdr USN Ret), and Ken Abraham. *The Right Thing*. Nashville: Integrity, 2002.

Wagner-Seavey, Sandra E. 'Effect of World War I on the German Community in Hawaii.' *Hawaiian Journal of History* (1980): 109–40.

Wallace, Mike. *Mickey Mouse History and Other Essays on American Memory*. Philadelphia: Temple UP, 1996.

Walsh, Craig W. 'The Forgotten Chapter: A Diplomatic Chronicle of the Seizure of the Hawaiian Islands by Lord George Paulet of H.M.S. Carysfort, 1843.' Diss. Rensselaer Polytechnic Institute, Troy, New York, 1970.

Walton, C. Dale. *The Myth of Inevitable U.S. Defeat in Vietnam*. London: Cass, 2002.

'Want Sculpture for War Memorial.' *Pacific Commercial Advertiser* Feb 28, 1919: 4.

Warfield, Charles Lamoreaux. 'History of the Hawaii National Guard From Feudal Times to June 30, 1935.' Masters Thesis. University of Hawai'i, 1935.

Warner, Dennis. 'Hanoi Troops Take Initiative.' *Honolulu Advertiser* June 17, 1967: B2.

Watabayashi, David. Letter. *Midweek* Feb 21, 2001: 4.

'Weak Welcome is Given to Soldiers: General Public is Not Turning Out to Meet Trains From Schoffield Barracks.' *Pacific Commercial Advertiser* Jan 30, 1919: 1.

Webb, Kate. 'Highpockets' in Tad Bartimus *et al. War Torn: Stories of War From the Women Reporters Who Covered Vietnam*. New York: Random House, 2002: 60–89.

Wells, Robert V. Rev. of *Before the Horror: the Population of Hawai'i on the Eve of Western Contact. Journal of Interdisciplinary History* 21.1 (1990): 159–60.

Weyeneth, Robert R. *Kapi'olani Park: A Victorian Landscape of Leisure*. Honolulu: Dept. of Parks and Recreation City and County of Honolulu, 1991.

'What Gathering Place is All About.' *Gathering Place* 1.1 (1971): 2.

'What's Happening?' *Roach* June 4, 1968: 10.

'What's Happening? Resistance Memo.' *Roach* June 18, 1968: 4.

White Geoffrey M. 'Emotional Remembering: The Pragmatics of National Memory' *Ethos* 27.4 (2000): 505–29.

*White Shadows in the South Seas*. Dir.W.S. Van Dyke and Robert Flaherty. With Monte Blue and Raquel Torres. Metro-Goldwyn-Mayer, 1928.

'Who is Nguyen Cao Ky?' *Gathering Place* 1.1 (1971): 15.

'Who Is The Real Enemy?' *Liberated Barracks* July–August 1972: 4.

*Who's Who in Marine Corps History* http://www.tecom.usmc.mil/HD/Whos_Who/Fuller_BH.htm Accessed July 11, 2009.

Wicker, Tom. 'Firepower versus South Vietnam.' *Honolulu Star-Bulletin* Feb 21, 1968: A23.

Wills, Gary. *John Wayne's America: The Politics of Celebrity*. Advance Uncorrected Reader's Proof. New York: Simon & Schuster, 1997.

Winslow, Anne Goodwin. *Fort DeRussy Days: Letters of a Malihini Army Wife, 1908–1911*. Ed. M. Winslow Chapman. Honolulu: Folk Press Kapiolani CC, 1998.

Winthrop, John. 'A Model of Christian Charity.' *Winthrop Papers*. Vol. II. Ed. Stewart Mitchell. Boston, 1931.

Witanek, Robert. 'Students, Scholars, and Spies: The CIA on Campus.' *Covert Action Information Bulletin*. Washington: Covert Action Publications, 1989: 25–8.

Wood, Houston. *Displacing Natives: The Rhetorical Production of Hawai'i*. Lanham, Md.: Rowman & Littlefield, 1999.

Wright, Theon. *Rape in Paradise*. Honolulu: Mutual, 1990.

Wyatt, Clarence R. *Paper Soldiers: The American Press and the Vietnam War*. New York & London: Norton, 1993.

Young, Marilyn. *The Vietnam Wars, 1945–1990*. New York: HarperCollins, 1991.

Zimmerman, Malia. 'Saluting UH's ROTC Program.' *Midweek* Jan 3, 2001: 5.

Zinn, Howard. *A Peoples History of the United States 1492–present*. Third edition. London: Pearson, 2003.

# Index